I0235264

Vergilius Redivivus:
Studies in Joseph Addison's Latin Poetry

Vergilius Redivivus:
Studies in Joseph Addison's Latin Poetry

ESTELLE HAAN

American Philosophical Society

Philadelphia · 2005

Transactions of the
American Philosophical Society
Held at Philadelphia
For Promoting Useful Knowledge
Volume 95, Part 2

Copyright © 2005 by the American Philosophical Society
for its *Transaction* series.
All rights reserved

Cover illustration: Isaac Fuller's Mural on the Last Judgment, Magdalen
College Chapel, Oxford (Engraving by Michael Burghers). By permission
of the President and Fellows, Magdalen College, Oxford.

ISBN–13: 978–0–87169–952–7
ISBN–10: 0–87169–952–4

Library of Congress Cataloging-in-Publication Data

Haan, Estelle.
Vergilius Redivivus: Studies in Joseph Addison's Latin Poetry / Estelle Haan.
    p. cm. — (Transactions of the American Philosophical Society ; v. 95, pt. 2)
English and Latin.
Includes bibliographical references (p.) and index.
ISBN–13: 978–0–87169–952–7 (pbk.)
ISBN–10: 0–87169–952–4 (pbk.)
    1. Addison, Joseph, 1672–1719—Criticism and interpretation. 2. Latin poetry, Medieval and
modern—England—History and criticism. 3. Addison, Joseph, 1672–1719—Knowledge—Language
and languages. 4. Addison, Joseph, 1672–1719—Knowledge—Rome. 5. English poetry—Roman
influences. 6. Virgil—Appreciation—England. 7. Virgil—Influence. I. Title: Studies in Joseph
Addison's Latin poetry. II. Title. III. Series.

PA8450.A32Z53 2005
824'.5—dc22

                                                                                    2005043569

For Tony

CONTENTS

PREFACE

It is hardly an exaggeration to say that Addison's Latin poetry has been virtually ignored by modern scholarship. Since the appearance in 1914 of Guthkelch's edition of his works[1] there has been no modern edition of the Latin poetry, with the exception of the hypertext version (together with brief notes) by Sutton.[2] And critical discussion is equally thin, amounting in fact to just two articles, one unpublished thesis, and a single chapter in another unpublished thesis.

As far back as 1938 Bradner, in an article that should have paved the way for further study, offered a comprehensive survey of factual problems surrounding the publication of several of Addison's Latin poems.[3] It is evident, however, that this discussion did not aim to offer a critical analysis. Almost twenty-five years later Schuch's dissertation on Addison and the poetry of Augustan Rome made some good observations,[4] but this focused on his vernacular rather than Latin writings, tracking down thematic parallels, while neglecting seventeenth-century appropriation of classical models. Nearly two decades later Wiesenthal in an unpublished thesis convincingly demonstrated that "Addison's Latin is both vigorous and energetic."[5] His chapter on the subject is particularly useful when set in the context of the other English Augustans whose Latin poetry he surveys. And more recently some

---

[1] A.C. Guthkelch, ed., *The Miscellaneous Works of Joseph Addison* (London, 1914), 2 vols.

[2] D.F. Sutton, ed., *The Latin Prose and Poetry of Joseph Addison: A Hypertext Edition* (The Philological Museum: California, 1997; revised 1998). Despite this very welcome and highly accessible version, it is clear that a new critical edition of the Latin poems, together with an English translation and detailed commentary, is long overdue. While this is not the aim of the present study, I have appended my own edition of the Latin poems discussed herein. See Appendices 1 and 2 below.

[3] Leicester Bradner, "The Composition and Publication of Addison's Latin Poems," *MP* 35 (1938), 359-367.

[4] Gerhard Schuch, *Addison und die Lateinischen Augusteer: Studien zur Frage der Literarischen Abhängigkeit des Englischen Klassizismus* (PhD thesis, University of Köln, 1962).

[5] A.J. Wiesenthal, *The Latin Poetry of the English Augustans* (PhD thesis, Virginia, 1979), 48-49. See in general 47-94.

insight into Addison's reworking of Virgil in his *Pax Gulielmi* has been
afforded by Williams and Kelsall[6] in an article which, as Sutton observes,
is "a model for the way Neo-Latin poetry can be discussed with profit."[7]

What is immediately apparent, nonetheless, is the fact that
Addison's Latin verse has failed to receive the critical attention it
deserves. And this seems to be the consequence of a number of factors.
Until very recently classical scholars have not ventured into the
immensely important domain of neo-Latin literature, important because it
illuminates our understanding of such issues as reception, the classical
tradition, and more generally the complexities of early modern culture.[8]
And English scholars (barring only a few exceptions) rarely cross that
linguistic divide between a poet's vernacular and Latin works,[9] despite
the fact that such an approach can and does prove mutually insightful for
both disciplines. It is unfortunate then that Bradner's observation made
well over half a century ago that "very little has appeared in the way of
critical study of these poems in relation to the literature of their time"[10]
still holds true today. Typical of its reception is the viewpoint of
Courthope, who could only remark that the Latin poems "are
distinguished by the ease and flow of the versification, but they are
generally wanting in originality."[11]

It is the aim of the present monograph to begin to fill this gap in
modern scholarship by examining the intricate intertextual relationships

---

[6] R.D. Williams and Malcolm Kelsall, "Critical Appreciations V: Joseph Addison, *Pax Gulielmi Auspiciis Europae Reddita*, 1697, lines 96-132 and 167-end," *G&R* 27 (1980), 48-59.

[7] Sutton, ed., *The Latin Prose and Poetry of Joseph Addison*, Introduction, 9.

[8] One clear exception is the excellent work of Dana Sutton, whose online bibliography of neo-Latin texts (compiled for The Philological Museum) has made hitherto neglected primary texts accessible to a wide readership.

[9] Among the few exceptions to this general trend are J.W. Binns, ed. *The Latin Poetry of English Poets* (London, 1974); *Milton Studies* 19 (1984), an important volume of essays on Milton's Latin poetry; Estelle Haan, *From Academia to Amicitia: Milton's Latin Writings and the Italian Academies* (Transactions of the American Philosophical Society 88.6: Philadelphia, 1998); Estelle Haan, *Thomas Gray's Latin Poetry: Some Classical, Neo-Latin and Vernacular Contexts* (Collection Latomus 257: Brussels, 2000); Estelle Haan, *Andrew Marvell's Latin Poetry: From Text to Context* (Collection Latomus 275: Brussels, 2003).

[10] Bradner, "Addison's Latin Poems," 359.

[11] W.J. Courthope, *Addison* (London, 1889; rpt 1911), 39.

between some of Addison's neo-Latin poems and the poetic corpus of one Augustan poet: Virgil (the *Georgics* in particular). While so doing it fully accepts nonetheless that Addison's Latin poetry also interacts, even if in a less overt or sustained way, with other Roman authors.[12] Offering a case study, as it were, of one neo-Latin poet's engagement with Virgil, it presents a series of chapter-length discussions, all of which, while clearly interrelated, may also, it is hoped, stand independently.[13] Throughout, the analysis is informed by a twofold aim: to assess how Virgilian texts were refined and redefined through appropriation to a contemporary context; to demonstrate on a representative level an apparent paradox: that in the case of Addison late seventeenth-century neo-Latin poetry, far from being "self-contained," was in virtue of its intertextual relationship with Virgil "traversed by otherness." [14] As such, the Addisonian Latin text exemplifies Kristeva's definition of intertextuality: "any text is a mosaic of quotations; any text is an absorption and transformation of another."[15]

Quotations from Addison's Latin and vernacular works are from Guthkelch's edition.[16] Quotations from *The Spectator* and *The Tatler* are from Bond's editions.[17] In all instances, both in the main text itself and in my edition of the Latin poems appended to this study, I have modernized spelling and punctuation.

---

[12] Sutton ed., *The Latin Prose and Poetry of Joseph Addison*, has compiled in his notes to the poems a detailed list of verbal echoes of several Roman authors. While some of these may be dismissed as mere tags, others (for example, Addison's Horatian echoes) may be significant pointers for critical readers. On Addison's appropriation of Horace in his Odes to Dr Edward Hannes and Thomas Burnet respectively, see Estelle Haan, "Twin Augustans: Addison's Neo-Latin Poetry and Horace," *N&Q*, forthcoming.

[13] Addison's *Pax Gulielmi*, although highly Virgilian, is not included in the present study since this precise aspect of the poem has already been surveyed at length by Williams and Kelsall, "Critical Appreciations V." See note 6 above.

[14] See Barbara Johnson, "Les Fleurs du Mal Armé: Some Reflections on Intertextuality," in *Lyric Poetry*, eds. Chaviva Hošek and Patricia Parker (Ithaca and London, 1985), 264-280, at 264: "Intertextuality designates the multitude of ways a text has of not being self-contained, of being traversed by otherness."

[15] See Julia Kristeva, *Desire in Language: A Semiotic Approach to Literature and Art*, trans. Thomas Gora, Alice Jardine and L.S. Roudiez (New York, 1980), 66.

[16] As cited in note 1 above.

[17] D.F. Bond, ed. *The Spectator* (Oxford, 1965), 5 vols; D.F. Bond, ed. *The Tatler* (Oxford, 1987), 3 vols.

ACKNOWLEDGEMENTS

The present monograph is in many respects a product of my ongoing interest in the Latin poetry of English poets, and more generally in the interrelationships between neo-Latin and the vernacular. I am very fortunate to have had the opportunity to cultivate such interests at Queen's University, Belfast as Lecturer and Senior Lecturer in Classics and more recently as Reader in English. At Queen's I have benefited greatly from discussions with Michael McGann. I am grateful to the anonymous readers for the Transactions Series of the American Philosophical Society for their very helpful suggestions.

I wish to thank the Queen's University Research and Scholarships Committee for funding trips to the British Library, London, and the Bodleian Library, Oxford, and the authorities of those institutions for permitting me to consult manuscripts and early printed books relevant to my research. I am indebted also to the Queen's University Library, especially its Special Collections and Inter-Library Loans divisions. Particular thanks are due to Robin Darwall-Smith, Archivist of Magdalen College, Oxford, for making available to me a wealth of material, and for answering my many queries. To Magdalen College, Oxford and the British Library, London I am grateful for permission to reproduce several drawings, engravings and frontispieces.

Finally I wish to thank my husband Tony Sheehan, Humanities Computing Officer at Queen's, not only for his brilliant assistance and advice in regard to the technical production of camera-ready copy, but also for his unfailing support and gentle care at all times. To him I dedicate this monograph as a small token of a very great love.

EH

ABBREVIATIONS

AJP	*American Journal of Philology*
BNYPL	*Bulletin of the New York Public Library*
CB	*Classical Bulletin*
CLS	*Comparative Literature Studies*
DNB	*Dictionary of National Biography*
ELH	*English Literary History*
G&R	*Greece and Rome*
HL	*Humanistica Lovaniensia:*
	Journal of Neo-Latin Studies
HSCP	*Harvard Studies in Classical Philology*
JHS	*Journal of Hellenic Studies*
JRS	*Journal of Roman Studies*
MH	*Medievalia et Humanistica*
MP	*Modern Philology*
N&Q	*Notes and Queries*
NLH	*New Literary History*
OLD	*Oxford Latin Dictionary*
RES	*Review of English Studies*
RS	*Renaissance Studies*
SEL	*Studies in English Literature*
SP	*Studies in Philology*

INTRODUCTION

Addison's current reputation rests almost exclusively on his role as the accomplished essayist of the *Spectator* and *Tatler* papers,[1] as the author of the drama *Cato*,[2] and as the composer of a body of minor English verse.[3] It is a reputation, however, that has hardly been served well by the passage of time. Thus Damrosch announces:

> His poems and his *Cato* lost favor rapidly as the eighteenth century went forward, and even the *Spectator*, which readers like Benjamin Franklin pored over as a guide to culturally approved language and manners, long ago passed into eclipse.[4]

---

[1] On Addison as essayist, see among others L.A. Elioseff, *The Cultural Milieu of Addison's Literary Criticism* (Austin, 1963); L.D. Bloom, "Addison's Popular Aesthetic: The Rhetoric of the *Paradise Lost* Papers," in L.L. Martz, Aubrey Williams, P.M. Spacks, eds. *The Author in His Work: Essays on a Problem in Criticism* (Yale, 1978), 263-281; Neil Saccamano, "The Sublime Force of Words in Addison's *Pleasures*," *ELH* 58.1 (1991), 83-106; William Walker, "Ideology and Addison's Essays on the Pleasures of the Imagination," *Eighteenth-Century Life* 24.2 (2000), 65-84.

[2] See among others M.M. Kelsall, "The Meaning of Addison's *Cato*," *RES* 17 (1966), 149-162; Taylor Corse, "An Echo of Dryden in Addison's *Cato*," *N&Q* 38.2 (1991), 178; Julie Ellison, "Cato's Tears," *ELH* 63.3 (1996), 571-601; L.J. Rosenthal, "Juba's Roman Soul: Addison's *Cato* and Enlightenment Cosmopolitanism," *Studies in the Literary Imagination* 32.2 (1999), 63-76; L.A. Freeman, "What's Love Got to Do With Addison's Cato?" *SEL* 39.3 (1999), 463-482.

[3] For the typical reception of Addison's English poetry, cf. the comment of Samuel Johnson in "Addison" (*Prefaces, Biographical and Critical, to the Works of the English Poets*, in Donald Greene, ed., *Samuel Johnson* [Oxford, 1984]), 666: "... It has not often those felicities of diction which give lustre to sentiments, or that vigour of sentiment that animates diction: there is little of ardour, vehemence, or transport; there is very rarely the awfulness of grandeur, and not very often the splendour of elegance." See in general S.J. Royal, "Joseph Addison (1672-1719): A Checklist of Works and Major Scholarship," *BNYPL* 77 (1974), 236-250.

[4] Leopold Damrosch, "The Significance of Addison's Criticism," *SEL* 19 (1979), 421-430, at 421.

The omission of any reference to Addison's Latin poetry even in this overly pessimistic assessment of his reception in general is all too typical of modern scholarship. And yet it was precisely in this field that he excelled. Or, in the words of Lord Macaulay, Addison, the neo-Latin poet, was "the man who does best what multitudes do well."[5]

In 1719 the author of the Preface to a bilingual edition of Addison's Latin poetry commented: "I will not say that it is absolutely necessary to be a good Latin poet in order to become a good English one."[6] Perhaps the antithesis of this statement is particularly pertinent in Addison's case: it is not absolutely necessary to be a good English poet in order to become a good Latin one. Addison's English verse can hardly be said to make him stand out from the "multitudes," and here the contrast with Milton or Marvell is glaringly obvious. Nevertheless, there is no doubt that his Latin poetry did set him apart from other seventeenth-century neo-Latin writers, perhaps even Milton included, as may indeed be implied by Macaulay's terms of praise. And where Milton's Latin poetry contains the germ of several ideas which would later come to fruition in his mature vernacular writings,[7] while Marvell skillfully experimented in the art of composing companion poems in both Latin and English,[8] Addison's Latin verse reveals the seeds of that articulate and wry mannerism which would shine through the prose works of a mature essayist who knew exactly how to appropriate classical sentiment to suit contemporary taste.[9] As neo-Latin poetry, moreover, it merits detailed study in its own right.

Macaulay's comment is perhaps all the more remarkable when it is remembered that in the late seventeenth and early eighteenth centuries

---

[5] Macaulay, "The Life and Writings of Addison," in *Critical and Historical Essays Contributed to The Edinburgh Review* (London, 1877), 736 (July, 1843).

[6] *Poems on Several Occasions with a Dissertation Upon the Roman Poets by Mr. Addison* (London, 1719), Preface, ix.

[7] See, for example, Macon Cheek, "Milton's *In Quintum Novembris*: An Epic Foreshadowing," *SP* 54 (1957), 172-184; Estelle Haan, *John Milton's Latin Poetry: Some Neo-Latin and Vernacular Contexts* (PhD thesis: The Queen's University of Belfast, 1987), 227-267. See in general E.S. Le Comte, *Yet Once More: Verbal and Psychological Pattern in Milton* (New York, 1953).

[8] Cf., for example, *Ros* and "On a Drop of Dew"; *Hortus* and "The Garden." See Estelle Haan, *Andrew Marvell's Latin Poetry*, 57-94.

[9] For links between the Latin poems and the *Spectator* and *Tatler* papers, see, for example, 35, 72, 74, 77, 79, 80, 86, 87, 109 below. Here I disagree with Wiesenthal, *The Latin Poetry of the English Augustans*, 52, who believes that there is almost no influence of the Latin poems upon the periodical essays.

Latin verse-composition, while existing as a universal pastime (later to be rewarded by prizes put forward on a regular basis by the *Gentleman's Magazine*), still retained its indubitable place in school and university curricula.[10] Partly as a consequence of an educational system that traced its origins back to the humanist ideals of the Renaissance, the true "gentleman" was rigorously schooled in the classics. On a broader literary level the inclusion of Latin quotations was frequently a quasi-ostentatious proof of learning. It was Latin poetry that would later come to head the *Tatler* and *Spectator* essays as though advertising the anticipated erudition of the magazines' envisaged contemporary readership. But the use of Latin still represented much more than this. The universities of Oxford and Cambridge continued to produce a seemingly incessant supply of Greek and Latin anthologies inspired by a multitude of contemporary events or royal and commemorative occasions,[11] and inclusion in such was frequently a means of self-advertisement on the part of a budding author. The expertise of the neo-Latin poet lay in an ability not to replicate skillfully, but to appropriate to a contemporary context or subject the very linguistic medium employed, for example, by the poets of Augustan Rome. Addison's prowess in this regard has indeed earned him not insignificant praise through the centuries.[12] Edmund Smith, for example, in the dedication of his *Phaedra*, published in London in 1714, described Addison's *Pax Gulielmi* as "the best Latin poem since the *Aeneid*,"[13] while Samuel Johnson would later say of the same poem that "the performance cannot be denied to be vigorous and elegant."[14]

But while Addison was seen to emulate the classical Latin poets whom he imitated, so too was he regarded as surpassing his peers.[15] Or to

---

[10] On the role of Latin in the seventeenth-century educational curriculum, cf. D.L. Clark, *John Milton at St Paul's School: A Study of Ancient Rhetoric in English Renaissance Education* (New York, 1948; rpt Hamden, 1964); W.T. Costello, *The Scholastic Curriculum at Early Seventeenth-Century Cambridge* (Cambridge, 1958).

[11] For example, after the return of Charles II Oxford published twelve such volumes between 1660 and 1700, and Cambridge produced ten. Cf. Leicester Bradner, *Musae Anglicanae: A History of Anglo-Latin Poetry 1500-1925* (Oxford, 1940), 206-207, at 206. For Addison's contribution to Oxford anthologies, see 14-29 below.

[12] Cf. Peter Smithers, *The Life of Joseph Addison* (Oxford, 1968), 11.

[13] *Phaedra and Hippolitus*: Dedication (to Lord Halifax), in *The Works of Mr. Edmund Smith* (London, 1714). Cf. Smithers, *The Life of Joseph Addison*, 38.

[14] Johnson, "Addison," 646. This is all the more striking when set alongside Johnson's severe criticism of three of Addison's other Latin poems, on which see 50 below.

[15] Cf. Thomas Tickell, ed. *The Works of the Right Honourable Joseph Addison* (London, 1721), I, vi (Preface): "He first distinguished himself by his Latin

approach this from a Macaulian perspective, so to speak: it is one thing for the multitudes to compose, but another to excel, to stand out from those multitudes. That Preface to *Poems on Several Occasions* (1719) proceeds to offer an interesting if somewhat unusual perspective of Addison among contemporary or near contemporary Latin poets, whereby he emerges as an Anglo-Latin poet taking his place alongside neo-Latin poets on the continent. The author begins by bewailing the fact that "since the general disuse and corruption of the Latin tongue, there are not many attempts in poetry in that language that retain the purity and graces of the Augustan age."[16] He then assesses the neo-Latin achievements of individual nations, highlighting among the Italians Vida as "the most pure and elegant, tho' some are offended at the perpetual imitation of his darling Virgil ... ,"[17] no one of significance among the French,[18] Grotius and Heinsius among the Dutch,[19] and Buchanan among the Scottish.[20] The analysis then shifts to Addison himself:

> As to our own nation, the occasional copies in the University collections are the best poems we have, the chief of which are published in the *Musae Anglicanae*, though I have read a great many more which deserve an equal honour. Out of these we have singled the poems of Mr Addison as the most shining ornaments of that work.[21]

Thus had Addison's reputation in this field already been established some one and a half centuries previous to Macaulay's pertinent observation.

The reference is to the *Musarum Anglicanarum Analecta* published at Oxford in 1699, an anthology of Anglo-Latin verse composed largely by scholars of Oxford University. To the second volume of this collection Addison contributed no fewer than eight Latin poems, and is generally

---

compositions ... and was admired as one of the best authors since the Augustan age in the two universities and the greatest part of Europe before he was talked of as a poet in town."

[16] *Poems on Several Occasions*, Preface, a2^r-a2^v.

[17] *Poems on Several Occasions*, Preface, vi. On Vida as affording Addison precedent for the mock-heroic neo-Latin "sports" poem, see 89-90 below.

[18] *Poems on Several Occasions*, Preface, vi: "The French have nothing considerable."

[19] *Poems on Several Occasions*, Preface, vii: "The Dutch themselves have some no mean Latin poems, as is evident from the works of Grotius and Heinsius."

[20] *Poems on Several Occasions*, Preface, viii. Buchanan is described as "the just boast of the Scots nation: he was a perfect master of the Latin tongue, knew all its strength and beauties, and very happily transfused them into his own poems."

[21] *Poems on Several Occasions*, Preface, ix.

regarded as the compiler and editor of the volume as a whole.[22] The circumstances of its publication betray the implicit esteem in which Addison regarded his Latin verse.

Addison's Latin poems first appeared without his permission in the *Examen Poeticum Duplex* (London, 1698). In response to this pirated edition he quickly issued (only six months later) the *Musae Anglicanae*,[23] in which he attacked in a Latin Preface Richard Wellington, the editor of the *Examen*. Addison's edition is pointedly described as a "genuine one, printed by the permission of its authors,"[24] while Wellington is presented as a money-maker seeking to capitalize at the expense of his authors' reputations. The poems included in the *Examen* are likened to deformed children, the product of gross disfiguration on the part of men, children thereby rendered unrecognizable to their parents, who would blush if by chance they did recognize them.[25] The metaphor is a telling one. For Addison, his neo-Latin poems constitute his "offspring," the product of careful nurturing. Indeed in the *Musae* he carefully signs eight poems as his own.

Addison's neo-Latin poetic voice was indeed nurtured, formulated and expressed at an early age. That he acquired a youthful fondness for things classical is attested by Macaulay's albeit overly enthusiastic comments that " at fifteen he was not only fit for the university, but carried thither a classical taste and a stock of learning which would have done honour to a Master of Arts,"[26] and that while at Queen's College, Oxford "the young scholar's diction and versification were already such

---

[22] Cf. Lucy Aikin, *The Life of Joseph Addison* (London, 1843), 61. Note, however, Bradner, *Musae Anglicanae*, 219, who correctly observes that the only evidence of Addison's editorship is "the signature to the dedication and a review in *Works of the Learned*, February 1699." Cf. Bradner, "Addison's Latin Poems," 359-360; Wiesenthal, *The Latin Poetry of the English Augustans*, 47.

[23] Cf. Smithers, *The Life of Joseph Addison*, 39: "Whether he was already at work upon a second volume of *Musarum Anglicanarum* in the capacity of editor, or whether he was goaded to undertake the task by the piracy, he produced such a book, which was registered on 9 February 1699."

[24] *Musarum Anglicanarum Analecta* (Oxford, 1699), II, a2^r: *Praefatio: sed illud et genuinum et auctorum permissu impressum.* (Hereinafter abbreviated to *Musae Anglicanae*).

[25] *Musae Anglicanae*, II, a2^r: *Praefatio: Londiniensi editori hanc laudem concedimus ut poetarum famae dispendio sibi quaestum faciat, illis parum invidentes qui opera adeo mutila et furtiva typis mandarunt ut deformes partus aut non agnoverint ipsi parentes aut agnitis erubuerint.*

[26] Macaulay, "The Life and Writings of Addison," 733.

as veteran professors might envy."[27] Johnson states that it was his Latin
verses that were responsible for Addison's first eminence at Magdalen,[28]
while Macaulay relays the interesting anecdote that the "ancient doctors
of Magdalen continued to talk in their common room of his boyish
compositions, and expressed the sorrow that no copy of exercises so
remarkable had been preserved."[29]

What has been preserved transcends the realm of mere pedagogy
to constitute a corpus of erudite and witty neo-Latin verse. As regards
volume, it should be remarked that when compared with the multiple
Spectator and *Tatler* papers, Addison's output of Latin poetry appears
slight. His extant Latin poems are eleven in number, and they total 915
lines.[30] The majority were composed between 1689 and 1694. Several are
occasional pieces: for example, the *Tityrus et Mopsus* celebrating the
inauguration of William III in 1689,[31] the *Pax Gulielmi Auspiciis
Europae Reddita 1697* on the Peace of Ryswick,[32] or Addison's
unpublished and hitherto overlooked Latin verses on the Vigo expedition
(1702), edited and discussed for the first time in the present study.[33]
Others treat of contemporary phenomena, pastimes, art or politics, be it
the barometer (*Barometri Descriptio*),[34] a potentially allegorical quasi-
mythological epyllion on Pygmies and cranes (*Proelium inter Pygmaeos
et Grues Commissum*),[35] a puppet show (*Machinae Gesticulantes*),[36] a

---

[27] Macaulay, "The Life and Writings of Addison," 734.

[28] Johnson, "Addison," 644: "Here he continued to cultivate poetry and criticism, and
grew first eminent by his Latin compositions, which are indeed entitled to particular
praise."

[29] Macaulay, "The Life and Writings of Addison," 734.

[30] This calculation includes four Latin epigrams (totaling 24 lines) on the Vigo
expedition, all of which are almost certainly by Addison (i.e. in addition to the 10-line
Vigo poem formally attributed to him). See the manuscript evidence discussed at 126-
129 below.

[31] See Chapter 1 below.

[32] For a good discussion of this poem, see the article by Williams and Kelsall cited at
viii above.

[33] Unpublished, these verses by Addison survive in a manuscript in the British
Library. See Chapter 7 below.

[34] See Chapter 2 below.

[35] See Chapter 3 below.

[36] See Chapter 4 below.

bowling green (*Sphaeristerium*),[37] or a mural in the chapel of Magdalen College, Oxford (*Resurrectio Delineata*).[38] For the most part they may be described as situation poems, and are lacking in any strong personal element.[39] In addition to these poems there are three further pieces which have at various times been attributed to him.[40]

When regarded in a neo-Latin context a number of factors emerge. Firstly, it is clear that the composition of Latin poetry was for Addison much more than "a harmless scholarly pastime."[41] Rather he seems quite consciously to have endeavored to achieve a reputation as a neo-Latin poet and not without the aim of self-promotion. Through the composition of Latin verse and the recitation of Latin prose he fitted into an academic Oxford community. That sense of place, of belonging, is reflected by the fact that he contributed Latin poems to University anthologies in 1689 and 1697. But far from being confined to the written word, Latin was also for Addison a vibrant oral and performative medium. In 1692 he delivered an eloquent essay on the Roman poets: *Dissertatio de Insignioribus Romanorum Poetis*.[42] One year later, at the University Encaenia of 7 July 1693, he, and two of his Magdalen colleagues,[43] delivered Latin prose orations[44] on the debate of old philosophy versus the new. Addison's work is colored by Ciceronian rhetoric, and obviously created an impression. When it was published posthumously by Curll, an

---

[37] See Chapter 5 below.

[38] See Chapter 6 below.

[39] The closest Addison comes to voicing personal sentiment is in the two Horatian Odes to Dr Edward Hannes and Thomas Burnet respectively.

[40] Two of these were included in the *Musae Anglicanae*, II: the *Proelium Navale* (136-139) and a piece on skating, entitled *Cursus Glacialis* (145-147). There is in fact quite a strong case for Addison's authorship of the first of these (see Bradner, "Addison's Latin Poems," 364-366). Finally, a Latin verse fragment included (without attribution) in *Spectator*, 412 may be the product of Addison's muse.

[41] Smithers, *The Life of Joseph Addison*, 11. Cf. Wiesenthal, *The Latin Poetry of the English Augustans*, 48.

[42] See Guthkelch, ed., *Miscellaneous Works*, II, 471-477. Contrast the unfavorable viewpoint of Wiesenthal, *The Latin Poetry of the English Augustans*, 51: "As a document of literary criticism, its only interest to us lies in its typicality of late seventeenth-century taste."

[43] Richard Smallbroke and Edward Taylor. Cf. Smithers, *The Life of Joseph Addison*, 20.

[44] These were published in the *Theatri Oxoniensis Encaenia, Sive Comitia Philologica Julii 7 Anno 1693 Celebrata* (Oxford, 1693), L2^v-N2^v.

advertisement proclaimed that Addison's piece (*Nova Philosophia Veteri Praeferenda Est*) was worth more than the price of the whole volume.[45] And it seems to be the case that this self-integration into an Oxford community was not unrewarded. Evidence would suggest that it was one of his earliest Latin poems that earned him an election to a demyship at Magdalen College.[46] Latin then would ultimately serve as a means of furthering the youthful poet's career. In a sense this could be viewed as a microcosmic equivalent of that career advancement of Milton and Marvell achieved largely in recognition of their abilities as Latinists. It is clear, moreover, that in the course of his continental tour Addison used the *Musae Anglicanae* as a passport, as it were, to erudite societies, as an important means of self-introduction and self-promotion.[47] Thus armed with this volume, did he seek perhaps to transcend the boundaries of both nationality and language.

In 1700 Addison met Boileau in Paris, to whom, according to Tickell, he presented a copy of the *Musae*. Boileau, in response, said "that he did not question but there were excellent compositions in the native language of a country that possessed the Roman genius in so eminent a degree."[48] Johnson, however, does not hold much store by Boileau's praise since the latter "had an injudicious and peevish contempt of modern Latin, and therefore his profession of regard was probably the effect of his civility rather than approbation."[49] Macaulay, by contrast, questions Johnson's viewpoint, arguing that Boileau was not "so ignorant or tasteless as to be incapable of appreciating good modern Latin."[50] In support of his argument he cites one of Boileau's letters, in which he praises a modern Latin poem sent to him as worthy of Vida and

---

[45] *A Dissertation Upon the Most Celebrated Roman Poets* (London, 1718). For a text of the work, cf. Guthkelch, ed. *Miscellaneous Works*, II, 467-469.

[46] See 14-15, 31-32 below.

[47] Cf. Courthope, *Addison*, 37: "It is characteristic both of his own tastes and of his age that he seems to have thought his best passport to intellectual society abroad would be his Latin poems."

[48] Cf. Tickell, ed., *The Works of the Right Honourable Joseph Addison*, I, vi-vii (Preface): "Our country owes it to him that the famous Monsieur Boileau first conceived an opinion of the English genius for poetry by perusing the present he made him of the *Musae Anglicanae* ... The true and natural compliment made by him was that those books had given him a very new idea of the English politeness."

[49] Johnson, "Addison," 644.

[50] Macaulay, "The Life and Writings of Addison," 741.

Sannazaro, but not of Horace and Virgil.[51] And by a strange paradox Boileau himself had used Latin verse as the medium for criticizing modern Latin.[52] For these reasons Macaulay believes that Boileau's praise was sincere,[53] and that "he entirely opened himself to Addison with a freedom which was a sure indication of esteem."[54] That the esteem was mutual is suggested by the brief character sketch of him provided by Addison in a letter to Bishop Hough written in November, 1700,[55] and by the references to Boileau in the *Spectator* essays.[56] All things considered, there is probably no valid reason to question the sincerity of Boileau's praise. Such perhaps was the power of Addison's Latin verse.

One of the chief hallmarks of that verse is its fusion of the contemporary and the classical. Now neo-Latin becomes the medium for modern descriptions of fireworks displays or puppet shows in late seventeenth-century London, or the mechanics of such inventions as the barometer, or the puppet, or the toy soldiers with which a young prince William plays as though in imitation of his father's real military exploits. Noteworthy too is a frequently mock-heroic tone characterizing, for example, the description of the moods and graces of a puny pygmy race

---

[51] Macaulay, "The Life and Writings of Addison," 741 : "Ne croyez pas pourtant que je veuille par là blâmer les vers Latins que vous m'avez envoyés d'un de vos illustres académiciens. Je les ai trouvés fort beaux, et dignes de Vida et de Sannazaro, mais non pas d'Horace et de Virgile."

[52] Macaulay, "The Life and Writings of Addison," 741, continues: "Indeed it happens, curiously enough, that the most severe censure ever pronounced by him on modern Latin is conveyed in Latin hexameters. We allude to the fragment which begins: *quid numeris iterum me balbutire Latinis/longe Alpes citra natum de patre Sicambro,/ Musa, iubes?*"

[53] Macaulay, "The Life and Writings of Addison," 741: "For these reasons we feel assured that the praise which Boileau bestowed on the *Machinae Gesticulantes* and the *Gerano-Pygmæomachia* was sincere."

[54] Macaulay, "The Life and Writings of Addison," 741.

[55] Writing from Marseilles on 29 November 1700, Addison states: "Among other learned men that I have waited on I had the good fortune to be introduced to Monsr. Boileau, who is now retouching his works and putting them out in a new edition. He is old and deaf, but talks incomparably well in his own calling. He heartily hates an ill poet, and puts himself in a passion when he talks of anyone that has not a high respect for the ancients" (*The Letters of Joseph Addison*, ed. Walter Graham, [Oxford, 1941], 25-26).

[56] For example, in *Spectator*, 183 (29 September 1711) Addison calls Boileau "the most correct poet among the moderns" (Bond, ed. II, 220) and in *Spectator*, 592 (10 September 1714) "a true critic" (Bond, ed. V, 26).

(as if in anticipation of Swift),[57] or the vivid powers of description evident in Addison's ekphrastic representation of a mural on the Last Judgment, which used to grace Magdalen College Chapel. Such poems pulsate with energy and color, invigorating their subject through the power of the word or, more specifically, the power of the Latin word.

Yet the appeal of Addison's Latin poetry lies not only in its refreshingly modern subject matter. Hand in hand with this is the appropriation of the language and imagery of classical, in particular Augustan, Latin poets. It is in this regard that Addison's Latin poetry when examined in relation to its so-called "classical" models is essentially parodic, its methodology anticipating that mock-heroic trend that would come to characterize much of eighteenth-century vernacular literature. Johnson refrained from identifying a single author as "influencing" Addison's Latin verse: thus "he has not confined himself to the imitation of any ancient author, but has formed his style from the general language, such as a diligent perusal of the productions of different ages happened to supply."[58] It is true that some of the Latin pieces engage with several Augustan poets, as is evident in their adoption of line endings from, say, Ovid or Tibullus. Similarly adaptation of the thought and meter of Horatian Odes (as in the Odes to Hannes and Burnet) indicates Addison's deep acquaintance with Horace. For the most part, however, his Latin poetry is distinguished by an unmistakable and frequently exuberant Virgilianism.

> Oh could the Muse my ravish'd breast inspire
> With warmth like yours, and raise an equal fire,
> Unnumber'd beauties in my verse should shine,
> And Virgil's Italy should yield to mine![59]

Thus proclaims Addison in his quest for inspiration, in his professed longing to emulate and surpass the greatest poet of Augustan Rome. Elsewhere he exclaims that Dryden's "lines have heightened Virgil's majesty."[60] But heightening Virgil's majesty is a skill possessed by Addison himself — at least by Addison the neo-Latin poet, for whom, it will be seen, Virgil constituted an important inspirational Muse. As Macaulay remarked:

---

[57] On links between Addison and Swift, see 65-66 below.

[58] Johnson, "Addison." 644.

[59] Addison, "A Letter From Italy" (1704), 51-54. See Guthkelch, ed. *Miscellaneous Works*, I, 53-54.

[60] Addison, "To Mr Dryden" (1693), 13. Guthkelch, ed. *Miscellaneous Works*, I, 3.

> Everybody who had been at a public school had written Latin verses with tolerable success, and were quite able to appreciate, though by no means able to rival, the skill with which Addison imitated Virgil.[61]

The present study will argue that this skill is most readily apparent in Addison's reworking of the *Georgics*, which, along with other Virgilian texts, functions as a major subtext of his neo-Latin poetry. And his regard for the *Georgics* is mirrored on a vernacular level also in, for example, his verse translation of most of *Georgics* 4 (1694),[62] in his *Essay on Virgil's Georgics* (1697),[63] prefixed to Dryden's translation (which in itself would prove extremely influential in gauging and determining the reception of Virgil's didactic poem in seventeenth-century England),[64] and later in the abundance of Virgilian quotations in his *Spectator* and *Tatler* essays.[65]

Addison's Latin prose dissertation on the Roman poets opens by according the highest place to Virgil: *omnium in re poetica maxime inclaruerunt Romani, et Romanorum Virgilius.*[66] His *Essay on Virgil's Georgics* reiterates such praise:

> ... And herein consists Virgil's masterpiece, who has not only excelled all other poets, but even himself in the language of his *Georgics.*[67]

And then more famously:

---

[61] Macaulay, "The Life and Writings of Addison," 736.

[62] "A Translation of All Virgil's Fourth *Georgic*, Except the Story of Aristaeus," first published in *The Annual Miscellany* (London, 1694), 58-86. See Guthkelch, ed. *Miscellaneous Works*, I, 7-18, and Appendix 3 below.

[63] Guthkelch, ed. *Miscellaneous Works*, II, 3-11. See Appendix 4 below.

[64] See John Chalker, *The English Georgic* (London, 1969), 17-30, at 17: "In form the *Essay* is modest enough, but its influence upon subsequent attitudes to the *Georgics* bore no relation to its size or scope. When discussing this type of didactic poetry both early and mid-century critics take Addison's dicta as their starting-point, and often do little more than vary his phraseology."

[65] See, for example, 34, 37 below.

[66] *Dissertatio de Insignioribus Romanorum Poetis*, Guthkelch, ed. *Miscellaneous Works*, II, 471.

[67] *An Essay on Virgil's Georgics* (1693) in Guthkelch, ed. *Miscellaneous Works*, II, 8. See Appendix 4 below. Cf. *Dissertatio: apud quemlibet Georgicorum librum inimitabili quadam sermonis elegantia res rusticae explicantur, sed ultimus de apum natura valde praeter ceteros animum delectat* (Guthkelch, ed. *Miscellaneous Works*, II, 471).

> He delivers the meanest of his precepts with a kind of grandeur, he
> breaks the clods and tosses the dung about with an air of gracefulness.
> His prognostications of the weather are taken out of Aratus, where we
> may see how judiciously he has picked out those that are most proper
> for his husbandman's observation; how he has enforced the expression,
> and heightened the images which he found in the original.[68]

In his Latin poems the reworking of the *Georgics* operates on several
complex levels: thus a whole series of weather signs afforded the cautious
farmer by the natural world (*Georgics* 1) is transmuted into weather
forecasts facilitated by the rising or setting of mercury in the barometer;[69]
elsewhere in, for example, the *Proelium inter Pygmaeos et Grues
Commissum* or the *Machinae Gesticulantes*, the bee community of
Georgics 4 is adapted to describe the nature and behavior of Pygmies[70] or
puppets,[71] beneath whose miniature size there lie an heroic grandeur and
an essentially warlike spirit.

But if the *Georgics* is perhaps the most pervasively Virgilian
subtext of Addison's Latin verse, it is not the only one. Addison also
turns to the *Eclogues* in, for example, his pastoral hymn *Tityrus et
Mopsus* celebrating the inauguration of King William and Queen Mary.[72]
And frequently surprising echoes of Virgilian epic occur in Latin poems
which are marked by their social, religious, political or military contexts.
Thus the games of *Aeneid* 5 are reborn in a seventeenth-century bowling
match;[73] aspects of the underworld of *Aeneid* 6 are inverted in the
Resurrectio Delineata to describe a Christian mural on the Last
Judgment;[74] the passion of Virgil's Dido, and the associated fire imagery,
are appropriated to a contemporary military context in a series of
epigrams on the Vigo expedition.[75]

---

[68] Guthkelch, ed. *Miscellaneous Works*, II, 9. See Appendix 4 below. Cf. Addison,
Spectator, 417 (28 June 1712: ed. Bond, III, 565): "In his *Georgics* [he] has given us a
collection of the most delightful landscapes that can be made out of fields and woods,
herds of cattle, and swarms of bees."

[69] See 43-49 below.

[70] See 55-62 below.

[71] See 80-87 below.

[72] See 21-27 below.

[73] See 94-103 below.

[74] See 113-116 below.

[75] See 130-137 below.

Addison's love of Virgil colors much of his Latin poetry, but he uses him merely as a springboard, as it were: as a "model" in only the most general of senses. Emulating his classical predecessor, he adapts Virgilian language and the contexts in which that language was employed, and does so to ironic effect. It is for this reason that a detailed textual examination of Addison's Latin poetry vis-à-vis Virgil can shed much light on the former's methodology. Such, it will be argued, reveals much more than the germ of that mannered erudition of the *Spectator* and *Tatler* papers. Paradoxically, it was through his inventive imitation and emulation of Virgil (and of the *Georgics* in particular) that Addison found an original Latin voice. It is a voice that would indeed set him apart from his contemporaries, enabling him to do "best what multitudes do well." Far from "passing into eclipse,"[76] Addison, the neo-Latin poet, could thereby emerge as a *Vergilius Redivivus* in late seventeenth-century England.

---

[76] Damrosch, "The Significance of Addison's Criticism," 421.

CHAPTER 1

Among the Oxford Shepherds: *Tityrus et Mopsus*

Addison's earliest extant Latin verses occur in a volume of poetry produced in 1689 by the University of Oxford in celebration of the accession to the throne of William and Mary. Entitled *Vota Oxoniensia Pro Serenissimis Guilhelmo Rege et Maria Regina M. Britanniae &c Nuncupata*, the collection is multilingual, consisting of Latin poems for the most part, but also including verses in Greek, Hebrew and English. Addison's poem, though untitled, has come to be known as *Tityrus et Mopsus* (a short title named after its two protagonists). The piece, consisting of 43 hexameters and occurring at folio O2ᵛ, is clearly attributed to its author, who is designated as of Queen's College: *Josephus Addison Commensalis e Coll. Reg.*, clear evidence of a date of composition preceding Addison's election as demy to Magdalen College on 30 July 1689.

And the verses may not be unrelated to that election. There is indeed a theory that it was this poem that occasioned Addison's election, a theory based upon dating alone, and the interpretation of a remark made by Addison's editor, Tickell. In his *Preface* to Addison's works Tickell had commented that the "accidental sight" of certain verses of Addison's in the hands of Dr William Lancaster, the bursar of Queen's College, led to Addison's election as demy.[1] That these verses may have been the *Tityrus et Mopsus* was first stated by Courthope,[2] who, however, based

---

[1] Tickell, ed. *The Works of the Right Honourable Joseph Addison*, I, v (Preface): "He had been there [Queen's College, Oxford] about two years when the accidental sight of a paper of his verses in the hands of Dr Lancaster, then Dean of that house, occasioned his being elected into Magdalen College." Cf. Johnson, "Addison," 644: "In 1687 he was entered into Queen's College in Oxford, where, in 1689, the accidental perusal of some Latin verses gained him the patronage of Dr Lancaster, afterwards provost of Queen's College; by whose recommendation he was elected into Magdalen College as a Demy, a term by which that society denominates those which are elsewhere called Scholars; young men, who partake of the founder's benefaction and succeed in their order to vacant fellowships."

[2] Courthope, *Addison*, 29-30.

his argument solely on dating, and was subsequently accepted by several Addison scholars.[3] Bradner, however, has rightly called this theory into question, stating that "it ignores the entirely mediocre quality of the poem itself,"[4] and proposing the Ode to Burnet or the *Barometri Descriptio* as much more likely candidates for the verses in question.[5] In defense of Courthope's theory perhaps is the obvious Queen's College connection and the proximity in terms of dates between the publication of the piece and Addison's election. In defense of Bradner's argument is the only slightly inferior (rather than "mediocre") quality of the poem itself when viewed alongside Addison's more masterful pieces such indeed as the Ode to Burnet and the *Barometri Descriptio*.

Modern scholarship, inasmuch as it has taken account of Addison's Latin verse,[6] regards the piece as no more than a juvenile, highly derivative and typically flattering exercise. Sutton passes it over in silence, making only the remark that it is "a competent but reasonably typical specimen of the sort of court flattery that served as the standard fare for academic anthologies."[7] Bradner suggests that Addison did not think the piece worth preserving since it was not included among his poems later anthologized in the *Musae Anglicanae*.[8] Whether or not this was the case, a close reading of the piece in relation to others in the volume and especially in terms of their reworking of Virgil suggests that in Addison's case at least what may appear at first sight to be purely derivative Virgilianism constitutes in fact a complex and highly self-

---

[3] See, for example, Smithers, *The Life of Joseph Addison*, 12-13, and especially his comment at 13: "'Tityrus et Mopsus' was something of a scholarship performance, and the subject would appeal to the restored Fellows of the college." Cf. Wiesenthal, *The Latin Poetry of the English Augustans*, 51.

[4] Bradner, "Addison's Latin Poems," 359. He continues: "Standards of Latin verse were too high at Oxford at this time to allow us to believe that this mechanical piece of congratulation, which neither Addison nor Tickell thought worth preserving, could have earned its author a coveted promotion."

[5] Bradner, "Addison's Latin Poems," 359. As Bradner notes, Addison's remaining Latin poems can be dated to later than 1689.

[6] See in general vii-viii, 1-2 above.

[7] Sutton, ed. *The Latin Prose and Poetry of Joseph Addison*, Introduction, 18.

[8] Bradner, "Addison's Latin Poems," 359. It is perhaps worth noting, however, that Addison, while not including his own poem on the subject, did anthologize in the *Musae Anglicanae* two of the *Vota Oxoniensia* pieces: Henry Aldrich, *Inauguratio Regis Gulielmi et Reginae Mariae* (*Musae Anglicanae*, II, 32-34) and Thomas Newey, *Inauguratio Regis Gulielmi et Reginae Mariae* (*Musae Anglicanae*, II, 52-55).

conscious reworking of his classical predecessor. While it may remain impossible to confirm or deny whether or not this actually was the piece that secured Addison's election to a demyship at Magdalen, the poem itself is not without interest on several counts. Not least among these is the fact that it reveals a seventeen-year-old undergraduate immersed in a close reading of Virgil, and as such foreshadows on a miniature level that all-pervasive Virgilianism exhibited by Addison's later writings. Yet even here, as elsewhere, the case is not one of slavish *imitatio* of a classical model. Instead an echo of, or allusion to, Virgilian pastoral may assume ironic force. Addison adapts phrases, evokes certain classical contexts, but only to lend an original layer of meaning to his own *retractatio*. In short, these earliest extant Latin verses reveal a poet who can skillfully manipulate a classical model, and who is most at home in the meter of the hexameter, the most prevalent meter of Addison's Latin verse. In addition to its inventive Virgilianism, moreover, is the light the piece sheds on a budding poet's role as an integrated member of an Oxford community and more generally on his early royalist allegiances. Central to a full appreciation of the merits or otherwise of these verses is a close examination of the literary context in which they first appeared. How does this work by a seventeen-year-old undergraduate compare with the pastoral poems of his peers and dons included in the *Vota Oxoniensia*? Perhaps a new reading of this hitherto neglected piece may reveal literary qualities unacknowledged by modern scholarship.

(i)   The *Vota Oxoniensia* and Virgilian Pastoral

Before discussing Addison's poem in relation to Virgil's *Eclogues*[9] (and to *Eclogue* 1 in particular) a brief survey of comparable Latin pastorals in the *Vota Oxoniensia* and a more detailed analysis of the more accomplished of these may help to place the piece in a wider contemporary context. The *Tityrus et Mopsus* is in fact one of six Latin pastoral poems scattered throughout the volume. The other five are contributed by Joseph Crabbe,[10] John Winter,[11] Bernard Gardiner,[12]

[9] On Virgil's *Eclogues* in general, see among others M.C.J. Putnam, *Virgil's Pastoral Art: Studies in the Eclogues* (Princeton, 1970); E.W. Leach, *Virgil's Eclogues: Landscapes of Experience* (Ithaca, 1974).

[10] *Vota Oxoniensia*, G1ᵛ-Giiʳ: *Carmen Pastorale: Interlocutores Tityrus et Corydon* by Joes. Crabb, A.M. *e Coll. Exon. Soc.* Of the two Joseph Crabbes listed in Joseph Foster, ed. *Alumni Oxonienses: The Members of the University of Oxford 1500-1866*

Benjamin Mander,[13] and James Buerdsell.[14] Even the most superficial of
readings would seem to suggest that although these pieces contain a wide
range of Virgilian echoes, their debt is primarily to *Eclogue* 1 (and also at
times to *Eclogue* 4). Of the five pieces in question three (by Crabbe,
Winter and Gardiner) likewise employ the name Tityrus for one of the
speakers, and use *Eclogue* 1 among their chief inspirational sources,
thereby providing an interesting context in which to view Addison's
treatment. For example, Gardiner's *Carmen Pastorale*, while briefly
echoing *Ecl*. 1 (for instance, the line ending *sub tegmine fagi* [*Ecl*. 1.1]
occurs at line 6), finds its main inspiration in *Eclogue* 4. This piece is
permeated by a sense of wonder felt by both character and landscape as
by way of pathetic fallacy the pastoral world gives several intimations of
the return of a golden age (*aurea nunc iterum nascuntur saecula mundo*
[26]). William is the *decus atque salus* (44), and his powers as conqueror
are emphasized. He is the *pater patriae* (53),[15] the guardian of the
countryside, while Mary is *veneranda* (57). Gardiner seems to rework

---

(London, 1891; rpt Nendeln, Liechtenstein, 1968), I, 344, one appears too old and the
other too young. The younger candidate did however matriculate at Exeter College (a
fact that accords with his signature in the *Vota Oxoniensia* as cited above), although
Foster records the date as 18 July 1691.

[11] *Vota Oxoniensia*, K2^r-L1^r: *Tityrus et Meliboeus Interlocutores* by Joh.Winter A.B.
Col. Mert. Probat. Soc. Winter matriculated on 30 March 1683, aged 16. He
graduated BA in 1686; was fellow of Merton College in 1688; MA in 1691. See
Foster, ed. *Alumni Oxonienses*, IV, 1662.

[12] *Vota Oxoniensia*, Q1^v-Qii^r: *Carmen Pastorale: Tityrus et Thyrsis Interlocutores* by
Gardiner, *ex Aul. Magd. Commensalis.* Gardiner matriculated on 7 November 1684,
aged 16. He graduated with a BA from Magdalen College in 1688. He subsequently
gained a BCL from All Souls College in 1693 and DCL in 1698. In his later career he
was Warden (1702-1726) and Vice-Chancellor (1711-1715). See Foster, ed. *Alumni
Oxonienses*, II, 546. See also *DNB* sv.

[13] *Vota Oxoniensia*, S1^r-S1^v: *Carmen Pastorale* (speakers Meliboeus and Corydon) by
B. Mander *e Coll Magd.* Benjamin Mander matriculated on 27 March 1685 and was
demy of Magdalen College 1686-1693. He received his BA in 1689; MA in 1691, and
was a Fellow 1693-1703. See Foster, ed. *Alumni Oxonienses*, III, 964.

[14] *Vota Oxoniensia*, T2^v (untitled): speakers Hylas, Meliboeus, and Lycidas by Jac.
Buerdsell A.B. *e C. Aen. Nas.* Buerdsell matriculated at Brasenose College on 10
April 1685, aged 15. He received his BA in 1688, Fellow and MA in 1692. See Foster,
ed. *Alumni Oxonienses*, I, 206.

[15] Gardiner applies to William the title bestowed (5 Feb., 2 BC) on Augustus by the
senate. Cf. Suetonius, *Divus Augustus* 58: *senatus te consentiens cum populo Romano
consalutat patriae patrem.*

Eclogue 4's presentation of a savior figure into a depiction of William as seventeenth-century equivalent. In its fusion of themes from more than one eclogue its methodology is not very dissimilar to that of Addison's poem. Particularly striking, as noted below, is the comparable identification of the King and Queen with the sun and moon respectively.[16] Likewise Benjamin Mander's *Carmen Pastorale* turns to *Eclogue* 4, but is not particularly Virgilian in its language. More political in its allegory, this is a hymn in honor of William as a rejuvenated Pan, guardian of the pastoral world, the patron to be praised by shepherds (*pastoresque suum debent laudare patronum* [51]), the bestower of *otia* (64), and the restorer of the golden age (*aurea Saturni veteris iam saecla redibunt* [65]).

John Winter's *Tityrus et Meliboeus* is, as its title suggests, very obviously indebted to *Eclogue* 1. The result, however, is a rather lackluster and highly derivative poem, which echoes almost verbatim several lines from Virgil. The piece is pervaded by a spirit of optimism as William is identified with Pan, the deity of the pastoral world, an identification made in a Latin poem by the Vice-Chancellor, Gilbert Ironside, prefixed to the volume: *te, deus, incolumes Pana fatentur oves* (14). In his presentation of William as Pan Winter draws upon *Eclogue* 1. Thus as Tityrus proclaims the benefits facilitated by the god (*ille meas errare boves (ut cernis) et agnos/ludere quo vellent campo permisit agresti* [25-26]), the lines are almost identical to *Ecl.* 1.9-10,[17] with Winter merely substituting *agnos* (25) for *ipsum* (9) and *campo* (26) for *calamo* (10). Tityrus' subsequent speech is again heavily indebted to Virgil. Thus at 31: *nuper ego patulae recubans sub frondibus ulmi* he echoes *Ecl.* 1.1: *Tityre, tu patulae recubans sub tegmine fagi*. The speaker recounts his sense of despair as wolves ravaged his flock and as Pan was apparently absent (*non ego vos posthac viridi proiectus in umbra/tondentes cytisum frondosa valle videbo* [54-55]) in the language of Meliboeus at *Ecl.* 1.75-76[18] and also 78.[19] The appearance of Pan, however, safeguards the sheepfold from the ravages of wolves, and the god can proclaim: *Tityre, ut ante, boves age, pasce et coge capellas* (59),

---

[16] See 22, 27 below.

[17] *ille meas errare boves, ut cernis, et ipsum/ludere quae vellem calamo permisit agresti* (Virgil, *Ecl.* 1.9-10).

[18] *non ego vos posthac viridi proiectus in antro/dumosa pendere procul de rupe videbo* (Virgil, *Ecl.* 1.75-76).

[19] *florentem cytisum et salices carpetis amaras* (Virgil, *Ecl.* 1.78).

borrowed from *Ecl.* 1.45.[20] The speaker's encomium of William is never made explicit, but only suggested on a quasi-allegorical level. On the whole Winter's piece lacks that skillful reworking and ironic adaptation manifested, as argued below, by Addison's methodology.

Where Winter's poem is informed almost exclusively by the optimistic sections of *Eclogue* 1, James Buerdsell presents a more balanced vision, in which the sorrows as well as the joys of the pastoral world come to the fore. In this respect his treatment more accurately reflects the tone of Virgil's poem. The piece is marked by that sense of despondency epitomized by the Meliboeus of *Eclogue* 1. As the poem opens Hylas asks Meliboeus the reason for his sorrow. The latter replies by lamenting the fact that an impious soldier has plundered his fields (*at nobis impius agros/diripuit miles* [4-5]), reminiscent of *Ecl.* 1.70.[21] Hylas by contrast, the equivalent of the Virgilian Tityrus, urges him to take heart, reassuring him that Pan will restore his plundered livestock. At last Meliboeus indicates his longing to repair his broken reedpipe (*iuvat reparare cicutam/quam nuper fregi* [21-22]). Buerdsell's debt to Virgil is suggested not so much by verbal echoes as by the use of contrasting shepherds, the tone of the whole, and the reassuring voice of one of the shepherds at least. But *Eclogue* 1 serves only as a point of departure, as the poem continues in a series of miniature hymns of Pan (William) and of Phyllis (Mary). Pan is braver than Mars; Phyllis conquers Pan with light. She surpasses queens as lilies do flowers.

Without doubt the most accomplished of these Virgilian pastorals is Joseph Crabbe's *Carmen Pastorale*. A close reading of this poem suggests an engagement with the *Eclogues* in general and with *Eclogue* 1 in particular, but the process of *imitatio* is rather more intricate than that exhibited by the poems discussed above. The piece takes as its subject two auspicious omens witnessed and narrated by the speakers Tityrus and Corydon. Corydon has had a vision of an ancient oak tree blooming with scarlet apples, with a golden inscription upon the foliage (*vigeat nova gloria ruris* [16]). In some respects this vision is the fulfillment of one of many prayers spoken by Damon in *Eclogue* 8. 52-53: *aurea durae/mala ferant quercus*.[22] Tityrus in reply announces that he has witnessed the Thames overflowing its banks. Both visions are regarded as auspicious

---

[20] '*pascite ut ante boves, pueri, summittite tauros*' (Virgil, *Ecl.* 1.45).

[21] *impius haec tam culta novalia miles habebit* (Virgil, *Ecl.* 1.70). Buerdsell has, however, converted prophecy into grim fact.

[22] Cf. Virgil, *Ecl.* 4.30: *et durae quercus sudabunt roscida mella*; *Ecl.* 3.70-71: *puero silvestri ex arbore lecta/aurea mala decem misi*.

omens.[23] Several of the statements made by the two shepherds echo Virgil on a thematic and less frequently verbal[24] level: the searching for a missing goat,[25] goats coming for milking twice a day,[26] the production of cheese,[27] and the proclamation of the name "Daphnis" by the pastoral landscape.[28] More importantly, it is the mood of optimism generated by the saving presence of a figure who will restore age-old values that links the poem to *Eclogue* 4, in which the birth of a child is envisaged as heralding the return of the golden age. Early in Crabbe's piece Tityrus can proclaim: *hic mihi laeta dies et luce sacratior omni* (5), while later he announces that both omens indicate future prosperity for the shepherds (*laetis pastoribus omnia cedent/prospera* [27-28]). This is rendered possible through a *patronus* (28), the unnamed William, who is seen as the agent for the return of *pietas* (*prisca redit pietas* [29]), and who by reinstating the Muses and laws is a major force of order in the poem as a whole and in the pastoral world in general (*Musas restituit veteres collapsaque iura* [32]). The poem, however, is even more closely related to *Eclogue* 1, in which Tityrus had enumerated a series of benefits provided by a *deus*,[29] benefits which appeared all the more precious when set against the pessimistic voice of Meliboeus. What Crabbe does is to negate several of Meliboeus' pessimistic statements, transforming them instead into pastoral privileges which can now be enjoyed. Thus *indoctus nec habet tam culta novalia miles* (33) negates the prediction

---

[23] The good omen of the Thames overflowing its banks can be contrasted with Horace's presentation of the inundation of the Tiber as an ill omen in *Odes* 1.2.13-20. For an inversion of the Horatian passage, see Milton, *Ad Salsillum*, 36-41.

[24] For example *cortice fagi* (59) is likewise the line ending at Virgil, *Ecl.* 5.13.

[25] *dum quaerebam errantem forte capellam* (Crabbe 12)//*vir gregis ipse caper deerraverat* (Virgil, *Ecl.* 7.7).

[26] *bisque die venient ultro ad mulctralia matres* (Crabbe 37)//*bis venit ad mulctram* (Virgil, *Ecl.* 3.30).

[27] *semper et exibit de magno caseus orbe* (Crabbe 38)//*pinguis et ingratae premeretur caseus urbi* (Virgil, *Ecl.* 1.34).

[28] *resonant en Daphnida silvae/hunc montes resonant et longo murmure valles* (Crabbe 44-45)//*Daphni, tuum Poenos etiam ingemuisse leones/interitum montesque feri silvaeque loquuntur* (Virgil, *Ecl.* 5. 27-28); *Daphninque tuum tollemus ad astra;/Daphnin ad astra feremus* (*Ecl.* 5. 51-52).

[29] *O Meliboee, deus nobis haec otia fecit./namque erit ille mihi semper deus, illius aram/saepe tener nostris ab ovilibus imbuet agnus./ille meas errare boves, ut cernis, et ipsum/ludere quae vellem calamo permisit agresti* (Virgil, *Ecl.* 1. 6-10).

made at *Ecl.* 1.70.[30] By contrast Corydon's announcement of the fall of Rome effected, it is implied, by William's campaigns (*atque equidem videor sonitus audire cadentis/Romae* [47-48]) is an ironic inversion of Tityrus' hymn to that rising city in *Ecl.* 1. 24-25.[31] Where the *deus* of *Eclogue* 1 was associated with the rising city of Rome, visited by Tityrus, the savior of Crabbe's poem is associated with that city's fall by means of the application of Rome as a metaphor for Catholicism.[32]

Perhaps only Crabbe's piece begins to come close to the methodology of careful fusion, appropriation and inversion exhibited by Addison's poem. Indeed when viewed in the context of the other Latin pastorals in the collection, Addison's youthful skill does seem to stand out: his echoes of Virgil are rarely verbatim. Instead he fuses several Virgilian lines, striking a whole series of parallels which in turn lend irony to his adaptation. Thus it could be argued that in terms of the *Vota Oxoniensia* Addison "does best what multitudes do well." The final impression is one of thoughtful *retractatio* rather than full-scale *imitatio*.

(ii)   Virgil Reinvented: From Eclogue to Encomium

Addison's poem is cast in the form of an amoebaean dialogue between two shepherds Tityrus and Mopsus.[33] As the poem opens, Tityrus invites Mopsus to sing with him the praises of heroes, unnamed at this point, but an obvious allusion to the royal couple William and Mary, in whose honor the poet is writing. Such singing, he states, can function as a means of passing the hours pleasantly (1-5). Mopsus replies in a similar vein, suggesting that they should repay pious gifts of praise to those who have given them leisure and peace, and that the woods should resound an encomium of those who have strengthened the realm (6-9). Here Addison's shepherd highlights central aspects of the pastoral landscape. But the *otium* they have been afforded transcends the merely pastoral to

---

[30] *impius haec tam culta novalia miles habebit* (Virgil, *Ecl.* 1.70).

[31] *verum haec tantum alias inter caput extulit urbes/quantum lenta solent inter viburna cupressi* (Virgil, *Ecl.* 1. 24-25).

[32] Similarly the reference to the French as *Gallus* (*nec minus infamis trepidat formidine Gallus* [52]) assumes an additional layer of meaning in that Gallus (Gaius Cornelius Gallus [69-26 BC], soldier and elegiac poet) is the singer of Virgil's tenth *Eclogue*. Cf. also Virgil, *Ecl.* 6.64ff.

[33] For a complete text and translation of this and other Latin poems of Addison discussed in the present study, see Appendices 1 and 2 below.

assume a meaning of political peace and stability.[34] Tityrus believes that his humble reedpipe can scarcely match the grand nature of his epic theme, but he makes the gnomic statement that in mighty matters to have the will is frequently sufficient. Hence he will sing the praises of William and Mary (now explicitly named), and echoing the words of the marriage ceremony in the Book of Common Prayer,[35] he proclaims that it is wrong to part those whom love has joined together (10-13). Now from four-line statements, the poem continues in a series of two-line quasi-epigrammatic pronouncements. Mopsus, likewise assuming the modesty topos, asks Phoebus and the Muses to be favorable to him as he sings, lest the honors of the King and Queen be diminished by the fault of his talent (14-15). In amoebaean fashion Tityrus picks up the theme and counters it in a rather surprising statement: he by contrast does not care for Phoebus or the Muses, and implies that he does not need their aid since he finds the subject matter, the theme (*lemma* [17]), conducive to his song (16-17). These preliminaries are followed by a series of encomia in which one shepherd strives to match or outdo the other in paired statements: William and Mary are ennobled by royal birth, but more so by their own virtues (Mopsus [18-19]); William possesses many realms – the heart, as well as literal kingdoms and seas (Tityrus [20-21]) (and here in the Latin word *maria* Addison as Tityrus may incorporate a punning reference to Mary). Mopsus takes up a new theme, now equating William with Mars, and Mary with Pallas, each of whom can inflict a wound though in very different ways: the one by his weaponry; the other by her beauty (22-23). Tityrus, perhaps embellishing that Mary/*maria* pun, remarks on how the ocean began to surge as they sailed upon its waters (24-25); in reply, Mopsus outlines the reaction of the pastoral landscape as the royal couple touched land, with shepherds sacrificing a lamb to Pan (26-27). Tityrus in turn observes that the fields resounded with music as shepherds and nymphs danced (28-29). Picking up and reworking his previous reference to a sacrificial lamb, Mopsus describes the sporting of a lamb in the fields (30-31). Tityrus states that William conquers hearts, the enemy, and even his very self (32-33). In reply, Mopsus states that Mary shares her virtue and her kingdom – she is worthy of three realms and indeed of her husband (34-35). Where in Tityrus' eyes William is the sun outshining the stars (36-37), Mopsus sees Mary as the moon resplendent amid lesser constellations (38-39).

---

[34] On the political connotations of *otium*, cf. *OLD* sv. 4: "(in political contexts) A state of public peace or tranquillity; peaceful relations (with another country)." Cf. Ter., *Andr.* 20: *in bello, in otio, in negotio*; Virgil, *Aen.* 6.813: *otia qui rumpet patriae*.

[35] As observed by Sutton, ed. *The Latin Prose and Poetry of Joseph Addison, ad loc.*

The whole concludes in a prayer that the royal pair may enjoy the peace
and quiet that they have bestowed upon their subjects (Mopsus: 42), and
a wish that their stars may shine long and late (Tityrus: 43).

Links between Addison's poem and Virgil's *Eclogues* are
unmistakable in this piece. Such are suggested not so much by verbal
echoes as by the device of contrasting shepherds, the tone of the whole,
and the reassuring voice of one of the shepherds at least. In particular, the
debt to *Eclogue* 1 is apparent, a debt matched indeed, as noted above, by
the majority of the other Latin pastorals included in the collection.[36]

Typical of Addison's methodology is his merging of a wealth of
Virgilian resonances. For example, the poem's opening line: *hic inter
corylos, umbrosa cacumina, densas* fuses two lines from the *Eclogues*
(*hic inter densas corylos* [1.14] and *tantum inter densas, umbrosa
cacumina, fagos* [2.3]). In so doing it adapts Virgil to a very different
context. In Addison, Tityrus is outlining the pastoral setting for the
shepherds' joyful song. The echo of Virgil is surely ironic given the fact
that in *Eclogue* 1.14 the speaker, Mopsus, was far from joyous: this was
the spot where his goat had in fact abandoned the hope of her flock, the
twin kids to whom she had given birth.[37] There the beauty of the normal
pastoral locale had been undermined by references to bare flint amid
hazels, the grim nature of the scene being epitomized perhaps by an
exclamatory *a!* (15). In Virgil, the whole was a visual embodiment of the
pessimism that is associated with the threat to the pastoral landscape so
prevalent in that *Eclogue*. Addison's echo of Virgil only shows how
different is the context in which his shepherds are singing their song. He
also incorporates the *umbrosa cacumina* from *Ecl.* 2.3, but again the
contrast is noteworthy. In Virgil, Corydon visited the landscape, the
dense beeches with their shady summits, but the purpose of his visit was
to sing a solitary song (*solus* [4]) and to utter his love lament to the
woods. Now by contrast solitude is displaced by companionship, while
the song that is to be sung is one of joy, not lovesickness, a hymn of
praise to a royal couple.

The apparent debt to Virgil continues in the following lines.
Addison's *nos cantare pares quoniam convenimus ambo* (2) again fuses
two lines from the *Eclogues* (*et cantare pares et respondere parati* [7.5]
and *cur non, Mopse, quoniam convenimus ambo* [5.1]). Addison has
borrowed the line ending straight from Virgil, as indeed does John

---

[36] See 16-21 above.

[37] *spem gregis, a! silice in nuda conixa reliquit* (Virgil, *Ecl.* 1.15).

Winter in his Latin pastoral included in this collection.[38] Indeed the fact
that the addressee in Virgil was likewise named Mopsus may lend further
weight to the borrowing. But once again the context is strikingly
different. In *Eclogue* 5 the theme of that particular song was death, as
Mopsus proceeded to sing of Daphnis, and the effect of his death upon
the pastoral landscape. The song sung by the Mopsus of Addison's poem
is by contrast one of the vibrant living and of the gift of pastoral *otium*
conferred by both William and Mary.[39] It could be argued then that the
explicit Virgilianism of these opening lines serves to demonstrate the
essential *difference* between Addison's shepherds and their Virgilian
counterparts. It is a contrast that is maintained as the poem progresses,
and again the whole is highlighted rather self-consciously.

Addison's piece is pervaded by a rather atypical theme: the *laudes
heroum* (3), all the more striking for its inclusion in these pastoral
surroundings, as though the singing shepherds can appropriate to their
own world those *heroum laudes* of the so-called messianic *Eclogue* 4,
essentially epic qualities to be recognized by the savior child (*heroum
laudes et facta parentis* [4. 26]). Viewed in this light Tityrus' statement
ut, Mopse, solemus (3) is surely ironic, for epic themes are certainly not
the norm in a pastoral world: in many respects they constitute the
exception rather than the rule. Even Virgil, after all, proclaimed when
including epic subject matter in *Eclogue* 4: *paulo maiora canamus!* (4.1).
There the pastoral landscape, its forests and lowly tamarisks, were unable
to please all – hence the elevation of the whole to a loftier plane. In view
of the echo of *Eclogue* 4 Addison's statement *tempora transibunt sic
laeta canentibus* (4) is double-edged. On the surface it refers to the way
in which singing can enable time to pass by quite happily, a theme found
in, for example, *Ecl.* 9.[40] But the whole notion of *laeta tempora* and of
their passing (*transibunt*) may also recall the ages predicted in *Eclogue* 4,
in particular the return of the Saturnian golden age (*redeunt Saturnia
regna* [6]) or *"talia saecla ... currite"* (46) as proclaimed by the Parcae,
or even *aderit iam tempus* (48) as the child is about to enter upon mighty

---

[38] John Winter, *Tityrus et Meliboeus*, 27 (*Vota Oxoniensia*, K2ʳ).

[39] The *otium* and *quies* under William and Mary (7 and 42) are paralleled by the *pax
aurea* in a Latin poem by Walter Moyle: *venit tandem pax aurea blandis/auspiciis,
venit alma quies, bellique recedit/horror* (*Vota Oxoniensia*, D1ᵛ, lines 7-9). Moyle
matriculated at Exeter College on 18 March 1688, aged 16. He would later become a
student of the Middle Temple (1690) and MP for Saltash (1695-1698). See Foster, ed.
Alumni Oxonienses, III, 1044.

[40] *saepe ego longos/cantando puerum memini me condere soles* (Virgil, *Ecl.* 9. 51-
52); cf. *cantantes licet usque (minus via laedet) eamus* (Virgil, *Ecl.* 9. 64).

honors. When viewed in relation to Virgil and especially in terms of the
heroum laudes of *Eclogue* 4, the *laeta tempora* seem to symbolize a new
age heralded by the accession of these royal figures, while hinting
simultaneously at the theme of the return of the golden age, a theme
which, although not mentioned explicitly by Addison, is a recurring
leitmotif in the other Latin pastorals included in the collection.[41]

To some degree the notions of epic praise, the benefits of a new
age, even the return of a golden age, underlie the poem as a whole. This
is suggested by the emphasis on the peace facilitated by the King and
Queen. And this *otium* is indeed a crucial gift bestowed upon the
shepherds, functioning not only as pastoral *otium*, but also as peace in a
more political/military context: Mopsus asks that pious gifts of praise be
rendered to those who have given *otium* and *quies* (6-7).[42] The theme will
be picked up in the poem's conclusion, and transformed into an eternal
peace that seems to transcend the merely mortal world: the prayer that
William and Mary receive the *aeternam ... quam donavere quietem* (42).
And the theme takes the poem full circle, as it were – back to the world
of *Eclogue* 1, a poem so central to Addison's conception. There after all
it was a god who afforded Tityrus his *otium* (*o Meliboee, deus nobis haec
otia fecit./namque erit ille mihi semper deus* [6-7]). Addison may be
drawing a subtle connection between the royal figures of his poem and
divinity itself. Later they will be compared to pagan gods. Again,
however, the potential for epic heroism is embedded amidst these
pastoral references. The phrase *munera laudum* (6) looks to the
exhortation to celebration as a consequence of Hercules' heroic defeat of
the monstrous Cacus in *Aeneid* 8.[43] William and Mary have certainly
provided the shepherds with *otium*, but it is much more than the normal
pastoral peace so central to the *locus amoenus*, a fact made evident in the
following quasi-prosaic line. Now the woods are to resound the
encomium of those who have deigned to *regni fulcire ruinas* (9). The
combination of *silvae* and *resonare* may echo *Eclogue* 1.5,[44] but the

---

[41] Cf. Walter Moyle, *Vota Oxoniensia*, D1ᵛ, lines 10-11: *iam redit et virgo, terras repetitque relictas/Astraea, et niveis caelo demittitur alis*; Richard Roach, *Vota Oxoniensia*, G2, lines 28-30: *auspice te vero redeunt Saturnia saecla,/aurea Libertas iterum rediviva triumphat/vexillis inscripta tuis*; Thomas Hanson, *Vota Oxoniensia*, Q2ᵛ, lines 28-29: *Pax aurea pennis/emicat, et pleno descendit copia cornu.*

[42] *nunc reddantur eis pia munera laudum/otia qui dederint nobis placidamque quietem* (6-7).

[43] *tantarum in munere laudum* (Virgil, *Aen.* 8. 273).

[44] *formosam resonare doces Amaryllida silvas* (Virgil, *Ecl.* 1.5).

praises of the beloved (which the woods were taught to resound) are now transformed into an encomium of royalty itself. Likewise the *regnum* here is more than *mea regna* (*Ecl.* 1.69) whose imminent loss Meliboeus had lamented.[45] Whereas in Virgil, a shepherd was virtually exiled from the world that was his kingdom, as he imagined it being possessed by an impious soldier, in Addison, the ruin of a kingdom is actually averted, as is indicated by the forceful *fulcire*.[46]

Despite his comment *ut ... solemus* (3) Tityrus states that such great themes do not suit his humble and slender reed (*tanta haud conveniunt humili tenuique cicutae* [10]): epic themes are not the customary shepherd song. Another neo-Latin pastoral had likewise indicated the possibility of epic material not befitting the pastoral pipe. In Milton's *Epitaphium Damonis*, a pastoral lament on the death of the poet's close friend Charles Diodati, composed some 50 years previously, the speaker Thyrsis when attempting *nescio quid grande* (155) had proceeded to convey how his pastoral reed had broken under the strain.[47] But the essentially British Arthurian epic proposed in that instance by Milton (as Thyrsis) becomes in Addison's poem a British epic on very different heroes: William and Mary.[48] Amid this heroic grandeur Addison turns to the world of Augustan lyric poetry, echoing Tibullus[49] and more strikingly, Horace. Now the traditional invocation for inspiration is shrouded in terms ironically evocative of Horace's renunciation of epic themes. As Mopsus asks for the favor of Phoebus and the Muses, he does so *ne culpa ingenii illorum minuantur honores* (15). In *Odes* 1.6 Horace by way of the device of *praeteritio* claims that he is incapable of singing the praises of Caesar on his unwarlike lyre.[50] The Muse will not permit

---

[45] *post aliquot, mea regna, videns mirabor aristas* (Virgil, *Ecl.* 1.69).

[46] In *Eclogue* 1 the *iuvenis* could in his own way avert that ruin as he stated *'pascite ut ante boves, pueri; summittite tauros'* (45), but significantly it took a god to safeguard this realm.

[47] *et tum forte novis admoram labra cicutis,/dissiluere tamen rupta compage, nec ultra/ferre graves potuere sonos* (157-159). Addison's *ipse ... canam* (12) finds precedent in Thyrsis' repeated *ipse etiam* (155) and *ipse ego .../dicam* (162-163).

[48] It is ironic that neither Milton nor Addison would eventually write the Latin epic poem envisaged in their respective Latin pastorals.

[49] Thus line 11 recalls Tibullus 3.7.6-7: *dictis ut non maiora supersint/est nobis voluisse satis.*

[50] Horace, *Odes* 1.6.8-12: *nec .../conamur, tenues grandia, dum pudor/imbellisque lyrae Musa potens vetat/laudes egregii Caesaris et tuas/culpa deterere ingeni.*

him to diminish the praises of Augustus through his own lack of talent. Addison inverts Horace, for instead of being forbidden by a Muse of lyric to sing the praises of a Caesar, Mopsus actually invokes the gods and the Muses to assist him in this endeavor and to compensate for any possible shortcomings in terms of his own poetic and pastoral talent. And echoes of Horace will indeed recur in the poem's closing lines.[51]

Tityrus' response is surprising: *ast ego nec Phoebum curo Phoebive sorores* (16): he does not need such inspiration since the theme suits his song, an inversion perhaps of a comment made by Menalcas in *Eclogue* 3 that Phoebus loves him, and his ensuing account of the honors he in turn bestows upon that god.[52] And yet Tityrus' comment is doubly ironic in view of the fact that later in the poem William himself is seen as a virtual sun-god, Phoebus himself. The lines proceed with a pun on Mary, the name of the Queen, and *maria* as the neuter plural "seas," a pun which may render a double meaning to the line. If a king is one who rules the vast tides of the heart (*immanes ... pectoris aestus* [20]),[53] *tum quot regna tenet Gulielmus quotque Maria!* (21): "how many kingdoms do William and Mary possess!" or perhaps, when re-punctuated, "how many kingdoms and seas does William possess!"[54] Indeed the latter meaning makes equally good sense given the context: William controlling the tides of the heart; William ruling over the seas.

In many respects the somewhat self-conscious pastoralism of the first half of the poem gives way in the second half to epic and to the equation of the royal figureheads with pagan gods: William as Mars

---

[51] See 28-29 below.

[52] *et me Phoebus amat; Phoebo sua semper apud me/munera sunt, lauri et suave rubens hyacinthus* (Virgil, *Ecl.* 3. 62-63).

[53] Cf. Dido at *Aen.* 4.531-532 *rursusque resurgens/saevit amor magnoque irarum fluctuat aestu*. For Addison's reworking of the imagery associated with Dido's passion, see his Latin epigrams on the Vigo Expedition discussed in Chapter 7 below.

[54] This possible pun on Mary/*maria* (21) may be paralleled elsewhere in the *Vota Oxoniensia*, in, for example, Christopher Hales: *mox, ubi se dubio credit Maria profundo/pinum glauca cohors; pinum omnes undique nymphae/caeruleis cingunt gyris* (*Vota Oxoniensia*, C1^r, lines 30-32) or in Robert Reeks: *ambo bono influxu, et concordi lumine nostra/et Maria et terras sidera cara beant* (*Vota Oxoniensia*, T1^v). Christopher Hales (later Sir) matriculated at Christ Church on 28 February 1688, aged 18. He would later become MP for Coventry. See Foster, ed. *Alumni Oxonienses*, II, 630. Robert Reeks matriculated at St Mary Hall on 23 November 1686, aged 15. He would receive his BA in 1691. See Foster, *Alumni Oxonienses*, III, 1243.

(*inclitus hic Mavors* [22]);[55] Mary as Pallas (*sapiens haec altera Pallas* [22]).[56] And as if to mark the transition there is a significant decrease in terms of the Virgilianism of the lines. Now there occur several topical references. William in search of the crown sailed from the Netherlands in November 1688, and the following February Mary crossed over. Developing perhaps the *maria*/Mary pun, Addison describes the surging of the ocean, but this is not the beginning of a storm to toss a second Aeneas, as it were; on this occasion it is with pride that the sea swells. The encomium continues upon land as *Arcades omnes* (26)[57] slaughter a tender lamb in honor of Arcadian Pan.[58] This traditional pastoral sacrifice is displaced later as lambs frisk in the fields, as do *haedi ... petulci* (31).[59] The William that concludes the poem constitutes in many respects a seventeenth-century equivalent of William the Conqueror (*Victor Gulielmus* [32]), overcoming hearts, foes, even himself. He is the sun surpassing the stars, while Mary (*qualis stellas micat inter luna minores* [38]) is described in language evocative of Horace's praise of the Julian star in *Odes* 1.12.[60] The final prayer that both royal figures be late in

---

[55] For William as Mars, cf. Henry Aldrich: *te duce Gradivum poscunt desueta triumphis/agmina* (*Vota Oxoniensia*, A2ʳ, lines 30-31), or Charles Goodall: "'Tis true we must allow the God of War/Victorious Mars, but you the brighter Star/He universal Monarch with his Arms/Submits as captive to your Sov'reign charms" (*Vota Oxoniensia*, Z1ʳ, lines 33-37). Henry Aldrich (1647-1710), an important figure, entered Christ Church in 1662. He was Dean in 1689, and Vice-Chancellor 1692-1695. See Foster, ed. *Alumni Oxonienses*, I, 13.

[56] For Queen Mary as Pallas, cf. the Vice-Chancellor's prefatory poem to the *Vota Oxoniensia*: *et tu cecropios [das] stare, Minerva, lares* (12) and Henry Aldrich: *ecce suos repetit, pulso bubone, penates/cecropiasque domos dilectaque moenia Pallas* (*Vota Oxoniensia*, A2ᵛ, lines 14-15).

[57] Cf. Ovid, *Met.* 3.210.

[58] For the prevalence of the character Pan in other Latin pastorals included in the collection, see 18-19 above.

[59] Contrast Virgil, *Georgics* 4. 10-11: *neque oves haedique petulci/floribus insultent.*

[60] Horace, *Odes* 1.12.46-48: *micat inter omnis/Iulium sidus velut inter ignis/luna minores.* For William as the sun and Mary as the moon, cf. the Vice-Chancellor's poem prefixed to the *Vota Oxoniensia*: *tu das nutantem firmari Delon, Apollo* (11) and *nulla intermissae patimur dispendia lucis/dum Phoebo sociam Cynthia iungit opem* (15-16). Cf. also Arden Adderley: *non aliter Phoebo currus moderamine fesso/orbem perlustrans luna ministrat opem* (*Vota Oxoniensia*, K1ʳ); Charles Goodall: *en vultu Phoebus splendidiore micat* (*Vota Oxoniensia*, Q1ʳ, line 10); Henry Bruges: "Thy Moon still rises, when thy Sun does set" (*Vota Oxoniensia*, X2ʳ, line 20); Thomas Mompesson: *sic agit currus rapidos Olympo/Phoebus et ponit sua iura*

adorning the sky (*et sero caelos exornet sidus utrumque!* [43]) recalls Horace's wish for Augustus/Mercury to linger on earth, returning only late to the heavens: *serus in caelum redeas.*[61] Now in the poem's concluding lines that *otium* afforded the pastoral world is reciprocated in a prayer and transmuted into eternal peace or indeed into an eternal rest after apotheosis.

Tityrus et Mopsus is a multilayered pastoral which engages with Virgil on several levels. But it also moves beyond Virgil. Addison is thereby enabled to produce his own song which emulates that of his classical predecessor. In so doing he encapsulates and epitomizes that boast of *aemulatio* proclaimed by the Vice-Chancellor, Gilbert Ironside, in his Latin verses prefixed to the Oxford volume as a whole:

> et pulso cedit sua Mantua vati
> o si par caneret rura recepta Maro.

For Addison *imitatio* and *aemulatio* are inextricably linked. That lost pastoral landscape has been regained in seventeenth-century England through the inauguration of William and Mary:

> "And Virgil's Italy should yield to mine!"[62]

---

mundo;/sic et alterna vice fulva regnat/Cynthia caelo (*Vota Oxoniensia*, O1ʳ, lines 25-28); a certain Trimnell: *surgit ad Antipodas Phoebi lux clarior Anglis/ordine et hoc volvit melior nata novato./luce tua attonitus, trepidus (Gulielme!) Iacobus/ceu tenuis nubes Aurora, evanuit aula* (*Vota Oxoniensia*, I2ᵛ, lines 38-41). Cf. also John Keate at *Vota Oxoniensia*, G3ʳ, line 2: *o lux Britannis debita naufragiis*; George Stratford at H2ʳ, line 2: *o lux secunda triumphis.*

[61] Horace, *Odes* 1.2.45-46: *serus in caelum redeas diuque/laetus intersis populo Quirini.*

[62] Addison, "A Letter from Italy," 54. See Guthkelch, ed. *Miscellaneous Works*, I, 55.

CHAPTER 2

A Georgic Weather Glass: *Barometri Descriptio*

The *Barometri Descriptio* takes its place within a miniature genre of neo-Latin verse treating of essentially "modern" scientific subjects. As such it stands apart from Addison's other Latin poems, although, as argued below, the methodology of appropriation of Virgil so characteristic of his Latin verse is likewise mirrored here. In many respects the poem can be seen to epitomize his "mastery over topics of common interest, a mastery which is normally thought of as coming to light only much later in the *Tatler* and *Spectator*."[1] It thus exhibits a key hallmark of neo-Latin literature: that ability to apply the language and frequently the sentiments of ancient Rome to suit a contemporary, and in this instance, scientific topic.

And other Anglo-Latin poets were to do the same. Thomas Bisse[2] chose Latin hexameters as a means of highlighting the advantages of the microscope. His Latin poem *Microscopium*, likewise included in the *Musae Anglicanae*,[3] may not be insignificant vis-à-vis Addison's Latin corpus as a whole.[4] And if the microscope could be celebrated in Latin verse, so too could the vacuum pump, which was the subject of Bisse's *Machina Pneumatica*.[5] A much later example of the genre can be found

---

[1] Bradner, *Musae Anglicanae*, 222.

[2] Bisse was educated at Corpus Christi College, Oxford, where he graduated BA in 1695, MA in 1699, BD in 1708, DD in Jan. 1713. He was an eloquent preacher in his later years. See *DNB*, sv.; Foster, ed. *Alumni Oxonienses*, I, 132.

[3] Bisse's poem occurs at *Musae Anglicanae*, II, 163-168.

[4] In its preoccupation with the miniature, for example, Bisse's *Microscopium* is not unrelated on a methodological level to two of Addison's Latin poems: the *Proelium Inter Pygmaeos et Grues Commissum*, and to his poetic account of a puppet show in *Machinae Gesticulantes*. As noted below (see 41-43), both Bisse and Addison turn to Virgil's epic depiction of miniature bees in *Georgics* 4, and adapt Virgilian sentiment and terminology to suit a modern topic.

[5] Thomas Bisse, *Machina Pneumatica*, *Lusus Poetici* (London, 1720), 27-30.

in Thomas Gray's stunning description of the powers of the telescope in *Luna Habitabilis*,[6] which may even echo aspects of Addison's treatment.[7] Bradner has defined the characteristic features of this genre of neo-Latin poetry, a genre virtually unparalleled in classical literature:

> A further extension of the descriptive type is the poem which gives an account of some scientific instrument ... The writers we are now concerned with did not have any serious purpose for or against science. They merely regarded new instruments as something of popular interest which might be made to yield a little amusement ... The point of these *jeux d'esprit* is in the polished style and the slightly supercilious tone of simulated wonder assumed by the author.[8]

True as this may be, it should be remarked nonetheless that the tone of Addison's piece suggests a serious interest in a relatively recent scientific phenomenon.[9] This interest is mirrored in some of his other Latin and vernacular writings, which do indeed reflect a "serious purpose for or against science." That is not to say that the poem is without humor. But the "jeux d'esprit" of this piece lie not in a frivolous attempt to amuse, but in an essentially literary playfulness as Addison sports with his classical Latin models, principally the weather signs section from Virgil, *Georgics* 1, a point to which this discussion will return.

While the date of Addison's poem remains unknown, it is likely that it was one of his earliest compositions. Bradner has even proposed it as a possible candidate for those verses that secured Addison's election to the demyship at Magdalen College.[10] In the absence of internal or external evidence it is impossible to determine, but it is worth remarking that the *Barometri Descriptio* is a piece of higher literary quality than the *Tityrus et Mopsus* suggested by Courthope as the vehicle for Addison's

---

[6] Cf., for example, *Luna Habitabilis*, 25-29 (on the magnifying capabilities of the telescope): *quin tete admoveas (tumuli super aggere spectas,/compositum) tubulo; simul imum invade canalem/sic intenta acie, caeli simul alta patescent/atria, iamque ausus lunaria visere regna,/ingrediere solo et caput inter nubila condes*. See Haan, *Thomas Gray's Latin Poetry*, 35-50. For further examples of scientific neo-Latin poetry, see Robert Percy Smith (1770-1845), *Cartesii Principia* and *Newtoni Systema Mundanum*. Cf. in general *Early Writings of Robert Percy Smith* (London, 1851). See Bradner, *Musae Anglicanae*, 304-307.

[7] *quin tete admoveas (tumuli super aggere spectas)* (Gray, *Luna Habitabilis*, 25) may echo Addison's exhortation: *quin age, sume tubum fragilem* (18).

[8] Bradner, *Musae Anglicanae*, 221.

[9] Cf. Sutton, ed. *The Latin Prose and Poetry of Joseph Addison*, Introduction, 10.

[10] Bradner, "Addison's Latin Poems," 359.

election,[11] and thus perhaps more likely to have caught the attention of Lancaster. Bradner also adduces as evidence that the poem is an early work (predating the *Sphaeristerium* at least) the abundance of changes (some 32 as well as the deletion of a five-line passage at the end) made by Addison to the *Examen* text of the poem in preparation for its subsequent publication in the *Musae Anglicanae*.[12] Perhaps the verses were composed to fulfill the requirements of a university exercise or perhaps as a performance piece on a university occasion.[13] In the absence of evidence only speculation is possible.

That Addison approached his subject with some degree of seriousness is suggested not merely by a close reading of the poem itself, but also by the fact that this was not his first time to use Latin to describe modern science. His youthful interest in the benefits of "new science" is evident in his Latin prose oration *Nova Philosophia Veteri Praeferenda Est* delivered at the Sheldonian Theater at the University Encaenia in 1693. Composed at the age of 21, the work convincingly argues the case for the advantages of new philosophy over the old,[14] and in so doing reveals its author as a man of his time, praising modern scientific techniques, and contrasting them with the limitations of the past. The speech begins by wondering how long will humankind follow in the footsteps of the ancients, religiously venerating the ineptitudes of antiquity.[15] This query is answered by a glowing encomium of a modern:

---

[11] See 14-15 above.

[12] As opposed to the mere six changes he made to, for example, the text of the *Sphaeristerium*. Cf. Bradner, "Addison's Latin Poems," 363-364.

[13] For quasi-scientific topics as the subject matter of university performance poems, cf. the likely Cambridge context of Milton's Latin poem *Naturam Non Pati Senium*. See W.A. Sessions, "Milton's *Naturam*," *MS* 19 (1984), 53-72; Estelle Haan, "Milton's *Naturam Non Pati Senium* and Hakewill," *MH* 24 (1997), 147-167.

[14] Addison's oration occurs at *Theatri Oxoniensis Encaenia Sive Comitia Philologica Julii 7 Anno 1693 Celebrata* (Oxford, 1693), L2ᵛ-M1ᵛ. See Guthkelch, ed. *Miscellaneous Works*, II, 467-469. It is answered by two further orations by Richard Smallbroke and Edward Taylor respectively: *Vetus Philosophia Novae Praeferenda Est*, M1ᵛ -N1ᵛ; *Quaeritur utrum Vetus Philosophia an Nova sit Praeferenda*, N2ʳ-N2ᵛ. On Curll's praise of Addison's piece, see 7-8 above.

[15] *quousque veterum vestigiis serviliter insistemus, Academici, nec ultra patres sapere audebimus? quousque Antiquitatis ineptias, ut senum deliria nonnulli solent, religiose venerabimur?* (Guthkelch, ed. *Miscellaneous Works*, II, 467).

Descartes, alias *Cartesius* (1596-1650),[16] who solved the difficulties of the universe; he destroyed the orbs of glass fixed by the whims of antiquity;[17] he searched the regions above, and discerned new suns and new worlds.[18] Later in the work Addison celebrates the advantages of new science as epitomized by the microscope, which enables us to scrutinize the tiniest of particles. In short, modern science renders our eyes much more penetrating: *usque adeo vel oculi acriores fiunt Neotericorum artibus.*[19] It is a telling statement, reflecting perhaps that preoccupation with the miniature which would come to characterize Addison's neo-Latin verse. It should be remembered also that Addison would include Bisse's Latin poem *Microscopium* in the *Musae Anglicanae*, a poem which, as argued below, contains several methodological points of contact with the *Barometri Descriptio* itself.[20] Much later in one of his *Tatler* papers the more mature Addison would likewise hail the benefits afforded by the microscope:

> I have lately applied myself with much satisfaction to the curious discoveries that have been made by the help of microscopes, as they are related by authors of our own and other nations. There is a great deal of pleasure in prying into

---

[16] Descartes (*Cartesius* is the Latinized form of his name) is frequently regarded as the father of modern philosophy. Addison's encomium pays tribute to his original contributions to a wide range of fields of study. Among these were mathematics, geometry, optics, psychology and physiology.

[17] *diffregit ille vitreos istos caelorum orbes quos veterum insomnia compegere.* (Guthkelch, ed. *Miscellaneous Works*, II, 467).

[18] *iuvat undique superiores caelorum tractus explorare novosque soles, et mundos inter sidera latentes detegere; iuvat immensas hasce aetheris plagas orbibus erraticis passim interspersas, terrasque per viam lacteam undiquaque discurrentes intueri, et machinae totius molem rectius metiri* (Guthkelch, ed. *Miscellaneous Works*, II, 467).

[19] *nec solum in caelis orbes novos, sed si in tellurem despiciatur, diversa animantium genera hodierna patefecit Philosophia, dum perspicilli ope oculorum acies intenditur, et obvios se produnt minutissimarum rerum partus, dum curioso intuitu animatas conspicimus materiae particulas, et reptiles miramur atomorum viventium acervos: usque adeo vel oculi acriores fiunt Neotericorum artibus, et opus, quod unum ex omnibus optimum voluit natura, emendatur et perficitur* (Guthkelch, ed. *Miscellaneous Works*, II, 467-468).

[20] Interestingly, the methodological affinities lie largely in both poets' appropriation of Virgilian language. See 41-43 below.

this world of wonders ... Your microscopes bring to sight shoals of living
creatures in a spoonful of vinegar.[21]

And if in a Latin oration the youthful Addison could eloquently proclaim
the benefits of the microscope, so would the more mature essayist sing
the praises of another relatively "modern" invention, namely, the
telescope:

> We see many stars by the help of glasses, which we do not discover with our
> naked eyes; and the finer our telescopes are, the more still are our
> discoveries.[22]

That "help of glasses," that "prying into this world of wonders" likewise
underlie the *Barometri Descriptio*.

Discovered in 1643 by Evangelista Torricelli (1608-1647), the
barometer surely constituted in Addison's eyes yet another relatively
recent example that *nova philosophia veteri praeferenda est*. Torricelli,
at the suggestion of Galileo, had used mercury in his vacuum
experiments. Filling a four-foot-long glass tube with mercury and turning
it upside down, he observed the existence of a vacuum in that some of
the mercury did not escape from the tube; this was followed by his
discovery that its movement was conditioned by changes in atmospheric
pressure. The invention would be celebrated by several contributors to
the *Tatler*,[23] while the metaphor of the barometer would later be applied

---

[21] *Tatler*, 119 (12 January 1710: ed. Bond, II, 205-207). It is interesting to note that
this letter bears the motto *In Tenui Labor* (from Virgil, *Georgics* 4.6). Cf. *ibid.* (II,
208): "I have been present at the dissection of a mite, and have seen the skeleton of a
flea; I have been shown a forest of numberless trees ... Your microscope can show
you in it a complete oak in miniature;" *Tatler*, 229 (26 Sept. 1710: ed. Bond, III, 187):
"A very ordinary microscope shows us that a louse is itself a very lousy creature." On
the microscopic magnification of insects, cf. Nicolaus Hobart, *Dioptrices Laus*, 52-54:
*cernis ut aversis Parthorum more sagittis/iratae minitentur apes, qua saeviat
oestrum/cuspide, vel muscam tutetur quanta proboscis* (*Musae Anglicanae*, I, 96).

[22] *Spectator*, 565 (9 July 1714: ed. Bond, IV, 530). Cf. Nicolaus Hobart, *Dioptrices
Laus*, 15-18: *scilicet hos, Galilaee, tibi debemus honores,/aethereas aperire domos,
acieque sagaci/astrorum servare vices sedesque deorum, et/naturae scrutari oculato
arcana cylindro* (*Musae Anglicanae*, I, 94-95).

[23] Cf. *Tatler*, 220 (5 September 1710: ed. Bond, III, 149): "It is well known that
Torricellus, the inventor of the common weather glass, made the experiment in a long
tube, which held thirty-two foot of water, and that a more modern virtuoso, finding
such a machine altogether unwieldy and useless, and considering that thirty-two
inches of quicksilver weighed as much as so many foot of water in a tube of the same
circumference, invented that sizeable instrument which is now in use;" *Postman*, 808

by Addison[24] and others[25] to the fluctuating world of politics, church and state.

In 1712 there was published at Frankfurt a Latin prose treatise by Petrus Weresmarti. Entitled *Dissertatio Philosophica ... de Phaenomenis Barometricis*, this work includes several observations likewise made by Addison in his Latin poem on the subject.[26] Thus, as might be expected, Weresmarti explains the link between the rising and falling of the

---

(26 September 1700, as quoted in Alexander Chalmers, ed., *The Tatler: A Corrected Edition* [London, 1806], IV, 256): "Next Tuesday morning [Oct. 1 1700] will be published the account of the alterations of wind and weather, by the discoveries of the portable barometer, from what quarter the wind will blow, clouds or rain, wind and weather, clear and cloudy, wet and dry, come every day and night for the month of October, all over England, and also when the quicksilver weather-glasses will rise in wet, and sink in fair weather, and rise and sink without any alteration at all."

[24] Thus Addison, *Tatler*, 214 (22 August 1710: ed. Bond, III, 126): "For the conduct therefore of such useful persons as are ready to do their country service upon all occasions I have an engine in my study which is a sort of a political barometer, or to speak more intelligibly, a state weather glass that by the rising and falling of a certain magical liquor, presages all changes and revolutions in government as the common glass does those of the weather;" Addison, *Tatler*, 220 (5 September 1710: ed. Bond, III, 148): "Having received many letters filled with compliments and acknowledgements for my late useful discovery of the Political Barometer, I shall here communicate to the public an account of my Ecclesiastical Thermometer, the latter giving as manifest prognostications of the changes and revolutions in Church as the former does of those in State;" Addison, *Spectator*, 281 (22 January 1712: ed. Bond, II, 595): "Nor must I here omit an experiment one of the company assured us he himself had made with this liquor, which he found in great quantity about the heart of a coquet whom he had formerly dissected. He affirmed to us that he had actually enclosed it in a small tube made after the manner of a weather glass, but that instead of acquainting him with the variations of the atmosphere, it showed him the qualities of those persons who entered the room where it stood."

[25] Cf. a certain T. Philomath, who asks: "Now Sir, what I humbly beg of you is that you would lend me your state weather-glass in order to fill up this vacant column in my works" (*Tatler*, 228 [23 September 1710]: ed. Bond, III, 184). Cf. *Tatler*, 228, (September, 1710: ed. Bond, III, 185): "This gentleman does not consider what a strange appearance his almanac would make to the ignorant, should he transpose his weather, as he must do did he follow the dictates of my glass. What would the world say to see summers filled with clouds and storms, and winters with calms and sunshine according to the variations of the weather, as they might accidentally appear in a State barometer? But let that be as it will, I shall apply my own invention to my own use; and if I do not make my fortune by it, it will be my own fault."

[26] These occur chiefly in the section: *Dissertatio Philosophica Quinta de Phaenomenis Barometricis eorumque causis, nec non de Barometri insigni commodo et usu terra marique.*

mercury and the changes in the weather, the fluid serving as an important
indicator of serene or cloudy weather, or rain, snow, hail, wind, storm
and clouds.[27] In treating *de phaenomenis Barometricis eorumque
significatione* the author propounds nine canons highlighting the
significance of the various risings and descents of the mercury.[28] Thus if
the mercury rises, that is a sign of good weather.[29] By contrast its swift
descent indicates a storm or squall;[30] its rising and sudden stalling
frequently indicate a less intense wind, lighter rain, hail or snow.[31] He
concludes with a succinct synopsis of the whole.[32] Later he outlines the
exceptional usefulness of the barometer at land and sea especially as a
means of predicting storms,[33] and cites Virgil's recommendation

---

[27] *Dissertatio Philosophica ... de Phaenomenis Barometricis* (Frankfurt, 1712), 4: *sive
varium ascensum et descensum mercurii in Barometro cum concomitantibus et
consequentibus aëris atmosphaerici mutationibus, sereno, nubilo, pluvia, nive,
grandine, vento, tempestate et procellis.*

[28] *Dissertatio Philosophica ... de Phaenomenis Barometricis*, 6: *ut de significatione
varii ascensus et descensus mercurii certius fiat iudicium, sive ut de imminente
tempestate ex vario mercurii ascensu et descensu certius iudicetur, Canones aliquot
constituimus, secundum quos iudicandum esse experientia satis longa nos docuit.*

[29] *Dissertatio Philosophica ... de Phaenomenis Barometricis*, 6: *Canon I: si
mercurius ascendat multum supra variabile, imo ad beau temps, sive notam serenae
tempestatis usque vel et altius indicat instantem vel praesentem maximam caeli
tranquillitatem et felicitatem. si ascendat ad summum, ventus ut plurimum est
Orientalis vel Boreus.*

[30] *Dissertatio Philosophica ... de Phaenomenis Barometricis*, 6: *Canon II: si
mercurius satis celeriter descenderit ad tempette, vel fere eo usque vel aliquot lineis
inferius, praenuntiabit tempestatem et procellam; maiorem vel minorem, prout
mercurius magis vel minus celeriter fuerit delapsus, et ex altiore vel humiliore loco
adeoque plus vel minus descenderit.*

[31] *Dissertatio Philosophica ... de Phaenomenis Barometricis*, 6 : *Canon IV: si post
aliquem ascensum subsistat mercurius nec tamen satis alte, indicat saepe ventum
minus intensum, tenuiorem pluviam, grandinem aut nivem rariorem.*

[32] *Dissertatio Philosophica ... de Phaenomenis Barometricis*, 8: *ascensus mercurii
satis celer et altus est certissimus serenitatis praenuntius, sed tempestatis sive
procellae eiusdem celerrimus delapsus ad infimos gradus. si mercurius haereat fere
circa notam serenae tempestatis, valde probabile est serenam fore tempestatem, et
nullam eo die fore pluviam; accidit tamen nonnunquam, licet rarissime, ut pluat
eodem die. similiter quando mercurius altus est, vel si inferius haereat post aliquot
graduum ascensum, magnam crastinae serenitatis facit spem.*

[33] *Dissertatio Philosophica ... de Phaenomenis Barometricis*, 43: *De insigni usu et
commodo Barometri terra marique.* Cf. *ibid.*, 44: *usus ergo et commoda, quae*

delivered at *Georgics* 1.50ff. on the advantages of ascertaining winds and climatic vicissitudes in advance of sailing:

> Hinc Mantuanus Poeta *Georg.* Lib I v 50 merito canit:
> *at prius ignotum ferro quam scindimus aequor,*
> *ventos et varium caeli praediscere morem*
> *cura sit.*[34]

The allusion in this Latin prose work to Virgil's didactic poem is particularly relevant to the present discussion, since it is the *Georgics*,[35] in particular book 1, that constitutes one of the most important subtexts of Addison's poem. The significance of the *Barometri Descriptio* lies not so much in the fact that it takes as its subject a modern scientific object, but in the way in which that abstract object is couched in Virgilian language. Thus the agricultural domain of Virgil's rustic farmer, and, more specifically, the didactic precepts issued to that farmer and especially the signs in nature to be observed by him, are applied to suit a contemporary scientific context. Indeed it is hardly a coincidence that the more mature Addison when applying the metaphor of the barometer to politics, would prefix to that particular *Tatler* essay two lines from Virgil's weather signs section.[36]

---

recensebimus, eum spectant qui rectum instrumenti usum novit, et prudenter secundum certos canones cum cura observationes habere, legitimumque de imminente tempestate iudicium ferre cupit. quinam autem sinit isti usus, et quanti momenti sint commoda quae Barometra rite et cum iudicio adhibita nobis adferre possint, facile quivis intelligit qui considerat quantum momenti saepissime in eo sit situm ut varias tempestatum vicissitudines praesciamus.

[34] *Dissertatio Philosophica ... de Phaenomenis Barometricis*, 44.

[35] On the *Georgics* in general, see among others P.J. Connor, "The *Georgics* as Description: Aspects and Qualifications," *Ramus* 8 (1979), 34-58; M.C.J. Putnam, *Virgil's Poem of the Earth: Studies in the Georgics* (Princeton, 1979); P.A. Johnston, *Virgil's Agricultural Golden Age: A Study of the Georgics* (Mnem. Supp. 60: Brill, 1980); Alexander Dalzell, *The Criticism of Didactic Poetry* (Toronto, 1996), chapter 4; Llewelyn Morgan, *Patterns of Redemption in Virgil's Georgics* (Cambridge, 1999); M.R. Gale, *Virgil on The Nature of Things: The Georgics, Lucretius and The Didactic Tradition* (Cambridge, 2000); Katharina Volk, *The Poetics of Latin Didactic* (Oxford, 2002), chapter 4.

[36] Addison, *Tatler*, 214 (22 August 1710: ed. Bond III, 124): *soles et aperta serena/prospicere, et certis poteris cognoscere signis (Georgics* 1. 393-394).

Now as the abstract and the descriptive coalesce so too do the realms of both science and poetry.[37] And more than that. Paradoxically nature's warning signs heralded by Virgil will ultimately be surpassed by the modern invention celebrated in Addison's poem.

(i)   Science and Metallic Showers

But the benefits of new science do not come without a price. The poem's opening description of mining conveys a tension between the wonders of discovery and the unscrupulous invasion of the pristine.[38] On one level mining can be seen as an instance of the advancement of humankind: after all, Lucretius, in a work pertaining to the didactic genre upon which this poem draws, had described the discovery of gold, silver and other metals as an integral part of the gradual development of civilization,[39] while Horace had pointed out that silver when left buried in the earth possesses no color.[40] On another level, however, could not the very act of mining be regarded as a perversion of the rustic farmer's occupation so central to Virgil's *Georgics*? If so, the poem's opening lines are marked by a series of ironies. Virgil's farmer undertakes the appropriate task of digging the soil. As such he is the true rustic *fossor*, as it were.[41] Addison's *fossor* (1) is altogether different. He is a miner, whose digging of the hidden caverns of the earth is described in disturbingly sexual terms: his penetration (*qua penetrat* [1]) of quasi-virginal caverns of the earth, which in turn are personified as "fecund with formless ore"

---

[37] Cf. *Poems on Several Occasions*, xiii: "The *Barometer* is a fine philosophical poem, describing the effects of the air on that wonderful instrument with great exactness, as well as in the most beautiful poetry."

[38] Compare the opening lines of Addison's *Sphaeristerium*, on which see 91-92 below.

[39] Lucretius, *De Rerum Natura* 5. 1241-1242: *... aes atque aurum ferrumque repertumst/et simul argenti pondus plumbique potestas...* Cf. 5. 1255-1256: *manabat venis ferventibus in loca terrae/concava conveniens argenti rivus et auri.*

[40] Horace, *Odes* 2.2.1-2: *nullus argento color est avaris/abdito terris.*

[41] *id venti curant gelidaeque pruinae/et labefacta movens robustus iugera fossor* (*Georgics* 2. 263-264). R.F. Thomas, ed., *Virgil: Georgics* (Cambridge, 1988), I, 204, states: "This is the first attestation of *fossor* in its neutral, agricultural sense (And V. uses it only here)." He cites Cat. 22.9-11, where *fossor* "appears as a synonym for 'country bumpkin.'"

(*metallo/fecunda informi* [1-2])[42] and gleaming with unworked veins (*rudibusque nitentia venis* [2]),[43] as though describing a young virgin in her puberty, but not yet grown to womanhood. Precedent for this is to be found in Pliny's pejorative account in *Historia Naturalis* 2. 158 of the penetration (*penetramus*) by men of the earth's innards as they dig (*fodientes*) for the veins (*venas*) of gold and silver, and the metals of bronze and lead, and search for gems and tiny stones. They drag out the earth's very innards so that a gem may be worn on the finger by which it was sought.[44] Addison nonetheless conveys the sense of wonder as the miner comes upon his find: he is astounded at hidden treasures and future coins (*dum stupet occultas gazas nummosque futuros* [3]). The line recalls the reaction of Aeneas to an ekphrastic representation[45] of the fall of Troy in *Aeneid* 1 (*dum stupet obtutuque haeret defixus in uno* [1. 495]), which included the doomed warrior huntress Penthesilea, beneath whose naked breast is buckled a golden girdle.[46] But whereas Aeneas beholds aspects of his and Troy's past, the miner literally looks at and indeed towards the future: those *nummos ... futuros.*

The miner's wonder contrasts harshly with the forcefulness of his act, as is conveyed by the positioning of *eruit* at the beginning of the hexameter,[47] and the strong consonantal sounds of line 4: *eruit argenti latices nitidumque liquorem.*[48] He is stunned at both his hidden treasure and that treasure's potential, which in turn is a symptom perhaps of the potential for the advancement of humankind. If so, this is highly

---

[42] Cf. Pliny, *NH* 2.207: *metallorum opulentia tam varia, tam dives, tam fecunda.*

[43] Cf. Caspar Barlaeus, *Britannia Triumphans*, 532-533: *hic stannum tibi vena vomit, pallensque metallum/eruit, et terrae scrutatur viscera fossor.*

[44] Pliny, *NH* 2.158: *penetramus in viscera, auri argentique venas et aeris ac plumbi metalla fodientes, gemmas etiam et quosdam parvulos quaerimus lapides scrobibus in profundum actis. viscera eius extrahimus ut digito gestetur gemma quo petitur. quot manus atteruntur ut unus niteat articulus!* Cf. Calp Sic., *Ecl.* 4.117-118: *iam neque damnatos metuit iactare ligones/fossor, et invento, si fors dedit, utitur auro.*

[45] On ekphrasis in Addison's Latin poetry, see *Resurrectio Delineata* discussed in Chapter 6 below.

[46] *aurea subnectens exsertae cingula mammae* (Virgil, *Aen.* 1. 492).

[47] For *eruit* at the beginning of a hexameter, cf. Statius, *Theb.* 4.438, *Appen Virg.* 117, Virgil, *G.*2.210, *Aen.* 2.612.

[48] Worthy of comparison perhaps is Seneca's account of the onset of the iron age as described in *Octavia*, 417-419: *sed in parentis viscera intravit suae/deterior aetas; eruit ferrum grave/aurumque, saevas mox et armavit manus.*

appropriate in a poem that celebrates the merits of a modern discovery, the barometer itself. But this meticulous excavation of "concealed" caverns (*caeca antra* [1]), this discovery of "hidden" wealth (*occultas gazas* [3]) is also to some degree an aberration against a natural order, a crime against virginal youthfulness. It seems to prepare the way for the analogy several lines later with Jupiter, whose assumption of a metallic shower, as it were, a shower of gold, was his means of seducing Danae. Such an analogy moreover is facilitated by the personification of abstract metal in these opening lines. Now the resplendently shining metal excavated by the miner is implicitly equated with that radiant shower of gold assumed by Jupiter in order to seduce Danae.[49] Jupiter is described as not shining more visibly when he enfolded Danae in his embrace, and rained (*depluit* [17]) his liquefied godhead in a shower of gold.[50] Here, as elsewhere, Addison reveals that tendency to equate abstract/inanimate substances with the animate. And by a tour de force that precious metal (*metallo* [1]) is equated with Jupiter, here significantly described as *pretiosus* (15) as he clads himself in a raiment of gold (*flavo ... amictu* [15]). Later his divinity is depicted as undergoing a smelting of sorts into gold (*liquefactum numen in auro* [17]).[51] That liquid silver (*argenti latices* [4])[52] discovered by the miner, a silver which possesses its own shining fluid (*nitidumque liquorem* [4]), is transmuted into another liquefied metal: Jupiter's shower of gold. But the description is not without pejorative undertones. Just as mining is a perversion of nature, so is this an act of intrusion, a cunningly stage-managed seduction. The liquid silver possesses a stealth of its own in that it fails to leave any vestiges of its path (5) and, as it rolls, does not mark the earth with any sign of dampness (6). Instead it almost seems to form a shower, breaking asunder into globules, and gathering itself into soft spheres, an action brilliantly conveyed by Addison's fusion of alliteration and hissing sibilants: *sed fractus sparsim in globulos formam usque rotundam/ servat et in teretes lapsans se colligit orbes* (7-8). The metal's stealthy progression culminating in a virtual shower now becomes Jupiter's

---

[49] Cf. Ovid, *Met.* 4.611: *quem pluvio Danae conceperat auro.*

[50] *nec deus effulsit magis aspectabilis olim/dum Danaen flavo circum pretiosus amictu/ambiit, et gratam suadente libidine formam,/depluit irriguo liquefactum numen in auro* (14-17).

[51] Cf. the oxymoronic juxtaposition of concrete and liquid in, for example, *argenti latices* (4) and *divitiasque fluentes* (12).

[52] Cf. Virgil, *Georgics* 2. 165-166: *haec eadem argenti rivos aerisque metalla/ostendit venis atque auro plurima fluxit.* Cf. also *Aen.* 8.445: *fluit aes rivis aurique metallum.*

deceptive seduction (*ambiit* [16]) of a female, and his cunning assumption of a shower to achieve that seduction. Both mining and seduction constitute an invasion of the *caeca antra* whether of landscape or of the female body, a perversion of virginal innocence.

But just as metal and rain can be joined through divine machination (*depluit irriguo liquefactum numen in auro* [17]), so too are they united in the form of the barometer itself. Here Addison assumes a quasi-kaleidoscopic methodology whereby image upon image undergoes a series of metamorphoses: the descent of the god Jupiter upon Danae (which took the form of a metallic shower of rain) is transmuted into another type of descent: that of another metal (mercury) in the barometer, and this in turn is inextricably connected with the descent of the rain that is betokened (*ut pluvia impendente metallum/mobile descendat* [20-21]). Indeed it is at this point too that the poem itself seems to descend, as it were, from the world of myth and the gods to the realism of modern science.

(ii)   From Bisse to Addison: the *Georgics* Reborn

What the *Barometri Descriptio* achieves above all is the successful couching of a scientific topic in poetic language,[53] and more precisely, in the language of Virgil. In this respect Addison's poem finds a parallel, albeit a less accomplished one, in the *Microscopium* by Thomas Bisse,[54] likewise included in the *Musae Anglicanae*.[55] Bisse uses Virgilian hexameters to create a picture of a world enlarged through the power of the microscope. The piece looks back to Virgil, as details of such tiny creatures as the louse, spider, fly, and ant are suddenly illuminated. The proemium to the poem seems to fuse that of *Georgics* 1 with *Georgics* 4.149-159. In the opening lines (1-6) the speaker catalogues his forthcoming subject matter: the minutiae of nature: the limbs and bones

---

[53] Wiesenthal, *The Latin Poetry of the English Augustans*, 49, comments: "Addison, following an ambition characteristic to the Augustan Age, sought to make new subjects the topic of poetry. The poems reflect ... an easy acceptance and extension of the late Latin tradition."

[54] On Bisse, see note 2 above.

[55] *Musae Anglicanae*, II, 163-168. Bradner, *Musae Anglicanae*, 224-225, observes: "The similarity of his work to Addison's and the appearance of his *Microscopium* in Addison's anthology suggests rather definitely a friendship between the two men."

of animals, leading to a crescendo in *expediam* (6).[56] Similarly the accumulation of relative clauses in a series of metamorphosed *qui* statements: *quas* (1), *quae* (3), *quos* (4), *quae* (4) is reminiscent of the exordium to *Georgics* 1: *quid* (1) *quo* (1), *quae* (3), *qui* (3), *quanta* (4). Among possible points of contact between Bisse and Virgil are: the disclosure of the *mores* of insects,[57] the metaphorical use of "arms,"[58] the description of the exiled louse,[59] which may recall the defeated and exiled bull of *Georgics* 3.225,[60] and especially the implementation of essentially Roman vocabulary to portray miniature creatures.[61] On the whole, however, the debt to Virgil is implicit rather than explicit, and is characterized by thematic points of contact: the observation of tiny insects (with implicit parallels with Virgil's bees); more generally the concept of size and the magnification of the miniature afforded by the microscope itself.[62] Thus the microscope is effective *rebus/...in exiguis* (1-2);[63] it can penetrate the inner details of its subject.[64] Noteworthy is

---

[56] *artes naturae varias, quas daedala rebus/pandit in exiguis, quales animalibus artus/ossaque concessit, quae serica texuit alis,/quos mores et quae pugnacibus addidit arma,/loricas galeasque et non imitabile tergum/expediam* (1-6). Worthy of comparison is Virgil, *Georgics* 4.149-150: *nunc age, naturas apibus quas Iuppiter ipse/addidit expediam.*

[57] *quos mores* (*Micro.* 4)//*mores et studia et populos et proelia dicam* (*Georgics* 4.5).

[58] *et quae pugnacibus addidit arma* (*Micro.* 4)//*dicendum et quae sint duris agrestibus arma* (*Georgics* 1.160).

[59] *tergique errat vagus exsul in oris* (*Micro.* 28).

[60] *victus abit longeque ignotis exsulat oris* (*Georgics* 3.225).

[61] *forte etiam leges condat parvumque senatum* (*Micro.* 105); *nam cum dimidio regno cumque urbibus amplis/tota in ieiunum fertur Respublica ventrem* (*Micro.* 110-111). Similarly Virgil's bees possess their own *penates* (*Georgics* 4.155). Cf. *Georgics* 4.43: *fovere larem*. This device is likewise implemented by Addison in *Machinae Gesticulantes*, on which see 84 below.

[62] On the concept of size in Virgil's presentation of the bee community and his frequent magnification of the miniature, see 80-82 below.

[63] At *Micro.* 7-8 all would remain concealed were it not for the microscope: *ni per saepta tubo transmissa sereno/induerant magnos artus et vix sua membra.*

[64] Likewise details of the nettle and its sting (66-73) are now visible under the microscope. Cf. in general Addison *qua penetrat* (1), *quin age, sume tubum fragilem* (18), *augurio hoc fretus* (59).

the detailed magnification of the spider (29-30),[65] its careful scrutiny of the web as it searches for a fly, which in turn is described as a magnified object.[66] And while the spider encapsulates the grotesquely predatory, he and his victims are also endowed with mock-heroic qualities. Bisse's description of the battle between the spider and the fly merits comparison in a general sense with the warring bees of *Georgics* 4.67-87, and also with the great battle scenes of the *Aeneid*. The fly/spider encounter emerges as in fact an epic battle.[67]

In terms of its reworking of Virgil, the *Microscopium* offers some interesting methodological parallels with the *Barometri Descriptio*. Addison's *imitatio*, however, is somewhat more sustained, as the following analysis hopes to illustrate.

On a general level, it is perhaps not insignificant that Addison locates the whole in an agricultural setting. Thus *arva* (28), *herbae* (32), *prata* (33), *pabula* (36), *prata* (43), *segetem* (43), *agricolae* (47) are highly appropriate in a poem that looks back to the farmer's world of *Georgic* 1. Unlike Bisse, however, he zooms in, as it were, upon a specific Virgilian passage: the account of the weather signs provided by nature (*G.* 1.351-392), while also drawing upon Virgil's account of the signs of fine weather (*G.* 1.392-423).

The Virgilian passage in question describes various indicators of heat, rain, winds, and cold provided by nature. These signs are to be observed by the prudent farmer. If a storm brews, the sea begins to swell, a din is heard on the hills, and moaning is heard in the woods (356-359). One should not attempt to set sail when gulls fly squawking towards the shore, coots sport on the sand, and the heron, abandoning its swamp, flies high above the clouds (360-364). Among other signs are shooting stars, falling leaves, and fluttering feathers (365-369). Thunderstorms are likewise signaled by a variety of signs: cranes taking refuge in the valleys, a heifer sniffing the breeze, a swallow circling a pond, frogs

---

[65] Bisse conveys the increasing sense of horror evoked by the magnification of its limbs: *dorsa tumere/incipiunt; crescit membris crescentibus horror* (*Micro.* 29-30).

[66] Bisse proclaims that thanks to the microscope we can learn that flies have eyes: *muscae tales (si credere vitro/fas) oculos natura dedit* (*Micro.* 53-54). Cf. his address to an awe-inspiring ant, whose details are revealed by the microscope: the little helmet, as it were, upon its head, the shoulders upon which it carries grain: *agnosco umeros, queis ferre solebas/aut viciae granum* (84-85). Cf. in general Virgil's comparison of the Trojans to ants at *Aen* 4.401-407.

[67] Cf., for example, *quo tremit et plures obiectis cruribus hostes/exspectat* (*Micro.* 57-58); *toties revoluta recumbit/hoste sub innumero longaque ita morte laborat* (*Micro.* 61-62); *exuviasque domum et spolia aurea portat arachne* (*Micro.* 63).

croaking in the marsh, an ant bringing her eggs out of her home, crows leaving the meadows en masse, and the various antics of birds (370-389); conversely other types of signs may also enable one to prophesy good weather: the stars and moon are bright, kingfishers remain in the deep, swine do not toss their straw, the clouds sink to lower levels, and the screech owl practices her lament (393-403). And once again the behavior of birds functions as a key signal to the prudent farmer (404-423).[68]

In many respects the specificity of Addison's sustained *imitatio* of Virgil at this point is rather atypical of his poetic practice. It can be viewed perhaps as both a product and a demonstration on a neo-Latin level of his esteem expressed elsewhere for precisely this weather signs section of Virgil's poem. In his *Essay on Virgil's Georgics* Addison singles out this passage for praise and comment:

> ... to set off his first *Georgic* he has run into a set of precepts which are almost foreign to his subject, in that beautiful account he gives of the signs in nature, which precede the changes of the weather.[69]

Later he states:

> His prognostications of the weather are taken out of Aratus, where we may see how judiciously he has picked out those that are most proper for his husbandman's observation.[70]

Addison's phrase "that beautiful account" may evoke for a modern reader of Virgil's poem that overly sentimentalized reaction to the lines best epitomized perhaps by Rand's enthusiastic critique:

> Where else in literature can one find the naturalist's clear sense of cause so charmingly combined with the poet's delight in the sounds and movements of all living things? Where else is such a sympathy, the true sympathy that includes both pathos and humor, with the life of dumb animals? There is more poetry in Virgil's science than in the romantic sentimentality that attributes human traits to birds and beasts.[71]

---

[68] On Virgil's depiction of animal behavior as foretelling the weather, see in general Gale, *Virgil on The Nature of Things*, 129-134.

[69] Guthkelch, ed. *Miscellaneous Works*, II, 4-5. See Appendix 4 below.

[70] Guthkelch, ed. *Miscellaneous Works*, II, 9. Cf. Guthkelch, ed. *Miscellaneous Works*, II, 8: "The reader is carried through a course of weather, and may beforehand guess whether he is to meet with snow or rain, clouds or sunshine in the next description."

[71] E.K. Rand, *The Magical Art of Virgil* (Harvard, 1931), 215.

What is beyond doubt, however, is that these lines constituted in Addison's eyes a Virgilian purple passage. The *Barometri Descriptio* reinvents and remolds key aspects of that passage, applying Virgilian language, sentiment, and methodology to an entirely different realm, thereby enhancing the "poetry in [Addison's] science."

One interesting methodological similarity between the two poets lies in the use of essentially didactic temporal signposting. In both instances this is achieved through emphatic repetition of *tum* or *cum* or *sin* etc. Thus:

Addison	Virgil, *Georgics* 1
tum (28, 36)	iam tum (45), tum (215, 278, 341, 342, 360, 395, 410)[72]
quando (57, 58)	
cum (34)	cum (288, 313, 314, 361, 362)
sin (30)	si vero (424); si (428, 430, 458); sin (432, 454)[73]

But the debt seems to extend to the nature of the weather signs catalogued, except that in this instance the barometer itself functions as the sole means of determining these in advance. A general statement that rain and heat are denoted by the respective descent or ascent of the liquid mercury in the barometer (19-23) is followed by a series of announcements: the rising of the fluid indicates good days and summer (26-29); its immoderate rising denotes parched grass and languishing meadows as the sun scorches the fields (30-33); the descent of the mercury denotes rain (34-44); its immoderate descent betokens storms and tempests (45-49). The lines are thus organized into two balanced sections denoting rising, immoderate rising; descending, immoderate descending, with the result that the poem's train of thought mirrors the potential fluctuations of the barometer itself.

Addison inverts the order of the weather signs included in the *Georgics*. For example, the winds/storms which constitute the first of Virgil's signs are now postponed until the end of the catalogue. In Virgil, the signs progress from winds/storms (birds providing signs) to rain, to good days, to signs provided by the sun. In Addison, the catalogue begins with good days, then proceeds to rain (heron passage) and signs of birds, and next to storms. Hence the Virgilian order is reversed. The effect is a

---

[72] On *tum* in *Georgics* 1 as a whole, cf. 1.45, 1.137, 1.139, 1.143, 1.181, 1.215, 1.305, 1.307, 1.341, 1.388, 1.410, 1.448, 1.455.

[73] For Virgil's use of *sin*, see also, *G.* 2.195, 2.234, 2.276, 2.483, 3.179, 3.504, 4.67, 4.239.

progression from rising to sinking fluid as indicative of certain weather
conditions. Addison moreover transposes Virgil's heron (used there as a
sign of winds) to his rain section:

VIRGIL		ADDISON	
1.351-352	Introductory statement re *aestus*, *pluviae* and signs	20-25	Introductory statement re *pluviae/aestus*
1.356-359	(a) Winds and storms at sea	26-33	(c) Good weather + signs: Rising liquid; parching sun
1.361-373	Associated birds: signs of storms/winds: gulls, coots, heron		
1.373-392	(b) Rain + associated animal/ bird signs: cranes, heifers, swallow, frogs, ants, birds	34-44	(b) Rain + associated signs lowering of liquid; behavior of heron
1.393-513	(c) Signs of good weather moon, sun, political dimension	47-54	(a) Storms and winds at sea

In highlighting the usefulness of the barometer, Addison explains how it
functions. Thus when rain is imminent, the pool of quicksilver settling at
the bottom of the tube will lower (*ut pluvia impendente metallum/mobile
descendat* [20-21]). This behavior of the liquid betokens the imminence
of rain. In *Georgics* 4 Virgil had likewise emphasized a sign (to be
observed by bees) of impending rain. Addison's *pluvia impendente* (20)
is taken directly from *Georgics* 4.191-192: bees do not retreat very far
from the hive when rain impends (*nec vero a stabulis pluvia impendente
recedunt/longius*); instead, they fetch water and attempt brief excursions.
While the verbal echo is evident, the more striking link is a thematic one,
for in *Georgics* 1 Virgil had given instances of signs (from nature) of
impending rain. Thus a shower can be forecast by the behavior of cranes,
or a heifer sniffing air through its nostrils, or a swallow circling a lake, or
a frog croaking in the mud (1. 373-378).[74] Addison's interest in cranes,
as attested by his Latin poem on the battle of Pygmies and cranes,[75] only
lends support to this possible parallel.

---

[74] *numquam imprudentibus imber/obfuit: aut illum surgentem vallibus imis/aëriae
fugere grues, aut bucula caelum/suspiciens patulis captavit naribus auras/aut arguta
lacus circumvolitavit hirundo/et veterem in limo ranae cecinere querelam* (*Georgics*
1. 373-378).

[75] See Chapter 3 below.

From ways and means of forecasting a shower the poem turns to the opposite extreme: *vel contra* (21): heat, which will cause the fluid to rise: *vel contra ubi postulat aestus* (21). In Virgil, the signs presented betoken both heat and rain: *atque haec ut certis possemus discere signis,/ aestusque pluviasque et agentis frigora ventos* (G.1.351-352). Virgil has winds and rain, and a transition from rain to heat: *nec minus ex imbri soles et aperta serena/prospicere et certis poteris cognoscere signis* (G.1. 393-394): thus stars appear in a clear sky. In a sense then Addison compresses into a mere two lines *Georgics* 1.351-423. From the detection of imminent rain and heat, he proceeds to state that the liquid itself advises of the sky's aspect and future temperature, able, as it is, to forecast frost and chill: *iam caeli faciem tempestatesque futuras/conscia lympha monet, brumamque et frigora narrat* (24-25). Verbally the lines look back to *Georgics* 1.252-253: *hinc tempestates dubio praediscere caelo/possumus*. Addison's notion of warning (*monet* [25]) can be compared to the warnings in Virgil provided by the moon (*moneret* [G. 1.353]) or by the sun (*monet* [G. 1. 465]).[76] Just as Virgil gives advice on signs of good as well as bad weather,[77] so Addison, signaling, as it were, his "days" section, proclaims: *tum laetos sperare dies licet* (28).[78] Now if the liquid begins to rise, the plants become parched (30-33). Line 32 (*iam sitiunt herbae*) draws upon *Georgics* 4.402 – a time favorable for the flock: *cum sitiunt herbae et pecori iam gratior umbra est* (Aristaeus episode).[79] In both, weather forecasts are denoted by the occurrence of the future participle of *venire*: Addison's *venturae pluviae* (36) may recall the bees of *Georgics* 4.156: *venturaeque hiemis memores*. In both, the behavior of the heron functions as a weather sign. In Addison, damp skies are indicated by the heron as it traverses the mid-region of the heavens, takes advantage of the thick air, and scatters the dewy clouds with its wings (37-40).[80] The specific reference to the heron echoes

---

[76] Cf. *Georgics* 1.457.

[77] *nec minus ex imbri soles et aperta serena/prospicere et certis poteris cognoscere signis* (*Georgics* 1. 393-394).

[78] On *dies*, cf. Virgil, *Georgics* 1.205, 1.276, 1.312, 1.434.

[79] Virgil had emphasized the importance of irrigation when the field is parched: *cum exustus ager morientibus aestuat herbis,/ecce supercilio clivosi tramitis undam/elicit* (*Georgics* 1.107-109).

[80] *nec certior ardea caelos/indicat umentes medias quando aetheris oras/tranando crassa fruitur sublimius aura,/discutit et madidis rorantia nubila pennis* (*Barometri Descriptio* 37-40).

Georgics 1. 364, in which this is but one of many birds who can prognosticate rain and winds.[81] Thus a bad time to sail is indicated by gulls flying out of the middle of the sea to shore (361) or by waterfowl sporting on dry land or by the heron deserting its familiar marshland and soaring above the high clouds: *notasque paludes/deserit atque altam super volat ardea nubem* (363-364).[82] Addison uses the image of the heron as a sign of rain, not wind. Both Virgil and Addison include signs of storms at sea. Thus in Addison farmers need to beware when the liquid sinks too low as this indicates a storm at sea with rivers overflowing their banks: *procellam* (46); *collectas hiemes tempestatemque sonoram* (49), even as the liquid *imo se condat in alveo* (51).[83] In the *Georgics* battling winds are the first occurrence: *ventorum ... proelia* (1.318), followed by a storm at sea (*aut freta ponti/incipiunt agitata tumescere* [1. 356-357]). This is a bad time to sail. Once again Addison inverts the order of Virgil. His concluding section highlights the time of year when it is possible to wear light clothing: *quando tenui velamine tutus/incedes* (57-58). Worthy of contrast perhaps is the Virgilian precept: *nudus ara, sere nudus* (1.299).[84] Addison emphasizes when one can look forward to fire: *quando sperabis frigidus ignem* (58), comparable perhaps with *Georgics* 1. 291-292: *seros hiberni ad luminis ignis/pervigilat*. And again he inverts the progression of Virgil's lines (cold to fire, to heat, to sowing) as he substitutes heat, which requires only slight clothing, to cold, to winter fire.

Having set up a series of parallels with Virgil's *Georgics*, the poem typically turns the whole upon its head in a final parting shot, which seeks both to emulate and to surpass its Virgilian model. One of the crucial precepts issued in *Georgics* 1 is that weather signs enable us

---

[81] *pluviasque et agentis frigora ventos* (*Georgics* 1. 352).

[82] Cf. R.A.B. Mynors, ed. *Virgil: Georgics* (Oxford, 1990), 79: "V ... introduces the 'heron' of Arat. 913 and 972 ... but in a new sign 'flying high above the clouds', vivid to those who know its great slow-beating wings and very close to a fragment of Aeschylus ... Serv. notes the supposed connection between the words *ardea* and *arduus*."

[83] Cf. Virgil, *Aen* 9.32 *et iam se condidit alveo* (of the river Nile).

[84] The precept is derived from Hesiod. Cf. Mynors, ed. *Virgil: Georgics*, 69: "Hesiod's famous precept was an exhortation above all to hard work ... V. uses it to contrast the open year, from the first ploughing (43ff.) to the end of the winter sowing (230) with the close season of winter, when a man must put on his *cucullus* before he ventures out." Mynors points out that *nudus* here = "'stripped' wearing only a *cinctus*, possibly a *tunica*."

to foresee storms,[85] the correct time for harvesting and sowing,[86] and when it is suitable to sail.[87] Addison concludes by stating that the advantages of the barometer are such that even if those weather signs *are* visible in nature, the behavior of this instrument alone should be able to function as an adequate indicator for the traveler or farmer. Whereas Virgil's catalogue of weather signs was characterized by his humanization of animals and birds, thereby adding "a new dimension to Aratus' relatively 'objective' account,"[88] Addison's reverts to the inanimate, as living creatures are now replaced by the barometer itself. So even though the black sky is bursting with clouds and threatening a dark day of rain (59-60),[89] if the instrument denies this and promises clear weather (61),[90] then the traveler can confidently make his journey despite looming clouds (62).[91] Similarly the reaper with no fear of a downpour can lay low crops in need of reaping (63-64).[92] In short, winter's cold falls harmlessly upon the earth since it strikes those already prepared for it. The whole is a subtle reworking of that Virgilian dictum: *numquam imprudentibus imber/obfuit* (*G.* 1. 373-374). All rely on an *augurium* (59), namely, a scientific instrument. The barometer thus renders its user entirely *paratus* in a way that far surpasses even the most meticulously diligent of Virgilian farmers. Such are the advantages of a modern invention. And such perhaps encapsulates on both a scientific and a poetic level that Addisonian dictum:

nova philosophia veteri praeferenda est.

---

[85] *hinc tempestates dubio praediscere caelo/possumus* (*Georgics* 1.252-253).

[86] *hinc messisque diem tempusque serendi* (*Georgics* 1. 253).

[87] *et quando infidum remis impellere marmor/conveniat* (*Georgics* 1. 254-255).

[88] Gale, *Virgil on The Nature of Things*, 133.

[89] *quamquam atri nubila caeli/dirumpunt obscura diem pluviasque minantur* (*Barometri Descriptio* 59-60).

[90] *machina si neget et sudum promittat apertum* (*Barometri Descriptio* 61). Noteworthy is the possible fusion of aspects of Virgil's description of the bees in *Georgics* 4. Virgil's bees, like the farmer, need foresight as to when it might rain. Virgil's *ver nactae sudum* (*Georgics* 4.77) (of the bees) becomes in Addison *sudum promittat apertum* (*Barometri Descriptio* 61).

[91] *audax carpat iter nimbo pendente viator* (*Barometri Descriptio* 62).

[92] *nec metuens imbrem, poscentes messor aristas/prosternat* (*Barometri Descriptio* 63-64).

CHAPTER 3

Virgilian Bees and Addisonian Pygmies

Addison's *Pugmaio-Geranomachia Sive Proelium Inter Pygmaeos et Grues Commissum* is perhaps his most sustained attempt at mock-epic poetry. This elaborately entitled piece has had a very mixed reception from critics of his Latin verse. Johnson famously referred to it as one of three Latin poems upon "subjects on which perhaps he [Addison] would not have ventured to have written in his own language,"[1] and continued:

> When the matter is low or scanty a dead language, in which nothing is mean because nothing is familiar, affords great conveniences; and by the sonorous magnificence of Roman syllables the writer conceals penury of thought and want of novelty, often from the reader, and often from himself.[2]

One might contrast the viewpoint of that eighteenth-century editor of *Poems on Several Occasions*, who proclaimed:

> *The Battle of the Pygmies and Cranes*, *The Puppet-Show*, and *The Bowling-Green* are of the mock-heroic kind, the subjects mean and trivial, seemingly incapable of poetical ornaments, but are raised to the heroic by a splendid boldness of expression, a pomp of verse, by metaphors, allusions and similitudes drawn from things of a higher class, and such as are suited by nature to convey ideas of greatness and magnificence to the mind.[3]

Likewise modern scholarship has reacted rather favorably. Bradner sees in the poem "an element of imaginative fancy which separates it from

---

[1] Johnson, "Addison," 645. The other two poems of which Johnson maintains an equally negative viewpoint are the *Barometri Descriptio* and the *Sphaeristerium*.

[2] Johnson, "Addison," 645.

[3] *Poems on Several Occasions*, Preface (xii).

other mock-heroics of its time,"[4] and regards it as "one of the most delightful mock-heroics ever penned."[5] Similarly Wiesenthal states: "nowhere does the neo-Latin rivalry with the ancients find a more comic exposition than here."[6] Sutton views it as affording Addison "a magnificent opportunity for indulging his delight in the world of the miniature."[7] It will be argued that as a mock-heroic the *Proelium*, far from exhibiting "penury of thought," is a highly imaginative and resourceful poetic exercise. Moreover, as argued below, the poem's mock-heroism and Virgilianism are inextricably intertwined. As Dalzell notes, "the mock-heroic has always been an element in the georgic tradition."[8] That Preface to *Poems on Several Occasions* had acknowledged this coexistence, while suggesting a contrast in terms of reader response:

> Virgil in his *Georgics* is the great master in this way, with this difference only, that *his* is a serious grandeur, *this* a mimic one; *his* produces admiration; *this* laughter.[9]

But perhaps it is in the marrying of "admiration" and "laughter" that Addison's real success lies.

In terms of genre the poem takes its place alongside several works inspired either directly or indirectly by the now lost Γερανομαχία falsely attributed to Homer by Proclus and authors of the *Vitae*.[10] Indeed it may well have been as a consequence of the popularity of that work that the theme of the Pygmies and the cranes resurfaces in the work of

---

[4] Bradner, *Musae Anglicanae*, 222.

[5] Bradner, *Musae Anglicanae*, 223.

[6] Wiesenthal, *The Latin Poetry of the English Augustans*, 75-76. One exception to Wiesenthal's statement might be Vida's *Scacchia Ludus*, a mock-epic on the game of chess, in which moves in the game are presented as military engagements. As such, Vida's poem may have provided an important neo-Latin precedent for Addison's *Sphaeristerium*, on which see 89-90 below.

[7] Sutton, ed. *The Latin Prose and Poetry of Joseph Addison*, Introduction, 12. This delight resurfaces in, for example, the description of the puppet world in *Machinae Gesticulantes*, on which see 80-82 below.

[8] Dalzell, *The Criticism of Didactic Poetry*, 118.

[9] *Poems on Several Occasions*, Preface (xii).

[10] Cf. Wiesenthal, *The Latin Poetry of the English Augustans*, 94.

several Greek writers.[11] That Addison's poem belongs to this genre is suggested not only by the Greek element in its title,[12] but also by the allusion in the poem proper to another pseudo-Homeric work in the same vein: the *Batrachomyomachia*, a mock-epic on the theme of frogs and mice.[13] In the spirit of generic *aemulatio* Addison states that Homer, when treating of the battle of frogs and mice, never sang of a war as memorable as this particular battle.[14] The allusion to Homer, the *Maeonius ... vates* (47),[15] is not without significance. In *Iliad* 3 advancing Trojan troops are compared to cranes inflicting death upon Pygmies:

> And when each of them was marshalled with their leaders,
> the Trojans went with a shriek and a war-cry,
> like birds, just as the shriek of cranes arises in the sky,
> the ones who, fleeing storm and endless downpour,
> fly with a shriek over the streams of Okeanos
> bringing slaughter and death to Pygmy men;
> high in the air, they provoke dread strife;
> but the Achaeans went in silence, infused with might,
> eager in their hearts to protect one another.
>
> (*Il.* 3.1-9)[16]

---

[11] Cf. Aristotle, *History of Animals* 7.12: "for they [cranes] move from the Scythian plains to the marshes above Egypt from where the Nile flows; this is the region whereabouts the pygmies live (for they are no myth, but there truly exists a kind that is small, as reported – both the people and their horses – and they spend their life in caves)." Translation is that of D.M. Balme, *Aristotle, History of Animals* (Cambridge Mass. [Loeb Class. Library], 1991), 11, 131-133.

[12] Cf. Wiesenthal, *The Latin Poetry of the English Augustans*, 75.

[13] Bradner, *Musae Anglicanae*, 7, notes that the *Batrachomyomachia* was often translated into English as an exercise by young poets of the Renaissance, and that it functioned as "the prototype of the prolific burlesque poetry of the Augustan Age in England."

[14] Cf. *Proelium*, 46-52: *non tantos motus nec tam memorabile bellum/Maeonius quondam sublimi carmine vates/lusit ubi totam strepituque armisque paludem/ miscuit : hic (visu miserabile!) corpora murum/sparsa iacent iuncis transfixa, hic guttere rauco/rana dolet pedibusque abscisso poplite ternis/reptat humi, solitis nec sese saltibus effert.* Wiesenthal, *The Latin Poetry of the English Augustans*, 79, notes that "The war here, as it is not in the *Batrachomuomachia* ... is fought between order and chaos, art and the destructive forces of nature."

[15] For Homer as *Maeonius ... vates*, cf. Ovid, *Tristia* 1.6.21: *tu si Maeonium vatem sortita fuisses.*

[16] Translation is that of Leonard Muellner in his excellent discussion of the subject in "The simile of the Cranes and Pygmies: A Study of Homeric Metaphor," *HSCP* 93

As Muellner has noted, these lines are related to several other bird similes in the epic, all of which are applied in a military context. The present simile follows one used of the Trojans at the end of *Iliad* 2. Worthy of comparison also is *Iliad* 2.459-468 (in which the march of Agamemnon's army is compared to a flock of birds including cranes). Likewise, at the end of book 15, Hector making for his ship is compared to an eagle preying upon birds (including cranes).[17] The point lies in the equation of predatory birds and their victims with epic warriors. And the military context in which such similes occur in Homer may shed some light on the possible allegorical subtext of Addison's poem.[18]

Turning from cranes to their victims, the Pygmies, it is important not to underestimate the popularity of the theme in contemporary vernacular literature. 1646 had seen the publication of Martin Lluelyn's *Men Miracles* (which included a section "Of Pigmies"),[19] and of Sir Thomas Browne's *Pseudodoxia Epidemica*, a chapter of which treated of the subject.[20] The theme recurs in Alexander Ross's *Arcana Microcosmi* published in 1652.[21] Several pertinent observations on the Pygmy race were made by Joshua Barnes in his *Gerania: A New Discovery of a Little Sort of People Called Pygmies* published at London in 1675,[22] and in 1699 by Samuel Garth in *The Dispensary*.[23] Such authors readily draw upon the representation of Pygmies in classical literature, and frequently provide a critique of their portrayal by a range of classical authors. For

---

(1990), 59-101, at 59. For the legend of the war between Pygmies and cranes, see among others W.H. Roscher and K. Ziegler, *Ausführliches Lexicon der Griechischen und Römischen Mythologie* (Teubner, 1884-1937), 3287 sv *Pygmaios* (and also 3291, [for Pygmies in art]).

[17] Muellner, "The Simile of the Cranes and Pygmies," 76, observes that "In the cranes and Pygmies simile ... the cranes have actually replaced the predatory eagle, falcon or vulture in other bird similes, and the Pygmies have replaced the cranes, swans or geese."

[18] See 58-59 below.

[19] Martin Lluelyn, *Men Miracles* (London, 1646), 17-34.

[20] Sir Thomas Browne, *Pseudodoxia Epidemica* (London, 1646) IV.xi.

[21] Alexander Ross, *Arcana Microcosmi* (London, 1652), Book II, chapter 3.

[22] Joshua Barnes, *Gerania: A New Discovery of a Little Sort of People Called Pygmies With a Lively Description of Their Stature, Habit, Manner, Buildings, Knowledge, and Government* (London, 1675).

[23] Samuel Garth, *The Dispensary* (London, 1699), 68-69. Cf. John Oldham, *Poems and Translations* (London, 1683), 40.

example, Browne sees Homer as the "primitive author" of a theme that has become particularly popular,[24] while Lluelyn summarizes the Homeric treatment of the theme, and likewise states that the subject is a famous one:

> Their war with Cranes who them annoy,
> As fam'd as is his war of Troy.
> Now he that in their story seekes,
> Finds Pigmies Trojans, Cranes the Greekes.
> But still the Pigmies did defie them,
> As if their King were Aged Priam.[25]

Although in generic terms at least Addison's poem seems to turn to the world of classical Greece, its treatment of the subject is closely linked to things Roman. Part of the poem's success lies in its engagement with classical Latin poetry, an engagement which is counterbalanced by interaction with contemporary literature on the topic. This twofold methodology, as it were, enables Addison to provide a rich texture of allusion through thematic and verbal reminiscence. As argued below, both factual and literary aspects of his treatment (for example, comments regarding the location and abode of the Pygmy race, their theft of eggs from cranes, the abduction of the Pygmy leader by a swooping crane, and the poem's final equation of Pygmies with fairies) mirror details found in Pliny, Juvenal, and also in seventeenth-century vernacular writings.

But while Addison's poem interacts with a broad range of texts, both Latin and vernacular, both classical and contemporary, its language looks to one author in particular: Virgil, especially the *Georgics*, and to a lesser degree the *Aeneid*. In short, his treatment of the subject mirrors on a more sophisticated level that Addisonian predilection for Virgil's poetry already observed above in the discussions of *Tityrus et Mopsus* and the *Barometri Descriptio*.

---

[24] Thomas Browne, *Pseudodoxia Epidemica*, ed. Robin Robbins (Oxford, 1981), I, 330: "The primitive author was Homer who using often similes, as well to delight the ear, as to illustrate his matter, in the third of his Iliads compareth the Trojans unto the cranes, when they descend against the Pigmies; which was more largely set out by Oppian, Juvenal, Mantuan and many poets since; and being only a pleasant figment in the fountain, became a solemn story in the stream, and current still among us." Cf. I, 330: "for though we meet herewith in Herodotus, Philostratus, Mela, Pliny, Solinus, and many more; yet were they derivative relators, and the primitive author was Homer." Cf. I, 332: "some write they fight with cranes, but Menecles in Atheneus affirmes they fight with partridges; some say they ride on partridges, and some on the backs of rams."

[25] Lluelyn, *Men Miracles*, 22.

(i)   The Georgic World of the Miniature

The title-page of Joshua Barnes' *Gerania: A New Discovery of A Little Sort of People ... Called Pygmies*, published in London in 1675, includes alongside a representation of a Pygmy and crane the following Latin hexameter: *ingentes animos angusto in corpore versant.*[26] The quotation, from Virgil's description of the warring bees at *Georgics* 4.83, is an apt one, suggesting an implicit equation between the Pygmy race and these insects. It will be seen that a similar identification underlies Addison's poem, and constitutes the core, as it were, of his Virgilian allusions. Once again he pries into that all-too-familiar world of the miniature, which in turn assumes epic proportions.

In this instance the miniature is represented by the Pygmy race itself. That the term "Pygmy" was derived from the Greek πυγμή meaning "cubit" is a point seized upon by such seventeenth-century vernacular authors as Browne,[27] Lluelyn,[28] and Ross.[29] The etymological link seems to be acknowledged in Addison's description of them as a *populus cubitalis* (141).[30] And emphasis upon the miniature is a leitmotif of his poem. In the proemium the speaker, proclaiming his subject matter and invoking his Muse, asks her to draw up his "small cohorts" (*parvas tu, Musa, cohortes/instrue* [2-3]). The cranes are described as indignant at their "puny campaign" (*pusillam/militiam* [4-5]).[31] Some ten lines later

---

[26] See Plates 1 and 2. Cf. the brief description of the Pygmy/crane battle included in Nicolaus Hobart's *Dioptrices Laus*, 60-65: *hinc Pygmaea cohors aucto cum corpore sumat/ingentes animos et dignos Marte furores;/iam truculenta novis incedat grandior armis,/Bistoniasque ad bella grues, gentemque rebellem/vindicta stimulante vocet; fremit aethere toto/hostis et attonitum dat Strymonis unda fragorem* (*Musae Anglicanae*, I, 96-97).

[27] Browne, *Pseudodoxia Epidemica*, I, 330, states: "By Pigmies we understand a dwarfish race of people, or lowest diminution of mankind, comprehended in one cubit, or as some will have it, in two foot, or three spans."

[28] Lluelyn *Men Miracles*, 20, can joke that they are "three palms high."

[29] Ross, *Arcana Microcosmi*, II, 3.3, describes them as "people of a cubit or two high." Ross however erroneously cites πoηωv not πυγμή as the Greek word for "cubit."

[30] Cf. Browne, *Pseudodoxia Epidemica*, I, 332: "so doth Cornelius construe *Pygmaei* or *viri cubitales*, that is not men of a cubit high, but of the largest stature, whose height like that of giants is rather taken by the cubit than the foot."

[31] With Addison's *pusillam* here and *pusillas ... umbras* (154-155) cf. Browne, *Pseudodoxia Epidemica*, I, 331: "Aristotle, whose words are these [*Hist. Animal.* 8.

the speaker, highlighting the novelty of his subject, announces that he
will sing of miniature combatants (*exiguosque canam pugiles* [16]). It is
a *parvula progenies* (30). Nowadays a traveler can see only the vestiges
of this campaign: valleys white with tiny bones (*valles ossibus albas/
exiguis* [25-26]), and marvel at *vestigia parva* (26). The language is
reminiscent of Virgil's treatment of the bees in *Georgics* 4, who are
frequently associated with such adjectives as *angustus*[32] or *exiguus*[33] or
parvus.[34]

Yet Virgil achieves a contrast between the puny size of these
insects and the might of their heroic undertakings. Similarly Addison's
Pygmies, though of small stature, possess an epic grandeur. Just as Virgil
could describe a battle within the bee community in heroic terms,[35] and
attribute to these creatures huge spirits (*ingentes animos angusto in
pectore versant* [83]), so Addison, through the device of *praeteritio*,
states that the huge hearts of heroes (*heroum ingentes animos* [6]) have
already been proclaimed in Latin verse. But what his own mock-epic will
achieve is precisely that notion of epic heroism, of great-souled
warriors.[36] This is achieved by following Virgilian precedent, describing
battles conducted by a miniature race, and drawing upon the *Aeneid* to
enhance that heroism or mock-heroism, as the case may be.

In fact epic grandeur and the novelty of his subject matter are
themes that underlie the poem's self-conscious proemium, which reworks
aspects of the proemium to *Georgics* 3. Here Addison rejects by
implication a whole series of classical epics:[37] the *Argonautica* of

---

12] ... That is, *Hic locus est quem incolunt Pygmaei, non enim id fabula est, sed
pusillum genus, ut aiunt.*" As noted by Robbins, *Pseudodoxia Epidemica*, II, 927,
Browne draws upon Scaliger's Latin version.

[32] Cf. *Georgics* 4.35 (of the beehive): *angustos habeant aditus*; *Georgics* 4.83 *angusto
in pectore*; *Georgics* 4.206: *angusti terminus aevi*. Cf. also *Georgics* 1.380: *angustum
formica terens iter*.

[33] Cf. *Georgics* 4.87 *pulveris exigui iactu*.

[34] Cf. *Georgics* 4.176: *si parva licet componere magnis*; *Georgics* 4.201 *parvosque
Quirites*.

[35] Cf. *Georgics* 4. 67ff.

[36] It is noteworthy that Addison's *Machinae Gesticulantes* contains (in lines 40-41) an
allusion to the war between the Pygmies and Cranes in what may well be a self-
conscious echo of his own *Proelium Inter Pygmaeos et Grues Commissum*. See 71
below.

[37] Worthy of comparison perhaps is Milton's rejection at *Paradise Lost* 9.13-19 of
epic heroes (Achilles, Aeneas, Odysseus) as the subject matter of his poem: "sad task,

Valerius Flaccus,[38] the *Iliad* of Homer (10),[39] Virgil's *Aeneid* (11),[40] the *Thebaid* of Statius (12),[41] and Lucan's *Bellum Civile* (12-13).[42] But sandwiched between these classical epic heroes is a seventeenth-century king, none other than William himself (*quem Gulielmi/gesta latent?* [11-12]). This is in all probability a self-conscious allusion on Addison's part to his own miniature epic poem *Pax Gulielmi*, which had indeed celebrated William's exploits.[43] He proceeds to state that he will be the first (*primus ego* [14]) to represent this particular war in poetry (14-15).[44] The claim of primacy and the language in which that is expressed are, as noted above, reminiscent of the proemium to *Georgics* 3. Here Virgil had likewise rejected commonplace subject matter, in his case, hackneyed Alexandrian/Callimachean themes: Eurysthea (4), Busiris (5),[45] Hylas (6),[46] Delos (6),[47] Pelops and Hippodamia (7-8).[48] He too had made the claim for primacy,[49] stating that he would be the first (*primus ego* [G.

---

yet argument/Not less but more heroic than the wrath/Of stern Achilles on his foe pursued/Thrice fugitive about Troy wall; or rage/Of Turnus for Lavinia disespoused,/Or Neptune's ire or Juno's, that so long/Perplexed the Greek and Cytherea's son."

[38] As denoted by *lectos Graium iuvenes et torva tuentem/Thesea* (9-10).

[39] This is encapsulated in the reference to the "fleet-footed Achilles" (*quis pedibus velocem ignorat Achillem?* [10]).

[40] This is symbolized by the phrase *dura Aeneae certamina* (11).

[41] As denoted by the phrase *fratres Thebani* (12).

[42] As denoted by *et flebile fatum/Pompeii* (12-13).

[43] The point is noted by Sutton, ed. *The Latin Prose and Poetry of Joseph Addison, ad loc*, who asks "Is this subtle self-congratulation?"

[44] *primus ego intactas acies gracilemque tubarum/carmine depingam sonitum, nova castra secutus* (*Proelium* 14-15).

[45] Cf. Callimachus, *Aetia* 2 (fr. 44 Pf). See Thomas, ed. *Virgil: Georgics*, II, 38; Mynors, ed. *Virgil: Georgics*, 179.

[46] A reference to Alexandrian and neoteric poetry, e.g. Ap. Rhod. *Arg.* 1.1207-1357; Theocritus, *Idyll* 13. See Thomas, ed. *Virgil: Georgics*, II, 38; Mynors, ed. *Virgil: Georgics*, 179.

[47] Cf. Callimachus, *Hymn* 4.

[48] Cf. Pindar, *Ol.* 1. See Thomas, ed. *Virgil: Georgics*, II, 38-39; Mynors, ed. *Virgil: Georgics*, 179.

[49] Virgil's claim to originality is paradoxically couched in language appropriated from Pindar, Callimachus, Ennius, and Lucretius. See Stephen Hinds, *Allusion and*

3.10]) to bring to Mantua Idumaean palms.[50] But Virgil's prophecy concerned a future, as opposed to the present, poem.[51] In Addison's case Pygmies and cranes (in the present poem) can take the place of epic subject matter (including his already composed epic, the *Pax Gulielmi*). It is as though his poetic career not only emulates, but, by means of this subtle inversion, surpasses that of his classical precursor.

The potentially epic quality of the battle between Pygmies and cranes underlies several vernacular treatments of the whole. Thus could Lluelyn proclaim: "for often wounded, often slaine/Was many an Agamemnon Crane."[52] Moreover the explicit reference to William in this proemium may lend support to the possibility of an allegorical reading of the poem. Sutton has perceptively asked:

> One might ... be tempted to wonder, at least momentarily, whether it is in any sense an allegorical interpretation of the contemporary War of the Grand Alliance. The Pygmies, who so mercilessly oppress the Cranes and then invite their own ultimate ruin, are at one point (143) described as a wicked race (*gentem nefandam*). Are they supposed to represent the French, and their doughty warrior-king Louis XIV? Is the great bird who eventually bears him off in his talons supposed to stand for William III?[53]

Sutton observes, however, that it is difficult to discern any hints of such allegory in the poem proper.[54] It could be argued, however, that such hints are indeed provided by way of intratextual links between this poem

---

Intertext: Dynamics of Appropriation in Roman Poetry (Cambridge, 1998), 52-55; Gale, *Virgil on The Nature of Things*, 11. Volk, *The Poetics of Latin Didactic*, 146, in commenting on this passage, remarks: "the only reason, one has to infer, why [Virgil] does what he does is because the other topics have been treated before."

[50] *primus ego in patriam .../Aonio rediens deducam vertice Musas* (Virgil, *Georgics* 3. 10-11). Cf. *primus ... referam* (*Georgics* 3. 12). On the topos of primacy, cf. Lucretius 1.117-119: *Ennius ut noster cecinit, qui primus amoeno/detulit ex Helicone perenni fronde coronam,/per gentes Italas hominum quae clara clueret*; Prop. 3.1.3: *primus ego ingredior puro de fonte sacerdos.*

[51] See Volk, *The Poetics of Latin Didactic*, 149-150.

[52] Lluelyn, *Men Miracles*, 23.

[53] Sutton, ed. *The Latin Prose and Poetry of Joseph Addison*, Introduction, 12. For the overtly political in Addison's Latin verse, see his epigrams on the Vigo Bay expedition discussed in Chapter 7 below.

[54] Sutton, ed. *The Latin Prose and Poetry of Joseph Addison*, Introduction, 12: "The principal objection to any allegorical interpretation is that authors of allegory usually plant hints inviting such a reading, and it is difficult to discern any in the poem."

and Addison's *Pax Gulielmi*. Common to both are the motifs of a farmer or traveler beholding the visual remains of a bygone race.[55] Both compare battles to the gigantomachia: the war between the Giants and Jupiter as they heaped Pelion on top of Ossa.[56] Such verbal and thematic parallels may strengthen the case for an allegorical reading of the poem.

Just as Addison's proemium owes a formally stylistic and thematic debt to that of the *Georgics*, so too does his presentation of the subject matter itself. It is hardly insignificant that in the *Georgics* cranes are cited as an example of pests who have the power to undo all the good work of a farmer.[57] They may, however, prove useful in that their behavior in flight can portend a storm.[58] Addison's locating of the cranes near Strymon,[59] the Mareotic marsh,[60] Cayster,[61] and the Scythian marsh[62] finds a parallel in Virgil's identification of those precise locales

---

[55] In *Pax* 10-13 the farmer digs these up in the now "deserted" ditches: *stat circum alta quies, curvoque innixus aratro/desertas fossas et castra minantia castris/rusticus invertit, tacita formidine lustrans/horroremque loci et funestos stragibus agros.* In *Proelium* 24-26 the traveler beholds the "deserted" abodes of the Pygmies, and valleys white with their tiny bones: *nunc si quis dura evadat per saxa viator,/desertosque lares et valles ossibus albas/exiguis videt et vestigia parva stupescit.*

[56] *Pax* 42-46: *sic postquam Enceladi deiecit fulmine fratres/caelicolum pater et vetuit contemnere divos,/divulsam terrae faciem ingentesque ruinas/mortales stupuere; altum hinc mirantur abesse/Pelion invertique imis radicibus Ossam.* Cf. *Proelium* 132-137: *talis erat belli facies cum Pelion ingens/mitteret in caelum Briareus solioque tonantem/praecipitem excuteret: sparguntur in aethere toto/fulminaque scopulique; flagrantia tela deorsum/torquentur Iovis acta manu, dum vasta Gigantum/corpora fusa iacent semiustaque sulphure fumant.* Cf. Lluelyn's presentation of the young Will at skittles: "And Mole with fist we know doth tosse a/Hill like a ball, Pelion on Ossa" (*Men Miracles*, 26). Cf. Homer, *Odyssey* 11. 315-316, and Addison, *Spectator*, 333 (22 March 1712: ed. Bond, III, 230): "Homer in that passage which Longinus has celebrated for its sublimeness and which Virgil and Ovid have copied after him tells us that the giants threw Ossa upon Olympus and Pelion upon Ossa."

[57] *Georgics* 1.120. Cf. Barnes, *Gerania*, 71: "For the cranes being the only causes of famine in our land, by reason they are so numerous that they can devour the most plentiful harvest, both by eating the seeds beforehand, and then picking the ears that remain."

[58] *Georgics* 1.383-387.

[59] *Strymonis unda* (*Proelium* 56).

[60] *stagnum Mareotidis* (*Proelium* 57).

[61] *uda Caystri/prata* (*Proelium* 57-58).

[62] *Scythica ... palude* (*Proelium* 58), *Istro* (*Proelium* 59).

as their abode.[63] On the other hand, his location of the Pygmies in India (19)[64] takes a firm stance upon a subject much debated among classical and Renaissance authors. Although Pliny had included the territory of the Indian Nomads as one of several possible locations in which Pygmies made their home,[65] a wide variety of sites was suggested by other authors. Thus, as Thomas Browne notes, the Pygmies were placed in Africa by Aristotle, in Asia by Philostratus, and in Scythia by Pliny.[66] India is seen as only one of several possibilities for the Pygmies' abode by Lluelyn[67] and Ross.[68] More specifically, Addison's comment that they dwell in valleys and caves (19-20)[69] is mirrored in Lluelyn's remark that they "liv'd of old, in Caves and Dens."[70]

Possible echoes of the *Georgics* continue to inform Addison's treatment. As the traveler traverses the present area, he sees valleys white with tiny bones, and marvels at the minute traces (24-26).[71] The lines

---

[63] *Strymoniaeque grues* (*Georgics* 1.120) (cf. *Aen* 10. 265: *Strymoniae dant signa grues*); *deserti ad Strymonis undam* (*Georgics* 4.508); *sunt et Mareotides albae* (*Georgics* 2. 91); *dulcibus in stagnis rimantur prata Caystri* (*Georgics* 1.384).

[64] *qua solis tepet ortu primitiisque diei/India laeta rubet* (*Proelium* 18-19).

[65] Cf. Pliny, *Historia Naturalis* 7.26: *super hos extrema in parte montium Trispithami Pygmaeique narrantur.*

[66] Browne, *Pseudodoxia Epidemica*, I, 332: "thus the relation of Aristotle placeth them above Egypt towards the head of Nile in Africa; Philostratus affirmes they are about Ganges in Asia, and Pliny in a third place, that is Gerania in Scythia."

[67] Lluelyn, *Men Miracles*, 19: "Pliny in Thrace some Pigmies puts,/And others up in Carea shuts./From India one his Pigmies takes,/And others neare to Nilus Lakes."

[68] Ross, *Arcana Microcosmi*, II.3.3: "Assertors of this opinion do not agree about the place of the Pigmies abodes; some placing them in India, some in Ethiopia, some in Scythia, some in Greenland." Cf. Barnes, *Gerania*, 1: "We were driven by a violent cold and dry North wind ... to ... the utmost borders of India;" Browne, *Pseudodoxia Epidemica*, I, 333: "... or what is delivered by Ctesias that they are negroes in the midst of India." Wiesenthal, *The Latin Poetry of the English Augustans*, 78, notes that "although Herodotus' description of the Pygmies would require an African setting, Addison moves the locale to India."

[69] *inter inhospita saxa/(per placidam vallem, et paucis accessa vireta)*(*Proelium* 19-20).

[70] Lluelyn, *Men Miracles*, 17.

[71] *nunc si quis dura evadat per saxa viator,/desertosque lares et valles ossibus albas/exiguis videt et vestigia parva stupescit* (*Proelium* 24-26). Addison's lines merit comparison with Alexander Ross's summary of George Buchanan's observation that the discovery in Scotland of Pygmy skulls and bones is proof that they once lived

transpose into the present what was in Virgil a grim prediction concluding *Georgics* 1. In lines 493-497 the speaker imagines a time when the farmer as he ploughs will come upon the weapons and bones of soldiers.[72] Addison has inverted Virgil in several ways: the prediction of future time (*tempus veniet* [493]) has become the *nunc* (24) of his poem; the *agricola* (494) is replaced by the *viator* (24); the discovery of huge bones in fields (496-497) has become the discovery in valleys of tiny bones and vestiges, remnants of the battle (24-26). In both instances it is a discovery that inspires wonder (*mirabitur* [497]; *stupescit* [26]).

While the miniature size of the Pygmies is emphasized by Addison, there is an irony in his comparison of this war to the gigantomachia.[73] This resulted in confusion, with rivers and rocks scattered into the air as Jupiter brandished his thunderbolt.[74] Worthy of comparison is *Georgics* 1. 281-283.[75] Obviously the tone of Addison's lines is mock-heroic, but it should be noted that for the comparison of minute creatures to giants, the other end of the extreme, Addison had precedent in Virgil himself. Thus the industrious bees of *Georgics* 4 are compared to the Cyclopes hard at work in the forge of Vulcan.[76] This drawing upon extremes, as it were, of comparing the tiniest with the

---

there: "Buchanan speaking of the Isles of Scotland, among the rest, sets down the Isle of Pigmies, in which there is a Church where are yet digged up divers small skuls and bones, answering to the report of the Pigmies little bodies; so that the inhabitants and neighbours make no question, but that Pigmies of old dwelt there" (Ross, *Arcana Microcosmi*, II.3.3). Cf. George Buchanan, *Rerum Scoticarum Historia* (Frankfurt, 1584), I, 31: *in hac [sc. Pygmaeorum insula] fanum est in quo credunt vicini populi olim Pygmaeos fuisse humatos. multi exterorum terra altius effossa repererunt, et adhuc deprehendunt capita parva et rotunda aliarumque corporis humani partium ossicula nihil famae vetustae derogantia.*

[72] *scilicet et tempus veniet, cum finibus illis/agricola incurvo terram molitus aratro/exesa inveniet scabra robigine pila/aut gravibus rastris galeas pulsabit inanis/grandiaque effossis mirabitur ossa sepulchris* (*Georgics* 1. 493-497).

[73] Addison proclaims: *talis erat belli facies cum Pelion ingens/mitteret in caelum Briareus solioque tonantem/praecipitem excuteret* (*Proelium* 132-134). For the description of the mythological assault of the Giants on Olympus cf. Addison, *Pax* 42ff.

[74] *flagrantia tela deorsum/torquentur Iovis acta manu, dum vasta Gigantum/corpora fusa iacent semiustaque sulphure fumant* (*Proelium* 135-137).

[75] *ter sunt conati imponere Pelio Ossam/scilicet atque Ossae frondosum involvere Olympum,/ter pater exstructos disiecit fulmine montis* (*Georgics* 1. 281-283).

[76] Cf. *Georgics* 4. 170-178: *ac veluti lentis Cyclopes fulmina massis/cum properant* ... etc. These lines are reworked at *Aen* 8. 449-453.

greatest of creatures is a methodology paralleled in vernacular treatments of the Pygmies. To some extent this arose out of a confusion in regard to the meaning of the Greek word πυγμή, which some misinterpreted as meaning "fist", not "cubit."[77]

(ii)   Transcending Virgil

It is not only in terms of their miniature size that Addison's Pygmies merit comparison with Virgil's bees. On more than one occasion they also seem to reproduce within their community several of those practices exhibited by Virgil's insects. Sometimes the significant use of a mere adjective is enough to signal a Virgilian context; in other instances there would appear to be a more full-scale adaptation of certain passages from *Georgics* 4.

As Addison emphasizes the former resilience of the Pygmies in the face of onslaughts from cranes, he describes a defender laying low his crane victim and bringing back upon his shoulders the huge booty (33-34).[78] This may be read as an ironic reworking of one aspect of the behavior of the bees of *Georgics* 4.217-218, who revere their king, frequently raising him upon their shoulders, and throwing their own bodies into battle on his behalf.[79] And the analogy works on another level

---

[77] Browne, *Pseudodoxia Epidemica*, I, 332, summarizes this: "Others expounded it quite contrary to common acception, that is, not men of the least, but of the largest size ... not taking Pygmies for dwarfs, but stout and valiant champions; not taking the sense of πυγμή which signifies the cubit measure, but that which expresseth pugils, that is, men fit for combat and the exercise of the fist." Ross, *Arcana Microcosmi*, II, 3.3, proclaims: "For if there have been giants, why not also Pygmies, nature being as propense to the least, as to the greatest of magnitudes: besides, the reasonable soul is not extended in the body of a giant, nor contracted in the body of a Pigmie; but can inform the one and the other without augmentation and diminution." Similarly Barnes, *Gerania*, A3ᵛ-A4ʳ, asks: "And why should it be thought improbable that Nature (who continually delightes to embroider this frame of being with variety of creatures) should somewhere produce men of a smaller character than our selves, considering those capital letters (Giants I mean) have been known so far to exceed us on the other side?"

[78] *umerisque reportat/ingentem praedam* (*Proelium* 33-34).

[79] *et saepe attollunt umeris et corpora bello/obiectant* (*Georgics* 4. 217-218). Furthermore the rhetorical repetition of *illum* as the bees revere their king: *ille operum custos, illum admirantur et omnes/circumstant fremitu denso stipantque frequentes* (*Georgics* 4. 215-216) may have inspired Addison's description of the Pygmy general: *ille gruum terror, illum densissima circum/miscetur pugna* (*Proelium* 118-119).

also, for as Addison's crane whets his talons for future strike (*exacuitque ungues* [61]), makes ready his sharp beak (*et rostrum parat acre* [62]),[80] and adapts his wings for flight (*fugaeque accommodat alas* [62]), the language draws upon the bees' preparations for battle as they sharpen their stings with their beaks and get their arms ready (*spiculaque exacuunt rostris aptantque lacertos* [*G.* 4.74]). The equation is further suggested in Addison's subsequent account of the cranes' passion for war and their zeal for vengeance, followed by their obtaining the proper springtime and brandishing their wings (63-64).[81] Addison's *ver nactus proprium* (64) may echo Virgil's *ergo ubi ver nactae sudum* (*G.* 4.77), likewise occurring in a military context: that of bees surrounding their king and calling upon the enemy: thus they rush forth into a great ball, and fall from the sky. And Addison's *tantus amor belli* is an ironic inversion perhaps of the bees' passion for generating honey: *tantus amor florum et generandi gloria mellis* (*G.* 4. 205).

But the poem also looks to other Virgilian animals. The Pygmies in former times took pleasure in devastating the cranes' nests and wreaking vengeance upon the chicks (35-36).[82] This act of destruction recalls a simile used of the grieving Orpheus of *Georgics* 4, whose lamentations are compared to a nightingale bemoaning the loss of her chicks, wrenched as fledglings from their nest by a cruel farmer.[83] Virgil's bird simile as an epitome of ultimate grief has become a reality

---

[80] Cf. *mortemque minantia rostra* (*Proelium* 3).

[81] *tantus amor belli et vindictae arrecta cupido./ergo ubi ver nactus proprium* (*Proelium* 63-64).

[82] *saepe improvisas mactabat, saepe iuvabat/diripere aut nidum aut ulcisci in prole parentem* (35-36). Pliny, *Historia Naturalis*, 7.26, describes how the entire band of Pygmies, mounted on the backs of rams and she-goats, and armed with arrows, goes in a body down to the sea and eats the eggs and chicks of cranes. This process, he states, lasts about three months: *fama est insidentes arietum caprarumque dorsis armatos sagittis veris tempore universo agmine ad mare descendere et ova pullosque earum alitum consumere; ternis expeditionem eam mensibus confici.* Cf. Lluelyn, *Men Miracles*, 18: "These Egges they caught with sweat and paines,/All from their neighbour Foes the Cranes;" Barnes, *Gerania*, 51: "Others that are of the militia are sent every Spring to the sea-side, to break the eggs of the young cranes, and kill the old ones, as many as they can;" 74: "he presented her with ... three hundred dozen of their eggs."

[83] *qualis populea maerens philomela sub umbra/amissos queritur fetus, quos durus arator/observans nido implumis detraxit* (*Georgics* 4.511-513). Cf. Gale, *Virgil on The Nature of Things*, 136: "Virgil's nightingale chicks seem entirely harmless, and the ploughman's act is apparently motivated by pure malice." At *Odyssey* 19.518-523 Penelope compares herself to a nightingale mourning her child.

in the Pygmies' ruthless treatment of the cranes and their young. Then, as the crane, having made one attack (99-100), gears itself up for a second onslaught (102-103),[84] the language recalls the behavior of Virgil's defeated bull at *Georgics* 3.235ff. There, fighting over a heifer, one bull is conquered (*victus* [225]), departs, but regains its strength and prepares for another attack.[85] And if a crane recalls Virgil's bull, so the defeated Pygmy recalls the behavior of Virgil's plague-ridden and already dying horse. As Addison describes the Pygmy summoning up many sobs and beating the ground with his feet (109-110),[86] the lines recall the horse of *Georgics* 3. 499-500.[87] In a single passage then Addison echoes several different animal scenes from the *Georgics* and does so for the purpose of ironic contrast: the contrast between the swooping crane with its aerial lightness and the sturdy bull; the contrast between the Pygmy's puny feet and those of a sturdy horse.

And a rather similar methodology can be seen to underlie Addison's reworking of Virgil's *Aeneid*. At times he seems to borrow Virgilian tags or line endings; at others to rework specific passages. Among verbal tags are: *sternit humi*,[88] *causae irarum*,[89] *mortis imago*,[90] *his accensa*.[91] It is noteworthy too that Homer's simile of the cranes is reworked by Virgil at *Aen*. 10. 264-266.[92] More generally, the swooping

---

[84] *mox defessa iterum levibus sese eripit alis/et vires reparata iterum petit impete terras* (*Proelium* 102-103). For the notion of the crane returning for a second attack, cf. Lluelyn, *Men Miracles*, 24: "For routed crane puts spur to wing,/And safe through empty aire doth fling,/And ere a baker make his tallies,/See crane returnes againe and rallies./But Pigmie wight must stand to list./Three inches stride would split his twist."

[85] *post ubi collectum robur viresque refectae,/signa movet praecepsque oblitum fertur in hostem* (*Georgics* 3. 235-236).

[86] *singultusque ciet crebros pedibusque pusillis/tundit humum, et moriens unguem exsecratur acutum* (*Proelium* 109-110).

[87] *pede terram/crebra ferit* (*Georgics* 3. 499-500). Gale, *Virgil on the Nature of Things*, 46-47, rightly notes that "the symptoms of the sick horse … pathetically mirror the characteristics of the healthy horse as described in 75-88."

[88] *Proelium* 33; *Aen*. 9.754; 10. 697.

[89] *Proelium* 43. Cf. Juno's *causa* (*Aen*. 1.8) and consequential *ira* (*Aen*. 1.11).

[90] *Proelium* 45. Cf. *Aen*. 2.369: *plurima mortis imago*.

[91] *Proelium* 55. Cf. *Aen*. 1.29 (of Juno).

[92] *quales sub nubibus atris/Strymoniae dant signa grues atque aethera tranant/cum sonitu, fugiuntque Notos clamore secundo* (*Aen*. 10. 264-266).

cranes at *Proelium* 121-125[93] and 128ff. merit comparison perhaps with the swooping Harpies of *Aen*. 3.225ff.[94] And at one point (76-77)[95] the Pygmy leader is described in terms that even seem to fuse aspects of Virgil's descriptions of Venus[96] and Dido.[97] The appropriation of the majesty of such female queenly figures lends an air of the grotesque to Addison's Pygmy leader. As always, more than one reading is possible, for Addison's lines are simultaneously endowed with a mock-heroic masculinity as if in anticipation of Swift's Lilliput.[98]

---

[93] Cf. Juvenal, *Satire* 13.167-173, in which a Pygmy warrior is snatched up into the sky by a hostile crane. The speaker remarks that this incident, if seen today, would provoke laughter: *ad subitas Thracum volucres nubemque sonoram/Pygmaeus parvis currit bellator in armis,/mox impar hosti raptusque per aera curvis/unguibus a saeva fertur grue. si videas hoc/gentibus in nostris, risu quatiare; sed illic,/quamquam eadem assidue spectentur proelia, ridet/nemo, ubi tota cohors pede non est altior uno.* In Addison, however, laughter is displaced by sorrow (*triste relatu* [122]) as *frustra Pygmaei lumine maesto/regem inter nubes lugent* (125-126). Juvenal's *bellator* (168) finds a parallel in Addison's *ductor* (115) and *bellator* (123). Both convey the suddenness of the abduction (*ad subitas* [167]//*subito appulsus* [120]//*ex inopino* [121]), and depict the warrior hanging poised between the crane's talons (*raptusque per aera curvis/unguibus a saeva fertur grue* [169-70]//*bellator ab unguibus haeret/pendulus* [123-124]).

[94] *at subitae horrifico lapsu de montibus adsunt/Harpyiae et magnis quatiunt clangoribus ales* (*Aen*. 3.225-226).

[95] *Pygmeadum ductor, qui maiestate verendus/incessuque gravis reliquos supereminet omnes* (*Proelium* 76-77).

[96] *Aeneid* 1.405: *et vera incessu patuit dea.*

[97] Cf. *incessit* (*Aen*. 1.497), and the comparison of Dido to Diana and her train, *gradiensque deas supereminet omnes* (*Aen*. 1. 501).

[98] Macaulay in "The Life and Writings of Addison", 736, proclaimed: "Swift boasted that he was never known to steal a hint … Yet we cannot help suspecting that he borrowed, perhaps unconsciously, one of the happiest touches in his Voyage to Lilliput from Addison's verses. Let our readers judge. 'The Emperor,' says Gulliver, 'is taller by about the breadth of my nail than any of his court, which alone is enough to strike an awe into the beholders.' About thirty years before *Gulliver's Travels* appeared, Addison wrote these lines: *iamque acies inter medias sese arduus infert/Pygmeadum ductor, qui maiestate verendus/incessuque gravis reliquos supereminet omnes/mole gigantea, mediamque exsurgit in ulnam.*" Wiesenthal, *The Latin Poetry of the English Augustans*, 94, is inclined to believe this interpretation. W.A. Eddy, *Gulliver's Travels: A Critical Study* (Princeton, 1923), 78, is much more skeptical: "Lord Macaulay felt sure that the passage in Addison's poem about the twenty-inch chieftain of imperial mien suggested the above to Swift, but I do not believe that this can be affirmed with any certainty," but supports (82) Macaulay's general claim that Addison's poem inspired Swift, adding nonetheless: "One would

Further Virgilian echoes serve to emphasize the bathos of the whole. This is most evident in a series of ironic points of reference to the underworld of *Aeneid* 6. For example, the Pygmies once possessed their own civilization (*hic varias vitam excoluere per artes* [22]). This phrase, used to denote a past world, as it were, echoes Virgil's description of the blessings of Elysium, which included *inventas aut qui vitam excoluere per artis* (*Aen.* 6. 663). In both instances the world in question is the world of the dead. And where a bygone Pygmy civilization recalls aspects of Virgil's Elysium, so the cranes seem to echo the birds of *Aeneid* 6. The inability of cranes to attack the Pygmy commander with impunity (83-84)[99] is not unlike those birds (*Aen.* 6. 239-240) who cannot fly with impunity over the Sibyl's cave.[100] And the actual

---

prefer to think, though, that Swift needed no such model to think of 'little men and big.'" Since Addison's poem was written by 1699 Swift may well have read it before he wrote the Voyage to Lilliput. And further points of contact are discernible. Common to both is the fact that one of a minute race seems taller than rest: *reliquos supereminet omnes* (Addison, 77); "he appeared to be of a middle age, and taller than any of the other three who attended him" (*Swift: Gulliver's Travels*, ed. Robert Demaria [Penguin, 2001], 25). Both describe cuts to the face: *hostilis nam insculpserat unguis/ore cicatrices* (Addison, 79-80); "sometimes they determined to starve me or at least to shoot me in the face and hands with poisoned arrows, which would soon dispatch me" (33); cf. 50: "the enemy discharged several thousand arrows, many of which stuck in my hands and face." In both, albeit in different ways, eggs are the prime cause of warfare: (Addison, 35-42); cf. 48 (between the Empires of Lilliput and Blefuscu): "It began upon the following occasion. It is allowed on all hands that the primitive way of breaking eggs before we eat them was upon the larger end: but his present Majesty's Grandfather, while he was a boy, going to eat an egg and breaking it according to the ancient practice, happened to cut one of his fingers. Whereupon the Emperor his father published an edict commanding all his subjects upon great penalties to break the smaller end of their eggs. The people so highly resented this law that our histories tell us there have been six rebellions raised on that account; wherein one Emperor lost his life, and another his crown. These civil commotions were constantly fomented by the Monarchs of Blefuscu; and when they were quelled, the exiles always fled for refuge to that Empire. It is computed that eleven thousand persons have at several times suffered death rather than submit to break their eggs at the smaller end." Indeed Swift (133) makes an explicit reference to Pygmies: "The sailors were all in amazement and asked me a thousand questions, which I had no inclination to answer. I was equally confounded at the sight of so many Pygmies, for such I took them to be, after having so long accustomed mine eyes to the monstrous objects I had left." Cf. 138: "I looked down upon the servants and one or two friends who were in the house as if they had been Pygmies, and I a Giant."

[99] *non illum impune volucris/aut ore aut pedibus peteret confisus aduncis* (*Proelium* 83-84).

[100] *quam super haud ullae poterant impune volantes/tendere iter pennis* (*Aen.* 6. 239-240).

Pygmy/crane battle likewise recalls Virgil's underworld. Thus as the Pygmies grow weary, some turn their backs in flight (*pars vertere terga* [139]) in a phrase borrowed from Virgil's description of the terrified reaction of the Greeks to the sight of Aeneas in the underworld (*Aen.* 6. 491). This is highly proleptic since by the end of the poem the Pygmies themselves, this tiny race, will indeed take their place in an underworld of their own.[101]

There is, however, one striking point of contrast between Addison's Pygmies and Virgil's bees. In *Georgics* 4, although individual bees live what is only a very short life,[102] still the bee community as a whole remains immortal,[103] as it creates the impression of a cycle of everlasting regeneration. Thus their *domus* is rendered secure for many years.[104] It is an intimation of immortality, so to speak, which is given its most articulate expression in the *bougonia* episode which concludes the whole. By contrast, the Pygmy race is now defunct. That this is the case is reiterated several times throughout Addison's poem: in the stark contrast between the *quondam* (21) of that once extant empire and the *nunc* (24) of a landscape that is now completely deserted and barren; and more strikingly in the emphatic collapse of the *Pygmaea domus* (144) which is now *tot bellis defuncta* (145) and, unlike that of Virgil's bee community, has utterly perished (*funditus interiit* [146]).[105] Addison proceeds to comment that all kingdoms come to an end in time (146-148).[106] As proof of such he cites the fall of the kingdoms of Assyria and Persia. The finality of the demise of the Pygmy kingdom is further suggested by Joshua Barnes, who ends his description of the Pygmies

---

[101] *Elysii valles nunc agmine lustrat inani/et veterum heroum miscetur grandibus umbris/plebs parva* (*Proelium* 151-153).

[102] *ergo ipsas quamvis angusti terminus aevi/excipiat* (*Georgics* 4.206-207).

[103] *at genus immortale manet* (*Georgics* 4. 208).

[104] *multosque per annos/stat fortuna domus* (*Georgics* 4.208-209).

[105] Cf. Lluelyn, *Men Miracles*, 22-23: "Full sundry Duels, sundry Fights/Were mannag'd by the Pigmie Knights,/And though at length they're kill'd and quiet, I think their Foes got little by it."

[106] *nempe exitus omnia tandem/certus regna manet; sunt certi denique fines/quos ultra transire nefas* (*Proelium* 146-148). Addison's language here is reminiscent of Virgil's description of the laws and conditions of the underworld: *nec portitor Orci/amplius obiectam passus transire paludem* (*G.*4. 502-503); *corpora viva nefas Stygia vectare carina* (*Aen.* 6.391).

with an "Epitaph of the Pigmie Governor's Son killed in Battle with Cranes:"[107]

> This Tomb doth hold
> A Pygmie bold;
> Who when alive
> In Arms did thrive;
> But a Crane's Bill
> My life did spill;
> And here I have
> A fitting Grave.[108]

Perhaps it is here that the Pygmies are clearly differentiated from Virgil's bees. In the closing lines of Addison's poem, however, the mere possibility of some sort of life after death for these miniature creatures is hinted at through the identification of these now deceased Pygmies with fairies. Thus, if old wives' tales are to be believed,[109] in the darkness of night shepherds have seen the tiny shades of disembodied Pygmies now safe from the cranes and forgetful of their sufferings, as they dance upon narrow paths and green rings, rejoicing in the name of fairies:

> laetitiae penitus vacat indulgetque choreis,
> angustosque terit calles viridesque per orbes
> turba levis salit et lemurum cognomine gaudet
> (*Proelium* 157-159)

Sutton remarks: "The final transformation of the dead Pygmies into *lemures* – surely to be translated 'faeries' – is the poet's own contribution to the tale."[110] But it is a contribution that may well have been suggested by seventeenth-century treatment of the Pygmy theme. Paracelsus in his *Liber de Nymphis, Sylphis, Pigmaeis et Salamandris* (1605) equates Pygmies with nymphs, salamanders, and other such spirits of fire and water, a point noted by Thomas Browne, who paraphrases Paracelsus' viewpoint as "his non-Adamical men, or middle natures betwixt men and spirits."[111] Barnes, in establishing the setting for his description of the Pygmies, proclaimed: "Some thought it was the land of the Fairies, and

---

[107] Barnes, *Gerania*, 109.

[108] Barnes, *Gerania*, 110.

[109] *si quid fidei mereatur anilis/fabula* (*Proelium* 153-154).

[110] Sutton, ed. *The Latin Prose and Poetry of Joseph Addison*, Introduction, 11.

[111] Browne, *Pseudodoxia Epidemica*, I, 332.

implored me to lead them back."[112] But perhaps the most striking parallel is to be found in a double simile used by Milton to equate demons with dwarfs in *Paradise Lost* 1.[113] Having depicted the congregated demons in mock-heroic terms, Milton suddenly shifts perspective:

> So thick the airy crowd
> Swarmed and were straitened; till the signal given,
> Behold a wonder! they but now who seemed
> In bigness to surpass Earth's giant sons
> Now less than smallest dwarfs, in narrow room
> Throng numberless.
>
> (*Paradise Lost* 1.775-780)

Voltaire's comment that this metamorphosis "heightens the ridicule of the whole contrivance to an unexpressible degree"[114] overlooks Milton's reworking of a passage from Virgil's *Georgics*. Having described a bee battle as an essentially epic contest, Virgil had likewise shifted perspective, stating that this great disturbance could be quelled by the sprinkling of a mere handful of dust.[115] There follows in Milton a double simile of both Pygmies and fairies:

> ... like that *pygmean race*
> Beyond the Indian mount, *or faerie elves*,
> Whose midnight revels, by a forest side
> Or fountain some belated peasant *sees*,
> *Or dreams he sees*, while overhead *the moon*
> Sits arbitress, and nearer to the earth
> Wheels her pale course, they on their mirth and dance
> Intent, with jocund music charm his ear.
>
> (*Paradise Lost* 1.780-787)[116]

---

[112] Barnes, *Gerania*, 11.

[113] It is noteworthy that Milton actually alludes to the battle of the Pygmies and the cranes at *PL* 1.573-576: "for never since created man/Met such embodied force, as named with these/Could merit more then that small infantry/Warred on by cranes."

[114] He proceeds to state: "Methinks the true criterion for discerning what is really ridiculous in an epic poem is to examine if the same thing would not fit exactly the mock heroic ... nothing is so adapted to that ludicrous way of writing, as the metamorphosis of the devils into dwarfs" (*Voltaire's Essay on Epic Poetry*, ed. F.D. White [Albany, New York, 1915], 137).

[115] *hi motus animorum atque haec certamina tanta/pulveris exigui iactu compressa quiescent* (*Georgics*. 4.86-87). Cf. Gale, *Virgil on The Nature of Things*, 50.

[116] Italics are mine. On Addison's later praise of this and other similes in *Paradise Lost* 1, cf. *Spectator*, 303 (16 February 1712, ed. Bond, III, 91): "If the reader

Yet a telling irony underlies Milton's presentation: the phraseology of "some belated peasant sees,/Or dreams he sees," coupled with the role of the moon at 784-785, draws upon Virgil's comparison of Dido's shade to the moon in *Aeneid* 6.[117]

The engagement of Addison's lines with Milton is signaled by a number of parallels: the location of India: "Indian mount" (781)/*India* (19) (with the Miltonian "mount" finding a parallel perhaps in *inter inhospita saxa* [19]); the timing of the whole in the darkness of night: "midnight revels" (782)/*per noctis opaca* (154); the observation of such by a "peasant" (783) or shepherds (*pastores* [154]); the abundance of joy and dancing: "mirth and dance" (786)/*laetitiae...vacat* (157), *indulgetque choreis* (157), *salit* (159).

As the poem concludes, the final image is of insubstantial creatures who may or may not be fairies, depending upon the credence given to that old wives' tale. This puny Pygmy race, like Virgil's bee community, is likewise immortalized, albeit in the spirit world. Or in Miltonic terms, that "Pygmaean race" has perhaps undergone a metamorphosis of its own into those "faerie elves."

---

considers the comparisons in the first book of Milton, of the sun in an eclipse, of the sleeping leviathan, of the bees swarming about their hive, of the fairy dance, in the view wherein I have here placed them, he will easily discover the great beauties that are in each of those passages."

[117] *obscuram, qualem primo qui surgere mense/aut videt aut vidisse putat per nubila lunam* (*Aen.* 6.453-454).

CHAPTER 4

Virgilian Bees and Addisonian Puppets: *Machinae Gesticulantes*

That predilection for the miniature, which characterizes so much of Addison's Latin verse, resurfaces in the *Machinae Gesticulantes*. Although there is no evidence as to when or where this poetical description of a puppet show was composed, that it probably postdates the *Proelium Inter Pygmaeos et Grues Commissum* is indicated by its paraphrase (in lines 40-49) of certain details from that poem.[1] Undoubtedly the most delectable of Addison's Latin poems, the *Machinae Gesticulantes* is, as Bradner notes, "a clever and amusing piece of work, in which the incongruity between the human appearance of the puppets and their actual wooden construction forms the basis of some excellent touches."[2] But the key to the poem's success lies in much more that this so-called incongruity. In its depiction of the craftsman's ability to manufacture and of the puppeteer's skill in giving life to the inanimate, the poem demonstrates a self-conscious awareness of the artist's power to create. As such it can be seen to epitomize that self-referentiality evident in several of Addison's other Latin poems.[3]

---

[1] At *Machinae Gesticulantes* 40-49 Addison seems to paraphrase *Proelium* 153-159. Common to both passages are: the equation of Pygmies with fairies (*parvi subsiliunt lemures* [*Mach.* 44]/*lemurum cognomine gaudet* [*Proel.* 159]); the notion of the imperviousness of this Pygmy/fairy band to the cranes themselves (*infensa gruum temnentes proelia* [*Mach.* 41]/*secura gruum* [*Proel.* 156]); the joy or laughter in which they now indulge (*indulgere iocis* [*Mach.* 42]/*laetitiae ... vacat* [*Proel.* 157]), and their dancing (*tenerisque vacare choreis* [*Mach.* 42]/*indulgetque choreis* [*Proel.* 157]) in narrow circles (*gyros/ducit et angustum crebro pede pulsitat orbem* [*Mach.* 45-46]/*angustosque terit calles viridesque per orbes/turba levis salit* [*Proel.* 158-159]). Cf. Bradner, *Musae Anglicanae*, 223.

[2] Bradner, *Musae Anglicanae*, 223.

[3] See, for example, the personification of the bowls in *Sphaeristerium*, discussed at 92-94 below, and the self-referential description of the craftsman giving them their individual markings, discussed at 100 below. A more conspicuous example lies in Addison's explicit equation between the painter and God as creator in *Resurrectio*

Part of the poem's own creative process lies in what may at first glance appear to be yet another "incongruity": the coexistence of two very different worlds set apart both temporally and culturally: the world of late seventeenth-century England, and that of ancient Rome. What the poem achieves, however, is a unification of these different time zones, so to speak, and it does so through adaptation and appropriation of an ancient civilization and its language: thus aspects of the Roman stage are adapted to suit a theater in miniature; more strikingly, features from Virgil's *Georgics*, most notably the description of the bees in book 4, and the construction of the plough in book 1, are now reborn in an account of puppets themselves: their size, their mock-epic behavior, and even the technicalities of their manufacture. In replicating the quasi-theatrical details of a contemporary entertainment or recreation (the ever popular puppet show) the poem itself "recreates," while offering some insight into performance in general and puppeteering in particular. At the same time, a Roman stage, a Roman poem, and the very language in which that poem was cast are transposed to a contemporary setting. Such indeed is the complexity of a text whose interaction with other texts is counterbalanced by some degree of topographical and performative realism.

(i)   *Romanitas* Recreated: Addison's Puppet Theater

An essential part of the poem's realism lies in its faithful description of those technical aspects of puppeteering that would later be attested by several contributors to *The Tatler* and *Spectator* papers. In many ways Addison reveals himself as an early "spectator" par excellence, but paradoxically the realistic spectacle that he watches and describes is conveyed in frequently Roman terms. Hence the poem is colored by its essential *Romanitas*, which in turn will undergo a metamorphosis of its own.

That such puppet shows were regular events in London is indeed evident from contemporary or near contemporary accounts. Cruikshank deduces evidence from Ben Jonson of the existence of two varieties: one with dialogue (as in *Bartholomew Fair*), the other without dialogue (as in

---

Delineata, and that poem's self-conscious delineation of the artistic process, discussed at 109-112 below.

Tale of a Tub).[4] The puppet show described in *Machinae Gesticulantes* is certainly a noisy affair, as is attested by references to a *stridula turba* (14), *rauca/voce strepens* (19-20), *crebro ... cachinno* (27). In this respect it exemplifies those puppet performances, the most skillful of which would later be engineered in London by a certain Mr Martin Powell.[5]

In the opening lines of Addison's poem the puppet show is located at the *compita* (5), traditionally a crossroads.[6] By application this is a likely reference to a sidewalk or a street corner[7] (probably in London), or, more generally perhaps, to "the place where people gather together."[8] Powell's puppet theater, for example, would be set up in Covent Garden, opposite St Paul's Church.[9] And something of the general atmosphere is conveyed in the emphasis upon the spectators' laughter (5)[10] as the actor gathers a crowd (5-6),[11] delighting his "gaping throng" by means of his

---

[4] George Cruikshank, *Punch and Judy* (London, 1828), 22. See in general Michael Byrom, *Punch and Judy: Its Origin and Evolution* (Aberdeen, 1972 rpt. London, 1979).

[5] See *DNB* sv. Until 1710 Martin Powell (fl. 1710-1729) held his puppet shows at Bath and other provincial towns, but as his fame spread to London he removed to the capital early in 1710. See George Speaight, "'Powell From the Bath': An Eighteenth-Century London Puppet Theatre," *Studies in English Theatre History in Memory of Gabrielle Enthoven* (London, 1952), 38-51. On the noise of such shows, cf. *Spectator*, 372 (7 May 1712: ed. Bond, III, 401): "this voluntary reparation which Mr Powell does our parish for the noise he has made in it by the constant rattling of coaches, drums, trumpets, triumphs and battles."

[6] Cf. *OLD* "A place where three or more roads meet, road-junction, cross-roads."

[7] As translated by Sutton, ed. *The Latin Prose and Poetry of Joseph Addison, ad loc.*

[8] Cf. *OLD*, citing Horace, *Serm.* 2.6.50: *frigidus a Rostris manat per compita rumor*; cf. Livy 34.2.12: *quid aliter per vias et compita faciunt?*

[9] Powell's shows were clearly much more advanced than the earlier form of the one-man puppet theater alluded to by Joseph Strutt in his *Sports and Pastimes of the People of England* (London, 1801): "In the present day the puppet-show man travels about the streets ... and carries the motion, with the theatre itself, upon his back. The exhibition takes place in the open air, and the precarious income of the miserable itinerant depends entirely on the voluntary contribution of the spectators, which, as far as one may judge from the squalid appearance he usually makes, is very trifling." As quoted by Cruikshank, *Punch and Judy*, 27.

[10] *compita qua risu fervent* (*Machinae Gesticulantes* 5).

[11] *glomeratque tumultum/histrio* (*Machinae Gesticulantes* 5-6).

buffoonery (6).[12] That "gaping" conveys an audience's desire to be surprised. Indeed the drawing power of such shows obviously lay in the joy or novelty which they could afford (*quotquot laetitiae studio aut novitate tenentur* [7]). Steele, in a later contribution to the *Spectator*, would likewise highlight novelty as a key part of the magnetism of the puppet show: "Thus he spends his time as Children do at Puppet-Shows, and with much the same advantage, in staring and *gaping at an amazing variety of strange things*."[13] In Addison, the audience comes together from all sides (*undique congressi* [8]). Indeed the popularity of puppet shows is frequently attested in the *Spectator* and *Tatler* papers. For example, in 1711 the sexton of St Paul's Church in a letter to the *Spectator* blames a puppet performance offered by Powell for thinning his church's congregation, lamenting: "I find my congregation take the warning of my bell, morning and evening, to go to a Puppet-Show set forth by one Powell under the Piazzas ..."[14] Fusing the classical and the contemporary, Addison conveys the fact that spectators were seated (*permissa sedilia complent* [8]),[15] simultaneously echoing Horace, *Ars Poetica* 205: *nondum spissa nimis complere sedilia flatu*. The echo is pertinent in that the Horatian context was likewise a theatrical one. But whereas Horace described the primitivism associated with early Roman theatrical performances[16] (hence it was only later that *accessit*

---

[12] *delectatque inhiantem scommate turbam* (*Machinae Gesticulantes* 6). On aspects of buffoonery as integral to the puppet theater, see Cruikshank, *Punch and Judy*, 42: "no doubt the drama consisted of 'gross buffooneries.'"

[13] *Spectator*, 364 (28 April 1712: ed. Bond, III, 368). Italics are mine.

[14] *Spectator*, 14, (16 March 1711: ed. Bond, I, 61). He continues by requesting that "Punchinello may choose hours less canonical. As things are now, Mr Powell has a full congregation, while we have a very thin house." In a subsequent letter (*Spectator*, 372 [7 May 1712]: ed. Bond, III, 400) it emerges, however, that Powell and his company have "given all the profits which shall arise to-morrow night by his play to the use of the poor charity-children of this parish." Cf. Cruikshank, *Punch and Judy*, 33. On puppet shows as rivaling other events, cf. the remark of the contributor to *Tatler*, 115 (3 January 1710: ed. Bond, II, 187) regarding Punch as an entertainment rivaling that of the theater: "I find for some nights past that Punchinello has robbed this gentleman of the greater part of his female spectators."

[15] Cf. Plautus, *Poenulus* 5: *bonoque ut animo sedeate in subsellis*.

[16] Hence the flute was not bound with silver and did not rival the trumpet, producing, as it did, few notes, and was simple in its form: *tibia non ut nunc orichalco vincta tubaeque/aemula, sed tenuis simplexque foramine pauco/aspirare et adesse choris erat utilis atque/nondum spissa nimis complere sedilia flatu* ... (Horace, *Ars Poetica* 202-205).

numerisque modisque licentia maior [211]), the implication of Addison's poem (whose puppet theater by contrast typifies the essentially modern) is that such *licentia* is already present not only in the general buffoonery (*scommate* [6]), but also and especially in the lascivious behavior of Punch himself (31-32).[17] We learn also that seats at the puppet show were variously priced (*nummo subsellia cedunt/diverso et varii ad pretium stat copia scamni* [9-10]). The language in which this fact is conveyed seems once again to transport the whole back to the ancient Roman theater.[18] The fact that seats are not randomly allocated (*nec confusus honos* [9]) may recall the custom in the Roman theater for certain seats to be reserved for (and thereby yielding to [*cedunt*]) important figureheads or senators.[19] By implication then Addison's spectators approximate a Roman audience, as though they have come to watch a drama by, say, Plautus or Terence. And the *Romanitas* of the whole continues: in the later Roman theater the curtain (*aulaeum*) was lowered at the beginning of a performance to reveal the stage,[20] a device echoed in Addison's *tandem ubi subtrahitur velamen* (11).[21] As readers we almost forget that the piece concerns itself with a miniature stage, so

---

[17] *nec raro invadit molles, pictamque protervo/ore petit nympham invitoque dat oscula ligno* (*Machinae Gesticulantes* 31-32).

[18] Cf. Plautus, *Poenulus* 24: *vel aes pro capite dent* (of slaves in the audience).

[19] For an insight into the conditions of staging, and arrangements for spectators etc., cf. in general the Prologue to Plautus, *Poenulus*.

[20] A curtain at the front of the stage was angled from the top of the *scaena*. At the beginning of a performance this was lowered into a slot and wound around a spindle, and raised at the end of the play. See William Beare, *The Roman Stage* (London, 1950), 259-266: "Appendix E: 'The Roman Stage Curtain.'" Cf. G.E. Duckworth, *The Nature of Roman Comedy* (Princeton, 1952), 84-85. Cicero, *Pro Caelio* 27.65, contains "the first mention of the *aulaeum* in literature" (see *Cicero: Pro Caelio*, ed. R.G. Austin [Oxford, 1952], 129). On the lowering of the *aulaeum* to mark the beginning of a performance, cf. Phaedrus 5.7.23: *aulaeo misso*; Horace, *Epistles* 2.1.189: *aulaea premuntur*.

[21] See Sutton, ed. *The Latin Prose and Poetry of Joseph Addison, ad loc.* Further classical undertones may color the phrase *humiles inter scaenas* (16), while the description of a laughing Punch: *et crebro solvit, lepidum caput, ora cachinno* (*Machinae Gesticulantes* 27) is generally reminiscent of the buffoonery of the Atellan Farce. Cf. Duckworth, *The Nature of Roman Comedy*, 12: "In many respects the plays [*fabulae Atellanae*] in situation and character were not unlike Punch and Judy shows." He notes (11) that "farcical situations were frequent, and cheating and trickery and general tomfoolery played a large part."

to speak, of small wooden puppets, as the poem itself now seems to "recreate" a magnified world.

As a puppet show, however, the theater of Addison's poem is probably very different from anything known of in the ancient world.[22] One such difference is the use of wires, which serve several purposes. It is clear from the poem and near contemporary accounts that several vertical wires hung from the front of the puppet stage, their purpose being to disguise the wires that were used to operate the puppets. For Addison, this is an instance of clever *fraus* (14). Thus as the audience scans the narrow aperture, several strings bisect their vision (12-13)[23] lest, if the gap is revealed with an empty façade (13),[24] the deception may be apparent (14).[25] That this skillful deception, as it were, was a particular hallmark of the successful puppet show is indicated by a remark made by a contributor to *The Tatler* in 1709. Speaking of Powell's puppet theater, he professes to know "very well the whole trick of his art," and that:

> it is only by these wires that the eye of the spectator is cheated and hindered from seeing that there is a thread on one of Punch's chops, which draws it up and lets it fall at the discretion of the said Powell, who stands behind and plays him, and makes him speak saucily of his betters.[26]

But if Powell could use several wires (*plurima ... fila*) to good effect, so too was he particularly adept at working the wires of the puppets themselves. Thus would Thomas Burnet proclaim him as:

> the great, the illustrious and the celebrated Mr. Powell, the Puppet-Show man, who has worthily acquired the reputation of one of the most dextrous managers of human mechanism, no English artist ever coming in vie with him – *His Wires are perfectly invisible*, his puppets are well jointed, and very apt to follow the motions of his directing hand.[27]

---

[22] See, however, Michael Byrom, *Puppet Theatre in Antiquity* (Bicester, 1996), which presents some possible evidence from Greek and Roman texts of the existence in the ancient world of internally strung marionettes.

[23] *qua plurima visum/fila secant* (*Machinae Gesticulantes* 12-13).

[24] *ne cum vacuo datur ore fenestra* (*Machinae Gesticulantes* 13).

[25] *pervia fraus pateat* (*Machinae Gesticulantes* 14).

[26] *Tatler*, 44 (21 July 1709: ed. Bond, I, 316).

[27] Thomas Burnet, *A Second Tale of a Tub or The History of Robert Powel the Puppet-Show-Man* (London, 1715), Introduction, xxvi-xxvii. Italics are mine. Cf.

Addison conveys something of the colorful splendor and spectacle of the puppet theater as the noisy puppets enter their *penates/... pictos* (14-15), whose walls are "rough with paint" (*moenia squalida fuco* [15]).[28] That splendor is mirrored in the puppets' costumes themselves, and Addison as neo-Latin "spectator" notes several points of detail. Often the troop of puppets appears glistening with gems (*gemmis rutila* [35]) and handsome in gold (*spectabilis auro* [35]),[29] as it takes pride in bright purple (*nitidisque superbit in ostris* [36]).[30] And the vivid account of the foremost puppet suggests that Addison is in fact describing either Punch himself,[31] as argued by Bradner,[32] or at least one of his ancestors, as suggested by Sutton,[33] among whom Harlequin would seem to be the likeliest contender.[34] Like Harlequin and his successor Punch, Addison's

---

ibid., xxxiii, Epilogue, lines 11-14. "He ne'er had spoke nor acted with such Fire,/Had not Lord POWEL stood behind the Wire./You can't imagine, Sirs, what Art can do;/'Twill make a Wooden Head, a Wise one too." Burnet substituted Robert for Powell's real name (Martin) "to render the obvious satire upon Robert Harley more effective." See *DNB* sv. Praise of Powell's skill is all the more striking when set against the criticism expressed by Joseph Strutt in *Sports and Pastimes of the People of England* cited by Cruikshank, *Punch and Judy*, 26: "In my memory these shows consisted of a wretched display of wooden figures, barbarously formed and decorated, without the least degree of taste or propriety: *the wires that communicated the motion to them appeared at the top of their heads*, and the manner in which they were made to move evinced the ignorance and inattention of the managers." Italics are mine.

[28] Cf. Addison, *Resurrectio* 11-12: *velamine moenia crasso/squalent obducta et rudioribus illita fucis.*

[29] On the gaudy apparel of puppets, cf. *Spectator*, 277 (17 January 1712: ed. Bond, II, 580): "The Puppet was dressed in a Cherry-coloured gown and petticoat ... her hair was cut and divided very prettily, with several ribbons stuck up and down in it."

[30] This passage (especially the use of purple and gold) combined with the earlier phrase *subnectit fibula vestem* (20) (used of Punch's costume) echoes the description of Dido in the hunting scene at *Aeneid* 4. 129-139.

[31] Cruikshank, *Punch and Judy*, 30, states: "the puppet-show of 'Punch and Judy' was well known and much admired 'while/Our gracious Anne was Queen of Britain's Isle.'"

[32] Bradner, *Musae Anglicanae*, 223.

[33] Sutton, ed. *The Latin Prose and Poetry of Joseph Addison, ad loc*, states that "this character may at least be reckoned as Punch's ancestor."

[34] On the origins of Punch in Italy, see Cruikshank, *Punch and Judy*, 7-18, who remarks at 13 that "the dress ... of Harlequin corresponds very much with the motley or parti-coloured habit of the clowns of the old dramatic poets," and concludes, at 15, that "Punch is one of the *familia Harlequini*." Cf. Addison, as quoted by Cruikshank,

puppet shouts in a hoarse voice (19-20), has exaggerated gestures (25), anticipating indeed Addison's later remark on "something so comical in the voice and gestures" of the Harlequin himself.[35] His costume is fastened by a larger pin (20), he has eyes that roll (21), he possesses a paunch (22), and has a humpback (22-23).[36] Such details are certainly comparable with a description of Punch[37] popularized in a ballad dating to as late as 1791:

> But not so handsome Mr Punch
>   Who had a monstrous nose, Sir,
> And on his back there grew a hunch
>   That to his head arose, Sir.
> But then, they say, that he could speak
>   As winning as a Mermaid,
> And by his voice – a treble squeak –,
>   He Judy win, that fair maid.[38]

While Addison does not mention Judy by name, he does depict this Punch-like puppet attacking gentle ladies, and planting kisses upon an unwilling female (31-32).[39] Similarly he shows irreverent scorn amid the

Punch and Judy, 14: "He tells us that in Italy 'Harlequin's part is made up of blunders and absurdities: he is to mistake one name for another, to forget his errands, to stumble over queens, and to run his head against every post that comes in his way.'" On the history of the Italian puppet theater, see Michael Byrom, *Punch in the Italian Puppet Theatre* (London, 1983). Cruikshank, *Punch and Judy*, 34, states that "the popularity of Punch [in England] was in the year 1711-12 completely established."

[35] Addison, *Travels in Italy*, as quoted by Cruikshank, *Punch and Judy*, 14.

[36] Cruikshank, *Punch and Judy*, 15, remarks on the fact that "the question arises to what circumstance he owes the deformity of his figure ... We can only answer that it pleased his inventor, Silvio Fiorillo, to make him so; and perhaps he did it in some degree with a view of rendering him more ridiculous, and to distinguish him more effectually from other characters of not dissimilar habits and propensities in the impromptu comedies: hence too, probably, the peculiar quality of his voice, to which Addison alludes."

[37] On descriptions of Punch, cf. *Tatler*, 45 (23 July 1709: ed. Bond, I, 322-323): "though Punch has neither a French nightcap nor long pockets, yet you must own him to be a pretty fellow, a 'very' pretty fellow;" *Musical Miscellany* VI (1731): "My cap is like a sugar-loaf,/And round my collar I wear a ruff." Cited by Cruikshank, *Punch and Judy*, 38.

[38] As quoted by Cruikshank, *Punch and Judy*, 47.

[39] *nec raro invadit molles, pictamque protervo/ore petit nympham invitoque dat oscula ligno* (*Machinae Gesticulantes* 31-32). *Spectator*, 115 reveals that Punch (Puncinello) had "a scolding wife." Cf. also Cruikshank, *Punch and Judy*, 32-33.

solemnity of an occasion (28-29).[40] However, as he hurls his insults amid laughter, his resilience shines forth. As Cruikshank succinctly summarizes:

> His good spirits, his self-possession and presence of mind never desert him; and these qualities, combined with his personal but prudal courage, carry him through every difficulty, and enable him to triumph over every adversary.[41]

Addison also captures something of the mock-heroic pageantry associated with some of the puppet shows themselves. These puppets reproduce whatever men do:[42] their encounters, battles and triumphs (17), and more specifically their wars: *bella, horrida bella* (51),[43] in which they wield such weapons as swords, powder-filled muskets, spears, and missiles (55-59).[44] By contrast they also enact biblical scenes: heroes of

---

[40] *quamquam res agitur sollemni seria pompa,/spernit sollicitum intractabilis ille tumultum* (*Machinae Gesticulantes* 28-29). Cf. *Tatler*, 45 (23 July 1709: ed. Bond, I, 323): "A young gentleman who sat next me (for I had the curiosity of seeing this entertainment) ... was enraged when Punchinello disturbed a soft love-scene with his ribaldry." Cf. *Spectator*, 14 (16 March 1711: ed. Bond, I, 64), in which under the Piazza in Covent Garden Mr Powell's hero danced a minuet with "a well-disciplined pig," while in the same show "King Harry (probably the Eighth) [laid] his leg upon the Queen's lap in too ludicrous a manner before so great an assembly." Cf. Cruikshank, *Punch and Judy*, 43.

[41] Cruikshank, *Punch and Judy*, 68.

[42] *quicquid agunt homines* (*Machinae Gesticulantes* 17). On puppets enacting human and topical themes, cf. Burnet, *A Second Tale of a Tub*, The Dedication, xxiv-xxv: "For what man, woman or child that lives within the verge of Covent-Garden, or what beau or belle visitant at the Bath knows not Mr Powell? Have not England, Scotland, France and Ireland; have not even the Orcades, the utmost limits of Caesar's conquest been filled with the fame of Mr Powell's mechanical achievements? The Dutch, the most expert nation in the world for Puppet-shows, must now confess themselves to be shamefully outdone. It would be trifling after this to recount to you how Mr Powell has melted a whole audience into pity and tears when he has made the poor starved children in the wood miserably depart in peace, and a Robin bury them ... It would be tedious to enumerate how often he has made Punch the diversion of all the spectators by putting into his mouth many bulls and flat contradictions to the dear joy of all true Teagues. Or to what end should I attempt to describe how heroically he makes King Bladud perform the part of a British prince?"

[43] On the Virgilian source for this phrase, see 83 below.

[44] Cf. *Spectator*, 31 (5 April 1711) on the portrayal of Alexander the Great in a puppet show.

old whom the "sacred page" (65) supplies,[45] processions of the ancient
Fathers with grey beards and wrinkled faces (68-70).[46] Such is the
versatility of this puppet band.

(ii)   Virgil Recreated: Puppets and Bees

Hand in hand with the potential realism of Addison's account of a puppet
show is the close intertextual relationship between his poem and Virgil's
Georgics. Frequently the poem's language shifts from that of stagecraft
to that of the beehive and its inhabitants.

     One of the key aspects of Virgil's description of the bee
community is the contrast between the minute stature of these insects and
their grandiose behavior. In his *Dissertatio* Addison remarks on the
contrast between the "slight theme" and the "solemn pomp" of
expression assumed by Virgil in the *Georgics*.[47] In the opening lines of
book 4 the speaker emphasizes the fact that his subject matter is slight (*in
tenui labor* [6]) yet marvelous (*admiranda tibi levium spectacula rerum*
[3]). The epic proportions of his slight subject are likewise emphasized
by *magnanimos ... duces* (4), who possess *mores/studia/populos/proelia*
(5).[48] The theme of size recurs as Virgil describes the site of the hive in
4.8ff. from the perspective of a tiny bee. Thus it is significant that shade

---

[45] *prisci heroes quos pagina sacra/suggerit* (*Machinae Gesticulantes* 65-66).

[46] That such biblical scenes, however, were frequently enacted irreverently is attested
by *Tatler*, 16 (17 May 1709: ed. Bond, I, 134), relaying the remarks of a
correspondent at Bath: "When we came to Noah's flood in the show, Punch and his
wife were introduced dancing in the ark. An honest plain friend of Florimel's, but a
critic withal, rose up in the midst of the representation and made many very good
exceptions to the drama itself, and told us that it was against all morality, as well as
rules of the stage, that Punch should be in jest in the deluge or indeed that he should
appear at all." Cf. also *Spectator*, 14 (16 March 1711): "of two ladies, Prudentia and
Florimel, who would lead the fashion, Prudentia caused Eve in the Puppet-Show of
'the Creation of the World' to be 'made the most like Florimel that ever was seen',
and 'when we came to Noah's Flood in the show, Punch and his wife were introduced
dancing in the ark.'"

[47] *ubi dum in tenui argumento procedit poema, solemnem quandam sententiarum et
verborum pompam studiose affectet poeta* (Guthkelch, ed. *Miscellaneous Works*, II,
471).

[48] Cf. Gale, *Virgil on The Nature of Things*, 228: "Within this short proem, the poet
plays repeatedly on the contrast between the smallness of the bees and their more
impressive qualities: they are 'light' but worthy of admiration."

for the hive should be provided by a "huge" olive tree (*ingens oleaster* [20]). The beekeeper should throw pebbles into the middle of the stream as a settling point for the bees as they stretch their wings to the summer sun. But these pebbles are described as "huge boulders" (*et grandia conice saxa* [26]). Once again we are regarding objects from the perspective of the bees themselves.

Addison's poem commences with what is virtually a verbatim quotation from *Georgics* 4.3, except that he substitutes *cano* for *tibi*.[49] Noteworthy also is the development of the Virgilian concept of *levitas*,[50] as Addison's race is described as an *exiguam gentem* (2). From the outset then the puppet community is described in terms evocative of Virgil's bees. But despite the sense of awe conveyed by the echo of Virgil's *admiranda*, this race constitutes a brainless people: *vacuum sine mente popellum* (2). One might contrast here the bees of *Georgics* 4 who possess *ingentes animos angusto in pectore* (83), and whose mental vigor is emphasized on more than one occasion: thus they are mindful (*memores* [156]) of winter even in the summer; they are motivated by *amor... habendi* (177); when their leader is safe *mens omnibus una est* (212); indeed they even have a share in the divine mind (*partem divinae mentis* [220]). Later, although their individual life span is brief, they create the illusion of immortality.[51] By contrast Addison's puppet race, at least initially, is mindless. But as the poem progresses it is the puppeteer who has the power to inspire this lifeless and brainless form, to provide it with a *mens* of its own. So while at the outset the puppets constitute a hollow wooden form,[52] the poem as a whole belies the notion that these are merely empty vessels.

That tiny creatures are much more than they seem is an implicit subtext of both *Georgics* 4 and Addison's poem. In his *Essay on Virgil's Georgics* Addison draws attention to Virgil's comparison of the bees to the gigantic Cyclopes:[53]

---

[49] *admiranda cano levium spectacula rerum* (1). Cf. *Aen.* 1.1 *arma virumque cano*.

[50] Cf. *levium ... rerum* (*Georgics* 4. 3; *Machinae Gesticulantes* 1).

[51] *ergo ipsas quamvis angusti terminus aevi/excipiat .../at genus immortale manet.* (*Georgics* 4. 206-208).

[52] Compare the detailed instructions provided in the poem's concluding lines regarding their manufacture — a passage which finds a parallel in Virgil's account of the building of the wooden plough at *Georgics* 1.160ff. See 85-87 below.

[53] In Addison's poem the theme of giant recurs on an altogether different level. One of the puppets, literally a dwarf (an *homuncio*: the hunch-backed Punch or one of his predecessors), is described as a giant who terrifies the rest of the puppet community,

And as in his *Aeneis* he compares the labours of his Trojans to those of bees and pismires, here he compares the labours of the bees to those of the Cyclops.[54]

That contrast in Virgil between the small stature of the bees and their huge and manifold emotions is borne out in Addison's poem, and works on several levels: between the physically puny theater, as it were, the *angusta claustra* (16), the *exiguo ... theatro* (18) and the grandeur of the scenes enacted. Upon this puppet stage, which in itself is described in terms reminiscent of Virgil's beehive, is performed a wealth of essentially human acts and emotions. And the performers are a *plebecula parva* (18), described as though they were a Roman *civitas*. In a sense Addison is making explicit what is implicit in Virgil's portrayal of the bees, namely, the personification of bee behavior.[55]

Like Virgil's bees, Addison's puppets are inclined to battle. In his *Essay on Virgil's Georgics* Addison notes the epic grandeur afforded Virgil's battling bees: "His verses are not in a greater noise and hurry in the battles of Aeneas and Turnus than in the engagement of two swarms."[56] Virgil describes on two occasions battles within the bee community – one is *discordia*, civil war; the other an account of the bees' patriotic willingness to go to war on behalf of their *rex*. And the language used is the language of epic. Thus two *reges* possess *discordia* (67-68)[57] with hearts trembling for war (69-70);[58] there is a martial trumpet blast

---

and inspires awe (*immanem miratur turba gigantem* [*Machinae Gesticulantes* 24]). Relying on his vast size he can hurl abuse at the other puppets.

[54] Guthkelch, ed. *Miscellaneous Works*, II, 10. Cf. *Georgics* 4. 176-177: *non aliter, si parva licet componere magnis/Cecropias innatus apes amor urget habendi.*

[55] Thus Addison proclaims: *quicquid agunt homines, concursus, bella, triumphos,/ ludit in exiguo plebecula parva theatro* (*Machinae Gesticulantes* 17-18). Worthy of comparison is the personification of the bees in the *proemium* to *Georgics* 4: *magnanimosque duces totiusque ordine gentis/mores et studia et populos et proelia dicam* (4. 4-5).

[56] Guthkelch, ed. *Miscellaneous Works*, II, 10. Similarly in the *Dissertatio*: *nec maiori carminum tumultu Aeneae et Turni recitat certamina quam hasce insectorum turmas inter se deproeliantes* (Guthkelch, ed. *Miscellaneous Works*, II, 471).

[57] *duobus/regibus incessit magno discordia motu* (*Georgics* 4. 67-68).

[58] *trepidantia bello/corda* (*Georgics* 4. 69-70).

(71).[59] The bees crowd round their *rex* and his tent, and summon the enemy (75-76).[60] One side will be the *victor* (85).

Addison, fusing the *Georgics* and the *Aeneid* at this point, refers to his puppets' *bella, horrida bella* (51), echoing the Sibyl's prophecy to Aeneas at *Aeneid* 6.86,[61] and the poet's assumption of similar language in book 7 to announce his so-called "Iliadic" half of the epic.[62] The use of the adverb *saepe* (51) recalls perhaps Virgil's point that the inclination to war on the part of certain bees is a frequent (*saepe* [*G.* 4. 67]) occurrence.[63] As in Virgil, the language employs the military terminology of civil war.[64] Where Virgil had described the bees' resolute determination to succeed in battle *usque adeo obnixi* (*G.* 4.84), Addison, using a similar phrase, conveys how war actually detracts from the pleasure of all (*usque adeo insincera voluptas/omnibus* [53-54]).[65] In Virgil, the bee battle was quelled by sprinkling dust (86-87). Such is not the case in Addison, but we do catch a glimpse of the aftermath when the passion of the puppet brawl has indeed calmed down: *sed postquam insanus pugnae deferbuit aestus* (62).

An essential part of Virgil's personification of the bees lies in his description of, as it were, their *Romanitas*. Frequently they are depicted in terms reminiscent of a Roman community. Thus they possess a commonwealth (*consortia tecta* [153]); they have their own *lares* (43),[66]

---

[59] *Martius ille aeris rauci canor increpitat* (*Georgics* 4. 71).

[60] *et circa regem atque ipsa ad praetoria densae/miscentur magnisque vocant clamoribus hostem* (*Georgics* 4. 75-76).

[61] *bella, horrida bella,/et Thybrim multo spumantem sanguine cerno* (*Aen.* 6. 86-87).

[62] *dicam horrida bella,/dicam acies actosque animis in funera reges* (*Aen.* 7. 41-42).

[63] *sin autem ad pugnam exierint - nam saepe duobus regibus incessit ... discordia* (*Georgics* 4. 67-68).

[64] Hence *pugnae* (53)/*ad pugnam* (4. 67); *hastae, fulgentiaque arma, minaeque* (56), *civilis crimina belli* (61)/*discordia* (4. 68). Cf. Thomas, ed. *Virgil: Georgics*, II, 159 (on Virgil's *incessit magno discordia motu* [68]): "the words recall 2. 496 *infidos agitans discordia fratres* (also 2. 459 *discordibus armis*), and suggest that the bees belong to a culturally 'advanced' society."

[65] This is perhaps a parody of the bees' pleasure in generating honey. Cf. *tantus amor florum et generandi gloria mellis* (*Georgics* 4. 205).

[66] *sub terra fovere larem* (*Georgics* 4. 43).

penates and *patria* (155).[67] As Addison's puppets appear on stage they are described as entering their painted *penates* (*mox stridula turba penates/ingreditur pictos* [14-15]) as though this were a Roman household. And the walls of the *penates* are rough with paint (*moenia squalida fuco* [15]). While *fucus* is used here to denote colored paint,[68] it is also the word for the glue used by bees to seal openings in the hive (4. 39).[69] Just as Virgil describes his bees as little Roman citizens (*parvosque Quirites* [201]),[70] so the puppet procession includes *exigui proceres parvique Quirites* (39).

In the *Georgics* the hive is to have a "narrow" entrance (*angustos habeant aditus* [4. 35]). Addison, having described his puppet theater in terms reminiscent of the Roman stage,[71] now appropriates Virgil's theme of narrowness to details of the staging itself, turning jussive subjunctives into factual statements. Virgil, having recommended a narrow entrance for the beehive, proceeds to explain why such is necessary: the winter cold congeals the honey while the sun melts it. In Addison, the narrow entrance (*angustos ... aditus* [12]) likewise has a specific purpose: that of maintaining the illusion of the puppet performance. If the gap (*fenestra* [13]) is presented with an unoccupied façade, that illusion is destroyed. Hence the need of wires as a means of bisecting the audience's vision (12-13).[72] This passing reference to a *fenestra*, however, is not without irony when it is remembered that this is a detail included in the *bougonia* episode of *Georgics* 4.

---

[67] *et patriam solae et certos novere penates* (*Georgics* 4. 155). Cf. Dalzell, *The Criticism of Didactic Poetry*, 122-123. Thompson, ed. *Virgil: Georgics*, II, 177, notes: "Virgil does not otherwise use *penates* of non-human beings, and it seems to be used elsewhere in this way only at Stat. *Silv.* 3.5.58-9."

[68] Cf. *OLD* sv 2: "A dyestuff, dye". Cf. Catullus 64.49: *pulvinar ... quod ... tincta tegit roseo conchyli purpurea fuco*; Horace, *Odes* 3.5.28: *neque amissos colores lana refert medicata fuco*. On Addison's use of *fucus* for paint, cf. its frequent occurrence in *Resurrectio Delineata*: *egregios fuci tractus* (1); *moenia .../rudioribus illita fucis* (11-12); *stagnantia fuco/moenia* (91-92); *o fuci nitor* (112). See also 109-112 below.

[69] *tenuia cera/spiramenta linunt, fucoque et floribus oras/explent* (*Georgics* 4. 38-40). Cf. *OLD* sv 3 "Bee-glue, propolis". Thomas, ed. *Virgil: Georgics*, II, 154, reads *fucoque et floribus* (39) as a hendiadys, "referring to *propolis* or 'bee-glue,' a resinous substance collected chiefly from the buds of trees and used to seal the hive." He continues: "As Page notes *fuco* implies something that can be 'smeared or daubed.'"

[70] *ipsae regem parvosque Quirites/sufficiunt* (*Georgics* 4. 201-202).

[71] See 74-76 above.

[72] See 76 above.

In Addison's puppet show, the *fenestra* plays an important role in that it helps create a particular illusion. In the *bougonia* episode, which is in itself an illusion of sorts (a miraculous means of reproducing a perennial supply of bees continuously emerging from the putrid carcasses of bulls), the *fenestra* functions as the setting for the entire scene. Four windows are added with slanting light set away from the four winds.[73] Next an ox is beaten to death, and it is from this carcass that the miracle bees emerge (308-309). Links between Addison's lines and this episode are also suggested by the juxtaposition of *mox* and *stridula turba* (14) as the puppets enter the stage, reminiscent of the description of *bougonia* at *Georgics* 4.310-311: *mox et stridentia pennis,/miscentur.* But that *bougonia* is replaced by another kind of resurrection: that of "useless wood" (*inutile lignum* [75]) into speaking puppets,[74] into wood moreover that has the power to enact human emotions or events. In the opening lines of the poem the puppet manufacturer was seen as a second Prometheus, with one important difference: instead of stealing fire from the gods for the creation of the human race, this artisan had utilized a skill that was innocent, thereby surpassing his classical precursor (3-4).[75] Now as the poem nears its conclusion the whole comes full circle via a flashback detailing the mechanics of a puppet's creation. The artisan (*opifex* [75]) forces sticks and wood into human shapes (*cogit in humanas species* [76]), binding legs to feet (*crura ligat pedibus* [78]), fitting arms to shoulders (*umerisque accommodat armos* [78]), joining limbs to limbs (*et membris membra aptat* [79]) and sewing joints to

---

[73] *... et quattuor addunt,/quattuor a ventis oblique luce fenestras* (*Georgics* 4.298-299). Cf. Thomas, ed. *Virgil: Georgics*, II, 199: "Virgil seems to be thinking of shelter, presumably from both wind and light. Cf. Lucretius 6.1110-11 (of the four climates)."

[74] Contrast *Tatler*, 44 (21 July 1709: ed. Bond, I, 317): "I shall command myself and never trouble me further with this little fellow, who is himself but a tall puppet and has not brains enough to make even wood speak as it ought to do. And I, that have heard the groaning board, can despise all that his puppets shall be able to speak as long as they live: but *ex quovis ligno non fit Mercurius.*"

[75] *quem non surreptis caeli de fornice flammis,/innocua melior fabricaverat arte Prometheus* (*Machinae Gesticulantes* 3-4). The lines find an interesting parallel in Nicolaus Hobart, *Dioptrices Laus*, 3-6: *quid, superi, querimur? reparans ecce omnia damna,/sanctior ars, nobis oculos melioraque praebet/lumina et antiqua vafri sine fraude Promethei,/arripit insontes caeli de fornice flammas* (*Musae Anglicanae*, I, 94).

joints (*et artubus insuit artus* [79]).[76] On one level this quasi-"technical" section of the poem finds a parallel in Virgil's description of the manufacture of the plough[77] in *Georgics* 1. 169-175, which in itself looks back to a more elaborate passage in Hesiod, *Works and Days*.[78] Virgil's farmer is told how to make an elm assume the curved shape of the stock (169-170); to the top of the stock he is to add an eight-foot pole, which in turn will connect with the yoke (171-172); at either side are attached two ears, in between which are fitted the share-beams (172); to the front of the share-beam is fastened the share. At the base of the stock is fitted the handle, which enables the plough as a whole to turn (173-174).

Developing the element of personification already implicit in Virgil's lines,[79] Addison applies this to a puppet, who approximates the human in a way that Virgil's plough cannot. Both convey the strength employed to bend or mould the wood (*magna vi flexa domatur* [169]/ *cogit* [76])[80] into the relevant shape (*curvi formam accipit ulmus aratri* [170]/*in humanas species et robore natam/progeniem telo efformat* [76-77]). The tying of the pole to the top of the stock becomes in Addison the binding of the puppet's legs and feet. The *binae aures* (172) attached

---

[76] For emphasis upon the wooden construction of the puppets and references to their manufacture, cf. *Tatler*, 115 (3 January 1710: ed. Bond, II, 188): "As for Punch, who takes all opportunities of bespattering me, I know very well his original, and have been assured by the joiner who put him together that he was in long dispute with himself whether he should turn him into several pegs and utensils or make him the man he is. The same person confessed to me that he had once actually laid aside his head for a nut-cracker. As for his scolding wife (however she may value herself at present), it is very well known that she is but a piece of crabtree. This artificer further whispered in my ear that all his courtiers and nobles were taken out of a quickset hedge not far from Islington: and that Dr Faustus himself, who is now so great a conjuror, is supposed to have learned his whole art from an old woman in that neighbourhood, whom he long served in the figure of a broomstaff."

[77] See among others A.S.F. Gow, "The Ancient Plough," *JHS* 34 (1914), 249-275; Robert Aitken, "Virgil's Plough," *JRS* 46 (1956), 97-106.

[78] Cf. Hesiod, *Works and Days* 427-436. Thomas, ed. *Virgil: Georgics*, I, 97, notes that Virgil "has radically trimmed the Hesiodic account, giving the necessary details, but removing all asides and poetic embellishments, almost as if his concern was to complete the description as soon as possible." Mynors, ed. *Virgil: Georgics*, 33, states that "Hesiod's lines on the mortar, the waggon, and the plough (*op.* 423ff.) were sufficiently prominent to demand something in that vein from any would-be *Ascraeum carmen*."

[79] Note, for example, *aures* (172), *dentalia* (172), *dorso* (172).

[80] Thomas, ed. *Virgil: Georgics*, I, 97, notes: "*domare* is a strong word, also used of man's exerting his will over trees at 2.62."

at either side[81] are now paralleled by arms fitted to the puppet's shoulders. Then the handle (*stiva* [174]), which sets the whole in motion (*quae currus a tergo torqueat imos* [174]),[82] becomes the pulleys which render the puppet mobile (*tunc habiles addit trochleas quibus arte pusillum/versat onus* [80-81]).[83]

But Addison fuses this technical passage with the miracle of *bougonia* itself. The stages of the coming to birth of his puppet, as limbs are gradually rendered mobile, seem to mirror the gradual emergence through *bougonia* of bees (*animalia* [309]), footless at first, but soon buzzing, tentatively taking to the air, and bursting forth in a rather monstrous birth.[84] Now in a different form of *bougonia* limb is joined to limb, while motion, dance, and voice engender the resurrection of that once useless wood (85-86). The whole is a self-referential encomium of the power of the artist to create and to recreate, to breathe life into his subject, and above all to give it a voice:[85]

> hinc salit atque agili se sublevat incita motu
> *vocesque emittit tenues et non sua verba.*
> (*Machinae Gesticulantes* 85-86).[86]

---

[81] Mynors, ed. *Virgil: Georgics*, 38, notes that "the 'ears' or wings seem to have been boards or stout pegs, of uncertain size and made of wood, which were fixed to the body of the plough to widen the furrow and throw up more soil ..."

[82] Mynors, ed. *Virgil: Georgics*, 39, identifies *stiva* as: "the handle or stilt fitted in various ways and at various angles onto the tail-end of the plough, with a crosspiece, *manicula*, at its top, on which the ploughman leans if the nose of the plough shows a wish to run itself into the ground, and with which he keeps a straight furrow, and steers his plough through 180 degrees when he reaches the headland."

[83] For a more elaborate example, cf. *Spectator*, 277 (17 January 1712: ed. Bond, II, 581): "As I was taking my leave the millener farther informed me that with the assistance of a watch-maker, who was her neighbour, and the ingenious Mr Powell, she had also contrived another puppet, *which by the help of several little springs to be wound up within it, could move all its limbs.*" Italics are mine.

[84] *trunca pedum primo. mox et stridentia pennis,/miscentur, tenuemque magis magis aera carpunt,/donec .../erupuere* (*Georgics* 4.310-313). Gale, *Virgil on The Nature of Things*, 230, perceptively remarks that "the footless insects emerging from the corpse have something about them of the monstrous births which are produced in the early days of the earth's fertility."

[85] Cf. Burnet, *A Second Tale of a Tub*, xxvii: "and as for Punch, who used heretofore to be nothing but a roaring, lewd, rakish, empty fellow, a perfect mohawk, he now speaks choice apothegms and sterling wit to the amazement of the applauding audience both in pit and boxes."

[86] Italics are mine.

CHAPTER 5

A Virgilian Game of Bowls: *Sphaeristerium*

In the second half of the seventeenth century there began to appear in England a miniature genre of neo-Latin poetry on contemporary sports and pastimes.[1] This is epitomized perhaps by Addison's inclusion in the *Musae Anglicanae* of poems on such activities as bullbaiting,[2] cockfighting,[3] and skating.[4] To this genre pertains his own Latin hexameter piece *Sphaeristerium*, on a bowling green and, more specifically, on the already popular game of bowls.[5] Nor indeed was Addison the first to treat of this topic. Latin hexameter verses by William Dillingham,[6] entitled *Sphaeristerium Suleianum* on a bowling green at Sulehay, directly precede Addison's poem on the subject in the *Examen*

---

[1] See Bradner, *Musae Anglicanae*, 221.

[2] Francis Knapp, *Taurus in Circo*, *Musae Anglicanae*, II, 80-84.

[3] Joseph Friend, *Pugna Gallorum Gallinaceorum*, *Musae Anglicanae*, II, 85-90.

[4] Philip Frowde, *Cursus Glacialis*, *Musae Anglicanae*, II, 145-147.

[5] On the popularity of the game of bowls cf., for example, John Evelyn's frequent references to the sport: *Diary*, ed. E.S. De Beer (Oxford, 1955), III, 68: "11 June 1652 About 4 in the afternoone, beeing at bowles on the Greene;" *Diary*, III, 219: "14 Aug 1658 We went to a challeng'd match to Durdens to Bowles for 10 pounds, which we wonn." That Addison witnessed bowling matches is indicated by his later comment in *Spectator*, 126 (25 July 1711: ed. Bond, II, 3-4): "Being upon the Bowling-green at a neighbouring market town the other day (for that is the place where the gentlemen of one side meet once a week)."

[6] William Dillingham (1617?-1689) is described in *DNB* as "a Latin poet and controversialist." He was admitted a sizar of Emmanuel College, Cambridge, 22 April 1636. He graduated BA in 1639, was elected Fellow in 1642, commenced his MA in 1643, and graduated BD in 1650, and DD in 1655. In 1658 he was elected Vice-Chancellor. His Latin poems are included in *Poemata Varii Argumenti, Partim e Georgio Herberto Latine (Utcunque) Reddita, Partim Conscripta a Wilh. Dillingham S.T.D.* (London, 1678). Cf. *Alumni Cantabrigienses*, ed. John Venn and J.A. Venn (Cambridge, 1922), II, 43.

Poeticum Duplex.[7] Both works moreover may owe some debt to Thomas Masters' *Mensa Lubrica* (1658), a Latin poem on the Shovel Board[8] (the ancestor of the modern American game of shuffle board). While such pieces are linked intertextually, they may also be regarded as the product of a rapidly evolving mock-heroic form, which would of course manifest itself more conspicuously in the following century in the vernacular writings of Pope and others. It is a form, however, that had already come to maturity in Italy, in Vida's *Scacchia Ludus* (1525),[9] describing in Virgilian language a chess game by Apollo and Mercury played in the presence of the other gods. Vida's poem was well known in England from the late sixteenth century onwards,[10] as indeed was his entire neo-Latin corpus,[11] and would be included in its entirety in the first neo-Latin

[7] The fact that Dillingham's poem precedes Addison's *Sphaeristerium* in the *Examen* (where it occurs at 29-33) may indicate that it was composed first, a point reinforced by internal evidence in the poems themselves. The piece was not anthologized by Addison in the *Musae Anglicanae*, which was based on the output of Oxford poets.

[8] *Musae Anglicanae* I, 17-19. Bradner, *Musae Anglicanae*, 204, overstates the question of "influence" by asserting that Dillingham's poem "was probably inspired" by Masters' piece, and that "either he [Dillingham] or Masters was, in turn, the cause of Addison's later *Sphaeristerium*." On possible points of contact, however, see 93, 95, 99, 100, 101, 102 below.

[9] See *The Game of Chess: Marco Girolamo Vida's Scacchia Ludus*, ed. with introduction and notes by M.A. Di Cesare (*Bibliotheca Humanistica & Reformatorica* 13: Nieuwkoop, 1975).

[10] The poem made some impact upon such neo-Latin works as Thomas Watson's *Amintae Gaudia* (London, 1592), which included as *Eclogue* 6 a battle between Jupiter and Pluto, and introduced the whole by the gift of a chess set, with the battle itself depicted in terms of the movements on a chessboard. Cf. Bradner, *Musae Anglicanae*, 48.

[11] For example, Vida was included in John Leland's *Principum ac Illustrium Aliquot et Eruditorum in Anglia Virorum Encomia, Trophaea, Genethliaca et Epithalamia a Ioanne Lelando Antiquario Conscripta* (London, 1589). That Vida's poetry was read in England is perhaps most notably manifested by echoes in Milton's Latin and vernacular poetry, of which Vida's *Christiad*, the *De Arte Poetica*, and Latin hymns constitute key neo-Latin intertexts. On Vida and Milton, see M.A. Di Cesare, "From Virgil to Vida to Milton," *Acta Conventus Neo-Latini Turonensis*, 1976 (Paris: Librairie Philosophique, 1980), I, 153-161; Gertrude Drake, "Satan's Councils in the *Christiad, Paradise Lost* and *Paradise Regained*," *Acta Conventus Neo-Latini Turonensis*, 979-989; Estelle Haan, "Milton's *Paradise Regained* and Vida's *Christiad*," *From Erudition to Inspiration: Essays in Honour of M.J. McGann* (Belfast: Belfast Byzantine Texts and Translations, 1992), 53-77; Estelle Haan, "From Helicon to Heaven: Milton's Urania and Vida," *RS* 1 (1993), 86-107; Estelle Haan, "'Heaven's Purest Light': *Paradise Lost* 3 and Vida," *CLS* 30.2 (1993), 115-136;

anthology (1678) to be published in England, an anthology compiled by William Dillingham no less.[12] Perhaps it was the novelty of its treatment that was particularly appealing. For, as Bradner notes, the skill of the neo- and in particular the Anglo-Latin sports poem lay in its presentation of a familiar object or pastime in a strange setting.[13]

(i)   A Virgilian Landscape?

For Addison that "strange setting" is perhaps more literary than topographical. The poem draws upon Virgilian language, fusing scenes from the *Eclogues*, *Georgics* and especially from *Aeneid* 5 (the anniversary games for Anchises). The consequences of this fusion are manifold: through recalling Virgilian pastoral Addison can highlight the pristine innocence of a rural landscape threatened by the heavy lawn roller which, in language reminiscent of a scene from the *Georgics*,[14] flattens the bowling green in preparation for the game. Then in the bowling match proper the context in which the whole is presented and the behavior of the competitors and spectators seem to recall those games of *Aeneid* 5. Later, as argued below, the poem comes full circle with the closing lines' appropriation and surprising metamorphosis of pastoral imagery.[15] Nothing is ever quite what it seems. Paradoxically, it is when Addison seems to echo Virgil that he is often at his most original. The poem describes a setting which, while unspecified, is in all likelihood an Oxonian one, that of Magdalen College, whose present Grove (Deer Park) used to be the site of bowling greens, orchards, and gardens.[16] With Dillingham, on the other hand, the case is rather different. Although he too, like Addison, looks back to the games in the *Aeneid*, he sets his

---

Estelle Haan, "Milton's Latin Poetry and Vida," *HL* 44 (1995), 282-304; Estelle Haan, "From Neo-Latin to Vernacular: Celestial Warfare in Vida and Milton," *Hommages à Carl Deroux: Christianisme et Moyen Âge: Néo-Latin et Survivance de la Latinité*, ed. Paul Defosse (Collection Latomus 279: Brussels, 2003), 408-419.

[12] *Poemata Varii Argumenti*, ed. William Dillingham (London, 1678).

[13] Bradner, *Musae Anglicanae*, 221.

[14] See 92 below.

[15] See 103 below.

[16] As shown in, for example, Radulph Agas' map of 1578.

poem in a precise location,[17] that of Sulehay, near Oundle in Peterborough.[18] In terms of its methodology, his poem acts as an important neo-Latin forerunner of Addison's piece, and there is indeed some evidence of interconnectedness. But Addison goes far beyond Dillingham in his inventive *imitatio* of Virgil, in his equation between the animate and the inanimate, and especially in his presentation of the essential *Romanitas* not only of the English bowlers, but surprisingly of the very bowls themselves. As such Addison's *Sphaeristerium* is a masterful, albeit neglected, neo-Latin sports poem.

The opening lines strike a contrast between the innocent pastoralism of the pristine plain (with its grassy surface, empty field, misty meadows, which do not yet acknowledge sunrise, and its dewdrops hanging upon the grass) and the cruel ruthlessness of firstly the scythe (*improba falx* [5]) cropping the previous night's small growth, and secondly the roller (*saxum versatile* [7])[19] pressing upon the protruding earth and wearing down the grass.[20] That contrast is reflected poetically also in the transition from the soft vowel sounds (especially the

---

[17] Bradner's judgment that the poem's "definite local setting" (*Musae Anglicanae*, 204), renders it more pleasing than both Masters' *Mensa Lubrica* and Addison's *Sphaeristerium* is certainly open to question.

[18] Dillingham was Vice-Chancellor of Cambridge University (1658-1660). Forced out of his mastership by the Act of Uniformity, he retired to Oundle, near Peterborough. It is here that he composed his Latin poetry. See *DNB* sv and Bradner, *Musae Anglicanae*, 204-205. Sulehay, is situated to the west of Oundle (eight miles west of Peterborough). The opening lines of the poem suggest that the bowling green is located on a raised level near a bridge at Wansford.

[19] Addison's lawn roller (*saxum versatile* [7]) finds a parallel in Dillingham's *volubile saxum* (12), which likewise flattens the plain, yet is described in terms which lack the pejorative undertones of Addison's lines. Instead the metaphor is one of careful polishing (*hanc bene detonsam ac ad vivum caespite raso/levigat atque polit subigitque volubile saxum,/labentem sphaeram ne qua fetusca moretur* [11-13]).

[20] Cf. Dillingham, who strikes a contrast between the surface as once tilled by farmers (*terra olim agricolae duros experta labores* [6]) and its present smoothness now that it has been re-covered with a fresh surface of grass, and endowed with a green "toga", as it were, of pure soil. This renders it suitable for the sport (*at postquam cincta est vivae munimine saepis/et viridi donata toga de caespite puro,/tota vacat ludo* [7-9]). In Virgil, *Aeneid* 5. 286-287 Aeneas, in choosing a site for a foot race, goes to a place with level turf: *tendit/gramineum in campum*. On possible echoes of Virgil's games in both Addison and Dillingham, see 94-103 below.

proliferation of *a* sounds) of lines 1-4[21] to the harsh consonantal sounds (especially *x, c, t, m, p*) of lines 5-8,[22] the latter reinforced by the forceful verbs *desecat* (6) and *deprimit* (8), and by the staccato rhythm of *tum motu assiduo saxum versatile terram* (7).[23] And the contrast is heightened by the intertextuality of this passage. Thus the line ending *in gramine guttae* (4) draws upon the Latin pastoral poetry of Calpurnius Siculus, a picturesque description of morning dewdrops glistening upon the grass.[24] But that seemingly pastoral landscape is under threat in the following lines, in which the choice of the adjective *improba* to describe the sickle (*falx* [5]) may recall Virgil's account in *Georgics* 1 of the necessary evil of work (*labor ... improbus* [*G.* 1. 145-146]) (and especially of agricultural work), imposed upon humankind by Jupiter in the iron as opposed to the golden age.[25] Similarly the line ending *surgentes atterit herbas* (8), depicting the forceful way in which the lawn roller wears down the rising blades of grass, is reminiscent of the behavior of the heifer in Virgil's fourth *Georgic*.[26] In Virgil, however, this occurs as part of a list of locations to be *avoided* by the beekeeper in his search for a suitable location for the site of his hive. In Addison, that dew will indeed be shaken off the grass, and the rising grass itself will be worn down by an inanimate lawn roller now implicitly equated with Virgil's animate heifer.

And if Addison's lawn roller resembles a living animal, so too in the following lines are the bowls themselves strikingly personified.

---

[21] *hic ubi graminea in latum sese explicat aequor/planities vacuoque ingens patet area campo,/cum solem nondum fumantia prata fatentur/exortum et tumidae pendent in gramine guttae* (*Sphaeristerium* 1-4).

[22] *improba falx noctis parva incrementa prioris/desecat, exiguam radens a caespite messem;/tum motu assiduo saxum versatile terram/deprimit exstantem et surgentes atterit herbas* (*Sphaeristerium* 5-8).

[23] For a rather similar contrast between the innocence of landscape and the ruthlessness of humankind, cf. the description of mining as a virtual rape of the earth in the opening lines of Addison's *Barometri Descriptio*, on which see 38-41 above.

[24] Calpurnius Siculus, *Eclogue* 5.55: *et matutinae lucent in gramine guttae.*

[25] *labor omnia vicit/improbus et duris urgens in rebus egestas./prima Ceres ferro mortalis vertere terram/instituit ...* (*Georgics* 1.145-148).

[26] *aut errans bucula campo/decutiat rorem et surgentes atterat herbas* (*Georgics* 4. 11-12).

Described as a "wooden throng" (*lignea ... turba* [9]),[27] they run over a verdant *palaestra* (9), and are "anointed" and "glistening with oil" (*uncta, nitens oleo* [10]).[28] Sutton, commenting on Addison's choice of the noun *oleo*, remarks: "It would seem intrinsically improbable that the balls were oiled to make them roll better: would this help? More likely Addison is describing them as being waxed, or perhaps varnished."[29] While the latter observation is correct, the choice of *oleo*, in conjunction with the reference to a *palaestra*, has a double-edged significance here. Firstly, it should be noted that Addison is using it metaphorically, equating these bowls with Roman wrestlers, whose custom it was to oil themselves before engaging in the *palaestra* (9).[30] Hence, for example, at *Aeneid* 3.281: *exercent patrias oleo labente palaestras*.[31] In fact the link between oil and wrestling was so close that *oleum* would become a metonym for that sport.[32] And the metaphor is an appropriate one, reflecting the competitive nature of the contest in which these bowls will participate. Once again Addison's predilection for personification (and especially for the personification of the miniature)[33] rears its head. But relevant also to the context of Roman exercising and Addison's

---

[27] Addison's *lignea percurrunt vernantem turba palaestram* (*Sphaeristerium* 9) may have been suggested by Masters' description of silver coins running along the shovel board (*pervolitant specie nummorum, argentea turba,/orbiculi* [*Mensa Lubrica*, 6-7; *Musae Anglicanae*, I, 17]). Likewise Masters' *orbiculi* (7; 50) finds a parallel in Addison's *orbiculus* (20; 48).

[28] It is noteworthy that the participants in Virgil's ship race, with which Addison's poem interacts (on which see 95, 96, 99, 101-103 below) have their shoulders smeared with oil to help their movement (*cetera ... iuventus/nudatosque umeros oleo perfusa nitescit* [*Aen.* 5. 134-135]). Cf. Homer, *Iliad* 23. 280-282 where Patroclus is described as accustomed to pouring olive oil on the manes of Achilles' horses.

[29] Sutton, ed. *The Latin Prose and Poetry of Joseph Addison, ad loc.*

[30] Cf. Dillingham's very brief reference to the *dignamque sua virtute palaestram* (81).

[31] Cf. Livy 21.55: *oleo ... per manipulos, ut mollirent artus, misso*. More generally, Addison's combined references to the *palaestra* and sunrise find a parallel in Plautus, *Bacc.* 424-425: *ante solem exorientem nisi in palaestram veneras,/gymnasi praefecto haud mediocris poenas penderes.*

[32] See, for example, *OLD*: "*oleum*: used, esp. by wrestlers to grease the skin; hence meton. for wrestling." See, for example, Catullus 63.64: *ego gymnasi fui flos, ego eram decus olei*; Seneca, *Ep.* 15.3: *homines inter oleum et vinum occupati.*

[33] Compare the personification of the wooden toy soldiers of the young William in *Pax Gulielmi*, 140-150, or of the wooden puppets in *Machinae Gesticulantes*, passim, on which see 85-87 above.

metaphorical use of the word *oleo* is the title of his poem. *Sphaeristerium* is a term used in classical architecture to denote a large space or room attached to the Roman baths (*thermae*). Here bathers would play ball games (usually prior to having a bath),[34] wash, and perhaps anoint themselves. Indeed Roman *thermae* possessed a *palaestra* of their own, a general peristylar sports area to which might be annexed the *sphaeristerium* itself.[35] Addison's *sphaeristerium* then, while obviously denoting a seventeenth-century bowling green, is also reminiscent of the games room of the ancient Roman baths.

(ii)   Bowling amid Virgilian Games

The methodology of personification continues in the following lines as the rolling bowls seem to recall the behavior of the human participants in the games of *Aeneid* 5. Here Addison, like Dillingham, uses the Virgilian scene as a point of departure (not without glancing back perhaps to Homeric precedent for that scene), and signals this by a series of verbal and thematic parallels. But his lines also seem to interact with Dillingham's poem itself. Hence in terms of its intertextuality the *Sphaeristerium*, as argued below, is infiltrated by a variety of texts, both classical and neo-Latin. At the same time it will be seen that both this piece and that by Dillingham are remarkable for the quasi-technical precision with which individual details of a bowling match are poetically cast in neo-Latin verse of the late seventeenth century.

In terms of its engagement with Virgil, Addison's poem is typically much less explicitly reminiscent than that of Dillingham.

---

[34] On ball games and Roman baths cf., for example, Pliny, *Epist.* 3.1.8 : *ubi hora balinei nuntiata est (est autem hieme nona, aestate octava), in sole, si caret vento, ambulat nudus. deinde movetur pila vehementer et diu; nam hoc quoque exercitationis genere pugnat cum senectute. lotus accubat et paulisper cibum differt*; Seneca, *Epist.* 56: *si vero pilicrepus supervenit et numerare coepit pilas, actum est.* On Augustus playing ball, cf. Suetonius, *Divus Augustus*, 83: *ad pilam primo folliculumque transiit.*

[35] On the association of sports with Roman baths, see John Ward, *Roman Era in Britain* (Methuen: London, 1911), 96: "Physical exercise was a concomitant of the bath. Even domestic baths sometimes had their tennis-court (*sphaeristerium*), as had Pliny's. In most of the public baths there was a spacious court (*palaestra*) with porticoes, exedrae, swimming-bath, etc., and other conveniences for outdoor recreation, ball-playing being a favourite pastime." See also Salvatore Aurigemma, *The Baths of Diocletian and the Museo Nazionale Romano*, trans. J. Guthrie (Fifth edition Rome: Istituto Poligrafico Dello Stato, 1963); Inge Nielsen, *Thermae Et Balnea* (Denmark, 1993).

Instead the use of a single word or phrase is enough to signal a Virgilian context. Both poets, for example, employ the term *meta* to describe the jack,[36] which now metaphorically assumes the role of the turning post in a Virgilian chariot or ship race. In *Aeneid* 5, prior to the ship race, Aeneas had established an oak marker as the *meta*,[37] and references to the *meta* recur in the course of the race proper.[38] In Addison, the jack, an *orbiculus* (20), flies forth to assume this function (*evolat orbiculus, quae cursum meta futurum/designat* [20-21]).[39] The juxtaposition of *meta* and *futurum*, which does not occur in Virgil, finds a parallel in Dillingham, as the jack, the *sphaera ... exigua* (35-36), functions as the *cursus ... meta futuri* (36), the "Helen" towards which every other shot is aimed.[40] And Dillingham reinforces the notion of the erotically seductive magnetism of the jack/*meta*/Helen through the associated image of embracing: hence the first bowl when cast "rests" in the *meta*'s "arms" (38),[41] while the next shot "clings" to its/her "embraces" (48).[42]

But as the *Sphaeristerium* progresses, verbal and thematic parallels with *Aeneid* 5 suggest that this bowling match, unlike that of

---

[36] Cf. Masters, *Mensa Lubrica*, 42: *summa gaudet consistere meta* (*Musae Anglicanae*, I, 19).

[37] *his viridem Aeneas frondenti ex ilice metam/constituit signum nautis pater* (*Aen.* 5. 129-130). Cf. Homer, *Iliad* 23.327-330, in which the turning post is none other than a tree stump: "There stands, about a fathom's height above the ground, a dry stump, of oak or pine, which rots not in the rain, and two white stones on either side of it are firmly set against it at the turning of the course." Translation is that of A.T. Murray, *Homer: Iliad*, rev. W.F. Wyatt (Harvard, 1999), II, 517. At 23. 334-336, Nestor tells Antilochus: "Pressing hard on it drive your chariot and horses close, and yourself lean in your well-plaited chariot a little to the left of your pair" (*ibid.*, 517). Cf. 23.338-340: "But let the near horse draw close to the post so that the hub of the well-made wheel seems to graze the surface" (*ibid.*, 519).

[38] Cf. *Aen.* 5. 159: *iamque propinquabant scopulo metamque tenebant.*

[39] Cf. *stipantque frequentia metam* (Addison, 27); *metae inclinata recumbit* (Addison, 47).

[40] *protinus emittit nullo molimine sphaeram/exiguam. haec Helena est, cursus haec meta futuri,/hanc ambire omnes* (Dillingham, 35-37). Cf. *seu circumducto metam contingere gyro* (Dillingham, 32); *stringere metam* (Dillingham, 44); *metaeque amplexibus haeret* (Dillingham, 48); *abducit metam* (Dillingham, 93).

[41] *illius requiescit in ulnis* (Dillingham, 38).

[42] *metaeque amplexibus haeret* (48). Dillingham continues the amatory metaphor in the depiction of the bowing motion of a bowler as though venerating a Nymph: *prono veneratur corpore Nympham* (40).

Dillingham's poem, encapsulates a whole variety of Virgilian games, which are now, as it were, merged into one. Common to all three poets is the phrase *radit iter*. In Virgil, Cloanthus in the ship race traces an inside path to the left (*radit iter laevum interior* [5. 170]), and steers in-between the ship of Gyas and the rocks themselves, thereby overtaking him.[43] In both Dillingham and Addison, this becomes a description not of a human competitor in a race, but of an advancing bowl that ends up clinging to the jack. Dillingham, closely following Virgil, describes a bowl which because of a smaller amount of lead can follow an inner left-hand path (*radit iter laevum interior* [47]) and, dislodging a previous bowl, can cling closely to the jack.[44] Whereas in Virgil, Cloanthus passed Gyas (who until then was in first position [*priorem* [170]) and left the *meta* behind (*metis ... relictis* [171]), Dillingham's bowl dislodges the leader (*priorem* [47]) from its space, and clings to the *meta*. In Addison, a weakly cast bowl traces a path (*radit iter* [24]), tending towards a slight curve until, its original force gradually expended, it comes to rest.[45] But his bowls are further personified in the ensuing lines. Addison's use of the verb *emicat* (25) to describe a series of bowls suddenly cast one after the other finds a parallel in Virgil's account of another sports game: the foot race. Here it is used of two of the participants, Nisus and Euryalus, who are also inseparable friends. Nisus takes the leading place, and darts ahead (*emicat* [5. 319]) in front of the others.[46] However, he trips and falls, and in so doing deliberately blocks the path of another contestant, Salius, so that his friend Euryalus can succeed. The latter thus darts ahead (*emicat* [5. 337]) to win the race.[47] Dillingham, while not using the

---

[43] *Aen.* 5. 169-171: *ille inter navemque Gyae scopulosque sonantis/radit iter laevum interior subitoque priorem/praeterit et metis tenet aequora tuta relictis.* The phrase recurs later in the ship race as Mnestheus is compared to a dove skimming its way in clear light without any movement of its swift wings: *mox aere lapsa quieto/radit iter liquidum celeris neque commovet alas* (*Aen.* 5. 216-217).

[44] Dillingham, 46-48: *hic sphaeram librat, minimi quae conscia plumbi/radit iter laevum interior, meliorque priorem/detrudit spatio, metaeque amplexibus haeret.*

[45] *Sphaeristerium*, 22-25: *at illa/leniter effusa exiguum quod ducit in orbem/radit iter, donec sensim primo impete fesso/subsistat.*

[46] *Aen.* 5. 318-319. In Homer's foot race Ajax likewise shoots ahead of the others (*Il.* 23. 759).

[47] *Aen.* 5. 337-338: *emicat Euryalus et munere victor amici/prima tenet, plausuque volat fremituque secundo.* In Virgil, however, the verb *emicat* serves perhaps as a proleptic irony when it is remembered that it can also mean "to shine brightly." In this, as in other details of the foot race, this scene ironically anticipates the ultimate downfall of Nisus and Euryalus in the night episode of book 9, in which Euryalus'

verb *emicat*, describes the first bowler (*primus ibi ante omnes .../descendit* [30-31]) in language reminiscent of Virgil's account of Nisus darting off into the lead (*primus abit longeque ante omnia corpora Nisus/emicat* [5. 318-319]), and actually names one of his competitors Nisus, who is presented as the bowler par excellence: thus no one is more outstanding than Nisus whether in casting a bowl, in reaching the jack, in dislodging an opponent's throw or in outrunning his opponent's shot.[48] As before, Addison's debt is less explicit, the Virgilian context merely signaled by the use of *emicat*.

And there are other more subtle links with Virgil. A close reading of Addison's poem suggests that his description of this particular bowling match reflects something of the quasi-orphic resonances which seemed to haunt Virgil's games, thereby endowing them with irony. Virgil's lines are in fact mutlilayered, as they seem to interact not only with the Orpheus/Eurydice episode proper in *Georgics* 4, but also with Virgil's reworking of that episode in other scenes in the *Aeneid* (such as Aeneas' loss of Creusa at the end of book 2 or indeed the tragedy of Nisus and Euryalus in book 9). In effect the games of *Aeneid* 5 present what is a frequently complex and essentially multifaceted Orphic subtext. And this manifests itself in a variety of ways and across a variety of games: in the similarity between the names Euryalus and Eurydice, in the use of the verb *respicere* in the ship race,[49] an action that proved Orpheus' undoing,[50] in the series of rhetorical questions of despair during the races,[51] paralleling perhaps the poignant questions posed to Orpheus by Eurydice.[52] Addison's lines, it could be argued, are likewise haunted

---

gleaming helmet gives him away. See *Aen.* 9. 371-374: *iamque propinquabant castris murosque subibant/cum procul hos laevo flectentis limite cernunt,/et galea Euryalum sublustri noctis in umbra/prodidit immemorem radiisque adversa refulsit.*

[48] Dillingham, 43-45: *excipit hunc Nisus, quo non praestantior alter,/sive globum versare manu seu stringere metam,/sive hostem turbare loco seu vincere cursu.*

[49] *Aen.* 5. 167-168: *et ecce Cloanthum/respicit instantem tergo.*

[50] Cf. Orpheus at *Georgics* 4.491: *victusque animi respexit.* Cf. Aeneas and Creusa at *Aen.* 2.741: *nec prius amissam respexi*, in a passage which draws upon and inverts the Orpheus/Eurydice episode of *Georgics* 4. Similarly of Nisus at *Aen.* 9. 389: *frustra absentem respexit amicum.*

[51] Cf., for example, *'quo tantum mihi dexter abis?'* (*Aen.* 5. 162); *'quo diversus abis?'* (*Aen.* 5. 166).

[52] Cf. *Georgics* 4. 494-495: *illa 'quis et me' inquit 'miseram et te perdidit, Orpheu,/quis tantus furor?';* cf. *Aen.* 9.390-391: *'Euryale infelix, qua te regione reliqui?/quave sequar?'*

by such resonances, suggested perhaps by his emphasis upon *vestigia*[53] (a theme prominent in Virgil's reworking of his Orpheus/Eurydice story in Aeneas' loss of Creusa at the end of *Aeneid* 2)[54] or in the use of the adverb *pone* (32) (used of Eurydice and Creusa, as they walk "behind" their husbands),[55] or in his association of *vestigia* with *pone* (32)[56] or the inclusion of mock-heroic recriminations on the part of unsuccessful bowlers against the layout of the bowling surface (34-35),[57] or at the "error" (41) of a shot,[58] or at their own bad luck, which they attribute to the gods (58).[59] But if gods can be intransigent in their cruelty, so too can the bowls themselves. The bowl that is deaf to laments is described as though it were a deity deaf to prayer (43).[60] By signaling a series of Virgilian passages Addison's lines present bowls or their bowlers sometimes as Orpheus, sometimes as Eurydice, following behind, tracing *vestigia*, uttering rhetorical questions about the futility of loss or failure, and proclaiming curses, laments or recriminations against the gods. Interestingly they may reflect Addison's insightful reading of Virgil.[61]

---

[53] Cf. *legens vestigia* (*Sphaeristerium* 21); *nimium vestigia plumbum/allicit* (*Sphaeristerium* 37-38).

[54] Cf. *Aen.* 2. 711: *et longe servet vestigia coniunx*; *Aen.* 2.753-754: *et vestigia retro/observata sequor.* Cf. also *Aen.* 9. 392-393: *vestigia retro/observata legit.*

[55] Cf. *Georgics* 4. 487: *pone sequens* (of Eurydice); *Aen.* 2. 725: *pone subit coniunx* (of Creusa).

[56] *pone urget sphaerae vestigia et anxius instat* (*Sphaeristerium* 32).

[57] *iniquam/incusat terram* (*Sphaeristerium* 34-35). Cf. Aeneas upon the loss of Creusa at *Aen.* 2.745: *quem non incusavi amens hominumque deorumque.* Cf. *obiurgatque moras* (*Sphaeristerium* 33) (cf. also *obiectasque moras* [Dillingham, 92]).

[58] *falsos/increpat errores* (*Sphaeristerium* 40-41). Cf. *Aen.* 2.739-740 (of Creusa): *erravitne via seu lapsa resedit.* Compare also Virgil, *Ecl.* 8.41: *ut me malus abstulit error!* and Dillingham: *quid reliquos memorem, varius quos abstulit error* (70); *devius errat* (75).

[59] *atque deos atque astra vocat crudelia* (*Sphaeristerium* 58). Cf. Virgil, *Ecl.* 5.23: *atque deos atque astra vocat crudelia mater.*

[60] *nullis ... movetur surda querelis* (*Sphaeristerium* 43). Cf. the intransigent gods of Orpheus' underworld: *nesciaque humanis precibus mansuescere corda* (*Georgics* 4. 470). On the futility of Orphic lamentation, cf. *Georgics* 4. 505: *quo fletu Manis, quae numina voce moveret?*; *Georgics* 4.515: *maestis late loca questibus implet* (Orpheus compared to a nightingale).

[61] Cf. Johnson's comment at "Addison," 663, that "of the Latin poets his *Dialogues on Medals* show that he had perused the works with great diligence and skill."

All three poets employ an epic simile to convey the speed or efficiency of the participants. In the case of both Virgil and Addison the simile is that of a chariot race.[62] In *Aeneid* 5, as the signal is given for the commencement of the ship race, the rowers advance. Their movement is compared to that of chariots.[63] In Addison, as a rival tries to get the upper hand against his opponent, whose hit is resting alongside the jack, he stoutly casts his bowl: its power and speed are compared to a charioteer leaving the starting gate at Elis, and seeing buildings whizzing past.[64] Dillingham's equivalent simile, however, is used of the defenders as opposed to attackers. Here bowls encircling the jack are compared to Roman youths in camp protecting their leader.[65]

Finally, it should be remarked that in terms of the details and technicalities of the bowling match, both Addison and Dillingham show their awareness of the rules and skills of the game. As such they take on the role of the observant "spectator". Both describe the division of the participants into teams, although Dillingham makes this more explicit. Thus whereas Addison alludes to a team division that may occur either intentionally or accidentally (*in partes turbam distinxerat aequas/ consilium aut sors* [18-19]),[66] Dillingham announces: *in partes itur* (16),

---

[62] Cf. *Georgics* 1.512-514, in which Rome, wracked by civil war, is compared to a chariot out of control: *ut cum carceribus sese effudere quadrigae,/addunt in spatia, et frustra retinacula tendens/fertur equis auriga neque audit currus habenas.*

[63] *non tam praecipites biiugo certamine campum/corripuere ruuntque effusi carcere currus* (*Aen.* 5. 144-145). Virgil continues: *nec sic immissis aurigae undantia lora/ concussere iugis pronique in verbera pendent* (*Aen.* 5. 146-147). Cf. *Iliad* 23. 362-372, in which the charging horses quickly leave the ships behind.

[64] *Sphaeristerium* 52-54: *haud ita prosiliens Eleo carcere pernix/auriga invehitur cum raptus ab axe citato/currentesque domos videt et fugientia tecta.* Cf. Masters, *Mensa Lubrica* 8-10: *Romani credas spatium te cernere Circi/aut stadium Elei, lustro redeunte, tonantis./utque coloratas mirata est Roma quadrigas* (*Musae Anglicanae*, I, 17); *Mensa Lubrica* 38-42: *vere ille argenteus orbis,/et dignus splendore suo qui carcere pernix,/evolat et (cursum accedens tenui stridore)/lineolam post se linquit, neque limine campi/contentus summa gaudet consistere meta* (*Musae Anglicanae*, I, 18).

[65] Dillingham, 64-69. While Dillingham's simile is very different from that of Addison and indeed Virgil, it is interesting to note that lines 67-68 (*tutaturque ducem, multoque satellite cingit./haud aliter Nisum socii fido agmine cingunt ...*) find a parallel in *Sphaeristerium* 55-56: *si tamen in duros, obstructa satellite multo,/ impingat socios.*

[66] Sutton, ed. *The Latin Prose and Poetry of Joseph Addison, ad loc*, states: "Addison writes as if it were simply a matter of each man competing on his own behalf, but lines 18f. suggest that somehow the participants are divided into two teams."

and proceeds to describe the opposing sides in allegorical terms as the rival Florentine political factions Guelphs and Ghibellines (17).[67] In other respects, however, Addison provides several details that are not to be found in Dillingham: for example, the fact that each bowl has its own peculiar markings (*quaeque suis incisa notis stat sphaera* [13]). The phrase is reminiscent of Horace, *Odes* 4.8: *non incisa notis marmora publicis*, and the context may not be unrelated to Addison's lines. In Horace, the speaker informs his addressee, Censorinus, that he would present his friends with bronze (*aera* [2]) and tripods (3-4) – that is, if he possessed them. However, he continues: *sed non haec mihi vis* (9). He states that even marble statues engraved with inscriptions cannot surpass the power of the Muses. Read in this context, Addison's phrase assumes perhaps an ironic twist as an Horatian negative becomes an Addisonian positive. For his bowlers *do* in fact possess bowls (is Addison punning here on the twin English sense of "bowls"?), each of which, like those statues which Horace does *not* possess, has a quasi inscription of its own. And he too had conveyed something of the workmanship of the "artist", the craftsman who designed those bowls (10-11).

Both Addison and Dillingham mention the various weights and consequential functions of certain bowls,[68] contrasting heavy with light. Hence a bowl which has a profusion of metal can roll in a curve.[69] By contrast, a bowl with a smaller amount of lead is lighter, and can advance in a straight line.[70] Both remark on the physical contortions of the bowlers,[71] and describe the variety of shots of which the game of bowls is comprised. There is the bowl that approaches in a stealthy manner,

---

[67] Dillingham, 16-17: *in partes itur; tu Guelfius esto,/hic Gibelinus erit, furiis tamen ante remotis.* On the implementation of the allegory, cf., for example, Deborah Parker's reading of the tenth canto of Dante's *Inferno* as a dramatized reconstruction of the political debate between Guelphs and Ghibellines (*Lectura Dantis: Inferno* X, in *Lectura Dantis*, I, No. 1 [Fall], [1987], 37-47).

[68] Cf. Masters, *Mensa Lubrica* 13: ... *et teretis facies non una metalli* (*Musae Anglicanae*, I, 17).

[69] *quae infuso multum inclinata metallo/vertitur in gyros et iniquo tramite currit* (*Sphaeristerium* 14-15)//*quas fusile plumbum/et docuit solidare gradus et ducere gyros* (Dillingham, 25-26). Cf. Masters, *Mensa Lubrica* 27: *seu plumbi ignavi massa est seu divitis auri* (*Musae Anglicanae*, I, 18).

[70] *quam parcius urget/plumbea vis motuque sinit procedere recto* (*Sphaeristerium* 16-17)//*minimi quae conscia plumbi/radit iter laevum interior* (Dillingham, 46-47).

[71] Hence *distorto corpore* (*Sphaeristerium* 40)//*corpore torto* (Dillingham, 58). Cf. also *prono veneratur corpore Nympham* (Dillingham, 40).

insinuating its way alongside the jack.[72] Then there is the rather sluggish shot, which the bowler, in an attempt to compensate for this weakness, follows as it rolls along, rebuking it for its delay.[73] Both employ the mock-heroic to describe the disappointment, frustration and even anger provoked by an unsuccessful bowl. Losing participants frequently curse the bowls, and even rebuke the gods as cruel.[74] Of course calling upon the divine was integral to the success or otherwise of sports participants in both Virgil[75] and Homer.[76] And such emotions can lead to anger.[77] But where anger is aroused in the participants, laughter is evoked in the spectators. And this too has precedent in Virgil. In the ship race Gyas pushes his helmsman Menoetes into the sea. The Trojans laugh at him as he tries to swim, choking the salt waters from his chest.[78] In Addison and

---

[72] *iam cautius exit/et leviter sese insinuat revolubile lignum* (*Sphaeristerium* 28-29)// *metaeque amplexibus haeret* (Dillingham, 48). In Dillingham, this is the culmination of a recurring motif. Cf. *seu circumducto metam contingere gyro* (32); *metae contiguus media requiescit arena* (42); *seu stringere metam* (44). Addison's *insinuat* (29) finds a parallel in Masters, *Mensa Lubrica* 50: *spatio summo sese insinuavit* (*Musae Anglicanae*, I, 19).

[73] *impressum subito languescere motum,/pone urget sphaerae vestigia et anxius instat,/obiurgatque moras currentique imminet orbi* (*Sphaeristerium* 31-33)// *currentem sphaeram manibus pedibusque fatigat/nunc festinantem vocis moderatur habena/ignavum et sine honore globum nunc increpat* (Dillingham, 55-57). With *languescere* (*Sphaeristerium* 31), cf. Dillingham, 72: *is medio languet.*

[74] In Addison, the losing bowler calls the gods cruel: *fortunam damnat acerbam,/atque deos atque astra vocat crudelia* (*Sphaeristerium* 57-58).

[75] Hence Cloanthus' prayer to the gods helps him win the boat race: *ni palmas ponto tendens utrasque Cloanthus/fudissetque preces divosque in vota vocasset* (*Aen.* 5.233-234); he promises the sea gods a sacrificial offering of a bull. Entellus after his victory in the boxing match prays (*Aen.* 5.474-476; 483-484); similarly in the archery contest Eurytion prays to his brother (*Aen.* 5.514).

[76] In Homer's foot race Odysseus prays to Athene, who hears him (*Iliad* 23. 768-772). Teucer in the archery contest had forgotten to promise sacrifice to Apollo. As a consequence he fails to hit the target (23. 862-865). Ajax blames Athene for his slipping in the foot race (23. 782-783).

[77] In Virgil, Aeneas has to intervene in the boxing match to quell the anger of Dares and Entellus (*procedere longius iras/et saevire animis Entellum haud passus acerbis* [*Aen.* 5.461-462]).

[78] *illum et labentem Teucri et risere natantem/et alsos rident revomentem pectore fluctus* (*Aen.* 5.181-182). On this passage, cf. Addison, *Spectator*, 279 (19 January 1712: ed. Bond, II, 589): "I remember but one laugh in the whole *Aeneid*, which rises in the fifth book upon Menoetes, where he is represented as thrown overboard and

Dillingham it is the simply dreadful shot that arouses laughter.[79] By contrast it is the bowl which eventually dislodges its opponent that wins the greatest acclaim and in effect concludes the contest and the poem. In Addison, the winning bowl despoils the opponent of his glory, and is met with a huge reaction of applause.[80] Dillingham, employing a military metaphor,[81] describes a bowl which has been cast with the force of lightning, dissipates the enemy ranks, causing death all about, and usurps the winning place.[82] As in Virgil's games, success is greeted by shouts and applause.[83] This din is mirrored in the surrounding landscape, which

---

drying himself upon a rock." In Homer, *Iliad* 23. 784 the Greeks laugh at Ajax who is covered in the slime in which he has slipped.

[79] *nec risus tacuere globus cum volvitur actus/infami iactu* (*Sphaeristerium* 36-37)//*vel devius errat/averso plumbo tota ridendus arena* (Dillingham, 75-76). Addison's *infami iactu* and the combined notion of consequential laughter finds precedent in Masters, *Mensa Lubrica* 29-30: *dextram comitatur inertem/et pudor et risus cassique infamia iactus* (*Musae Anglicanae*, I, 18).

[80] *partoque hostis spolietur honore,/turba fremit confusa, sonisque frequentibus, 'euge,'/exclamant socii; plausu strepit omne viretum* (*Sphaeristerium* 60-62). Cf. Masters, *Mensa Lubrica* 59-60: *neque deflevere cadentem/moerentes socii, plausu super aethera tollunt* (*Musae Anglicanae*, I, 19).

[81] On the military metaphor in Dillingham and Addison, see their description of bowls as arms: *eadem ludentibus arma ministrat* (Dillingham, 28)//*quisque suis accingitur armis* (Addison, 19), and of an opponent as the enemy: *hostem turbare loco seu vincere cursu* (Dillingham, 45)//*hostis at haerentem orbiculo detrudere sphaeram/certat* (Addison, 48-49). Overall the metaphor is more prominent in Dillingham. Cf. *ducis laudes* (52), *triumphi* (53), and, in particular, the simile of a Roman camp at 64-69 (although note *Sphaeristerium* 55-56).

[82] *at evolat illa/fulminea vibrata manu ruptasque phalanges/dissipat hostiles, huc illuc funera spargens,/obiectasque moras cursum molita per omnes,/abducit metam et summa consistit arena* (Dillingham, 89-93).

[83] In Virgil, as the rowers proceed, the whole grove resounds with applause and shouting: *tum plausu fremituque virum studiisque faventum/consonat omne nemus, vocemque inclusa volutant/litora, pulsati colles clamore resultant* (*Aen.* 5.148-150); in the boat race Sergestus strikes his boat on rocks: the crew leaps up and exclaims: *consurgunt nautae et magno clamore morantur* (207); as Mnestheus catches up with Cloanthus the shouts redouble: *ingeminat clamor cunctique sequentem/instigant studiis, resonatque fragoribus aether* (227-228); as Euryalus wins the foot race *plausuque volat fremituque secundo* (338). There ensue cheers of approval when Hippocoon's lot jumps out for the archery test: *clamore secundo* (491); further applause as his arrow sticks in the mast: *ingenti sonuerunt omnia plausu* (506). Cf. the *lusus Troiae*, which is greeted by applause: *excipiunt plausu pavidos* (575). Cf. also Homer's foot race in which the Achaeans cheer Odysseus. Likewise at Polypoetes'

reacts in a sort of pathetic fallacy as the neighboring mountain groans. The shattering effect upon the pastoral world is perhaps best epitomized by the trembling reaction of Dillingham's *Nympha loquax* (96).[84] However, in the closing lines of Addison's piece pastoral is reinstated, if somewhat transformed, by a reworking of the poem's opening. Those swelling dewdrops (*tumidae ... guttae* [4]) hanging upon the grass have now become the salty droplets of sweat[85] exuded by the bodies of the exhausted bowlers gripped by the heat of Sirius, the Dog-star (*et salsas exsudant corpora guttas* [64]). As they wipe the flowing moisture from their faces (66),[86] the bowlers seek out what is in effect a pastoral landscape: those breezes that breathe gentle coolness, and the much longed-for shade that is so integral to the pastoral world[87] (*lenia iam zephyri spirantes frigora et umbrae/captantur* [65-66]).[88] And as if to highlight the reinstatement of the pastoral Addison recalls Virgil, *Eclogue* 2.8: *nunc etiam pecudes umbras et frigora captant*. Thus does the poem come full circle, its very "form" mirroring that craftsmanship epitomized by its subject: those artfully rounded bowls themselves:

<blockquote>
formae quibus esse rotundae
artificis ferrum dederat facilisque moveri (10-11).
</blockquote>

---

throw of the discus there is loud applause; similarly the Achaeans roar as Teucer's arrow severs the string, and the bird hovers.

[84] *protinus it caelo clamor totusque remugit/mons circum; trepidat mediis exterrita silvis/Nympha loquax, dubitans tanti quae causa triumphi,/quanto non meminit celebrari funera cervi* (Dillingham, 94-97).

[85] Cf. the description of the sweating rowers in Virgil's ship race: *tum creber anhelitus artus/aridaque ora quatit, sudor fluit undique rivis* (*Aen.* 5.199-200). In Homer's chariot race (*Iliad* 23. 507-508) sweat pours to the ground from the necks and chests of Diomedes' horses.

[86] *vultuque fluens abstergitur umor* (*Sphaeristerium* 66).

[87] Cf., for example, Virgil, *Ecl.* 1.1: *Tityre, tu patulae recubans sub tegmine fagi*; *Ecl.* 1. 4: *tu, Tityre, lentus in umbra.* See also 18 above.

[88] The theme of shade sought by the bowlers occurs in a rather different sense in the earlier part of Dillingham's poem. This shade constitutes the *domus*, which affords *gratissima fessis/umbra viris* (27-28). That this is a reference to the bowling club-house is indicated by the statement that it is from here that the boy brings out the balls, and here that he stores them again at night (*hinc puer expromit sphaeras, hic nocte recondit* [29]).

CHAPTER 6

Artistic Rebirth: *Resurrectio Delineata*

The *Resurrectio Delineata ad Altare Col. Magd. Oxon* is certainly the most accomplished example of Addison's use of ekphrasis.[1] The context of these neo-Latin hexameter verses is an Oxonian one, the verses themselves having been composed in all likelihood while Addison was still demy at Magdalen College.[2] Hitherto it has been assumed by a majority of scholars that the poem describes the altarpiece of the College Chapel.[3] Upon closer examination, however, it emerges that it delineates not an altarpiece, but in fact a mural on the Last Judgment which used to grace most of the east wall of the chapel, but which is no longer extant. The mural was painted in c. 1664[4] by Isaac Fuller (1606-1672),[5] among

---

[1] On ekphrasis in general, see among others Robert Druce and J.D. Hunt, eds. "Poems on Pictures," *Word & Image* 2.1 (1986), 45-103; John Hollander, "The Poetics of Ekphrasis," *Word & Image* 4.1 (1988), 209-219; D.P. Fowler, "Narrate and Describe: The Problem of Ekphrasis," *JRS* 81 (1991), 25-35; Murray Krieger, *Ekphrasis: The Illusion of the Natural Sign* (Johns Hopkins, 1991); James Heffernan, "Ekphrasis and Representation," *NLH* 22.2 (Spring 1991), 297-316; James Heffernan, *Museum of Words: The Politics of Ekphrasis from Homer to Ashberry* (Chicago, 1992), 119-124; W.J.T. Mitchell, "Ekphrasis and the Other," *Picture Theory and Essays on Verbal and Visual Representation* (Chicago, 1994), chap. 5.

[2] On Addison's election to a demyship at Magdalen College, see 5-6, 14-15, 31-32 above.

[3] Sutton, ed. *The Latin Prose and Poetry of Joseph Addison, ad loc.*, incorrectly states that the piece describes the chapel's main west window.

[4] Robin Darwall-Smith, archivist of Magdalen College, informs me that no documents about the creation of the mural seem to have survived.

[5] Fuller was well known in his day as a painter of rather large works, whose subject matter was for the most part biblical, historical or mythological. His style was generally characterized by exaggerated muscularity and very strong coloring. According to Bainbrigg Buckeridge, *An Essay Towards an English School of Painters*, appended to Richard Graham's translation of Roger de Piles, *The Art of Painting and the Lives of the Painters* (London, 1706), 374, "he studied many years in France under Perrier, and understood the anatomical part of Painting, perhaps equal to

whose Oxford works was another on the same theme painted above the altar of All Souls College.[6] Both murals constituted to some degree Anglicized pastiches of Michelangelo's famous Last Judgment.[7] In the 1660s the remains of the fifteenth-century reredos of Magdalen College Chapel, which had sustained much damage during the Reformation, had been plastered over, and it was upon this surface that Fuller undertook the work in question.[8] The College's nineteenth-century historian John Rouse Bloxam states:

> "After the ravages of the rebellious usurpers", says Ingram, "it became necessary to repair the injury which the sacred edifice, the Chapel, had sustained in its internal appearance. But the conflict of contending sects and parties in England had gradually introduced a taste for foreign art to the neglect and disparagement of our ancient architecture. Hence a large picture of the Resurrection, painted by Isaac Fuller, who had studied under Perrier in France, was thought a good expedient to cover the mutilated remains of the old tabernacle-work over the Altar."[9]

But the commission was not without controversy. Apparently the College, having paid the artist, complained about the tardiness of his progress, and proceeded, though unsuccessfully, to take an action against him. Fuller seems eventually to have extracted his due payment for the

---

Michael Angelo, following it so close, that he was very apt to make the muscling too strong and prominent. Among his works, there are several fine pieces in many great taverns in London, which are not esteemed the worst of his performance." The best modern survey of Fuller's life and works is that of M.J.H. Liversidge, "Prelude to the Baroque: Isaac Fuller at Oxford," *Oxoniensia* 57 (1992), 311-329. For earlier discussions, see Ellis Waterhouse, *Painting in Britain 1530 to 1790* (London, 1978), 58-59; Edward Croft-Murray, *Decorative Painting in England 1537-1837* (London, 1962), I, 43-44.

[6] Cf. Kerry Downes, "Fuller's 'Last Judgement,'" *Burlington Magazine* cii (1960), 451-452.

[7] On general resemblances between Fuller's Last Judgment (in Magdalen College) and that of Michelangelo, see 117-122 below.

[8] See Robin Darwall-Smith and Roger White, *The Architectural Drawings of Magdalen College — A Catalogue* (Oxford, 2001), xxxv. Cf. Roger White's useful introduction for an explanation of the context for Fuller's work in the general alterations undergone in the Chapel in the course of the seventeenth century.

[9] John Rouse Bloxam, *A Register of the Presidents, Demies ... of Saint Mary Magdalen College in the University of Oxford* (Oxford, 1857), II, cxxxii.

whole.[10] An account of the mural included in the *New Oxford Guide* for 1759 suggests that it was never properly finished:

> The altar-piece was performed by Isaac Fuller, about 90 years ago. It represents the resurrection, and, I suspect, never received the last finishing. It evidently wants grace and composition, and has too much of the Flemish colouring and expression. Many of the figures are however finely drawn.[11]

It is likely, however, that this anonymous observer of the work simply misinterpreted as evidence of its supposed incomplete state that rawness of coloring which, as noted below, characterized this and Fuller's other works in general. At any event the mural seems to have remained in place until as late as c. 1828, at which time the whole Chapel was gutted and rebuilt in accordance with a more "correct" Gothic style. Such a gutting, however, entailed sweeping away all the encrustations of previous centuries.[12]

Fortunately, however, the story does not end here. Fuller's mural, which is obviously so central to a reading of Addison's *Resurrectio*, is not entirely lost to us. In fact it is possible to catch a rather good glimpse of what it actually looked like from two visual sources among the archives of Magdalen College: (i) an engraving by Michael Burghers,[13] a Dutch engraver (1640-1723), who had emigrated from Amsterdam to

---

[10] Bloxam, *Register*, II, cxxxii-iii, continues: "At this time, therefore, Fuller commenced his labours, and received £100 for Arrah [for Arrab, or Arra, or Arrha – an abbreviation for Arrhibone, earnest money, or a sum paid down for current expenses before he commenced the work]: in 1665 £78; in 1666 £72; but the College became discontented at the slow progress of the work, and brought an action against Fuller for not having completed it. He however seems to have gained the cause, and the College were compelled to give up £63.10s for payments due to him, besides the amount of their legal expenses in prosecuting the suit."

[11] Anonymous, *The New Oxford Guide or Companion Through the University* (Oxford, 1759), 21. The author proceeds to note that "the painting is elegantly celebrated by Mr Addison, formerly a student of this House, in a Latin poem, printed in the *Musae Anglicanae*." Cf. Liversidge, "Prelude to the Baroque," 315.

[12] I am grateful to Robin Darwall-Smith for answering several queries on the history of the mural.

[13] Again I am grateful to Robin Darwall-Smith for alerting me to the existence of this engraving among the Magdalen archives, and to Michael McGann for fruitful discussion.

Oxford.[14] This engraving is virtually contemporary with Addison's poem;[15] (ii) a very clear drawing (albeit in ink and sepia wash) made in c. 1817 by G.C. Cooper.[16] As argued below, comparison with these iconographical representations serves to highlight the accuracy and artistic skill of Addison's ekphrasis. Neither, however, can convey any sense of the very strong coloring which seems to have characterized the mural, an aspect central to Addison's ekphrastic representation. For this it is necessary to turn to written accounts and reactions, both near contemporary and later, which highlight and for the most part criticize the rawness of Fuller's coloring and also the exaggerated muscularity of his figures. John Evelyn mentions, though only in passing, the piece as viewed by him on 25 October 1664 (and hence only very recently finished), describing it as "a Last Judgment on the wall by Fuller, as is the other [at All Souls], somewhat varied."[17] In contrast to the seeming neutrality of Evelyn's viewpoint is that of Buckeridge in 1706, who, while proclaiming Fuller as "an English history painter of good note," continues:

> He had a great genius of drawing and designing history, which yet he did not always execute with due decency, nor after an historical manner; for he was too much addicted to modernise and burlesque his subjects, there being sometimes a rawness of colouring in them, besides other extravagancies suitable to the manners of the man: but notwithstanding all that a critic may find fault with in his works, there are many perfections in them, as may be seen by his Resurrection at All-souls college Chapel at Oxford, to which that at Magdalen college, though performed by the same hand, cannot in the least compare.[18]

Worthy of comparison is Horace Walpole's scathing criticism of the work:

---

[14] Burghers settled in Oxford in 1673 where he worked under David Loggan, whom he eventually succeeded as the University's official Engraver. He was the engraver of the *Oxford Almanack* from 1676 until 1716.

[15] See Plate 3.

[16] See Plate 4.

[17] See Evelyn, *Diary*, ed. De Beer, III, 386.

[18] Buckeridge, *An Essay Towards an English School of Painters*, 374. See Liversidge, "Prelude to the Baroque," 312-313.

> In his historic composition Fuller is a wretched painter; his colouring was raw and unnatural, and not compensated by disposition or invention ... His altar-pieces at Magdalen and All Souls colleges in Oxford are despicable.[19]

while Chalmers states of the Magdalen piece:

> As an imitation of Michael Angelo, it falls far short of the sublime, although sometimes wild, imagination of that great artist; nor is the colouring harmonious or natural.[20]

A more recent critic, however, has succinctly summarized the nature and possible merits exhibited by the Magdalen work:

> ... Taking into consideration the date it is nonetheless a remarkable performance for an Englishman, as much in its scale as in its content. There can have been few, if any, religious paintings as large carried out in England since the Reformation, and without the benefit of any kind of local pictorial tradition on which he could draw Fuller at least managed a not altogether unworthy attempt.[21]

What then was Addison's opinion of this mural? A careful reading of his *Resurrectio* reveals a speaker doubtlessly impressed by an almost breathtaking profusion of color, a speaker who indeed acknowledges the meticulous skill of the artist. For the demy Addison, gazing upon a relatively recent work (a mere twenty-five years old, in fact), this is "a picture fertile in colors" (*fecunda colorum/...pictura* [6-7]). His eyes are obviously drawn to its radiant center as he describes (correspondingly in the center of his poem)[22] the resurrected Christ suffused in serene light (*sereno/lumine perfusus* [54-55]), showered with pointed rays (*radiisque inspersus acutis* [55]), with "tranquil flames" (*tranquillae ... flammae* [56]) poured about his head, and fire gleaming in his eyes (*nitet ignis

---

[19] Horace Walpole, *Anecdotes of Painting in England* (1761), ed. Ralph N. Wornum (London, 1888), II, 80.

[20] Alexander Chalmers, *History of the Colleges, Halls and Public Buildings Attached to the University of Oxford* (Oxford, 1810), 214. He continues with the probably anecdotal comment: "Some of the figures, however, are correctly drawn; and he has at least imitated the temper of Michael Angelo with success, in introducing among the damned the portrait of an hostler at the Greyhound Inn, near the College, who had offended him." Cf. Liversidge, "Prelude to the Baroque," 315-318.

[21] Liversidge, "Prelude to the Baroque," 318.

[22] On structural points of contact between Addison's poem and the bands of the Fuller mural, see 119-124 below.

ocellis [57]). His majesty shines forth (*plurimaque effulget maiestas numine toto* [58]). Later as the College's founder Waynflete rises from his tomb, the speaker asks: *quis tamen ille novus perstringit lumina fulgor?* (81). And such emphasis upon brightness and color becomes more explicit as the poem reaches its climax. The effusive outburst in the closing lines constitutes a virtual hymn to the mural's abundant colors, whose grace surpasses the colors of the very rainbow (108-111).[23] Nor does Addison conceal that admiration. Already suggested by the above descriptions, it is highlighted through the use of hyperbolic exclamation: these are "beautiful colors" which, the speaker hopes, will endure (*o pulchri durate colores!* [112]).

In such emphasis Addison manifests the sensitive alertness to the beauty and power of color that, as the mature essayist of the *Spectator* and *Tatler* papers, he would later reveal in such comments as: "Among these several kinds of beauty the eye takes most delight in colours,"[24] or "colours speak all languages, but words are understood only by such a people or nation,"[25] or, perhaps most notably:

> I at first amused myself with all the richness and variety of colours, which appeared in the western parts of heaven: in proportion as they faded away and went out, several stars and planets appeared one after another, till the whole firmament was in a glow. The blueness of the ether was exceedingly heightened and enlivened by the season of the year, and by the rays of all those luminaries that passed through it. The galaxy appeared in its most beautiful white ... [26]

But the *Resurrectio* presents color as the culmination of a very painstaking and carefully wrought artistic process. From the poem's opening lines the speaker highlights the material side of artistic creation: the labors of the artist's "pencil" (*calamique labores* [1]), a pencil later

---

[23] *quanta colorum/gratia se profert! tales non discolor Iris/ostendat vario cum lumine floridus imber/rore nitet toto et gutta scintillat in omni* (*Resurrectio* 108-111). On the abundant colors of the rainbow as epitomized by the goddess Iris, see, for example, Virgil, *Aeneid* 4.700-702: *ergo Iris croceis per caelum roscida pennis/mille trahens varios adverso sole colores/devolat*. Cf. Addison, *Spectator*, 265 (3 January 1712: ed. Bond, II, 532) (of a coquet) "who intends to appear very suddenly in a rainbow hood like the Iris in Dryden's Virgil, not questioning but that among such a variety of colours she shall have a charm for every heart."

[24] Addison, *Spectator*, 412 (23 June 1712: ed. Bond, III, 544).

[25] Addison, *Spectator*, 416 (27 June 1712: ed. Bond, III, 559).

[26] Addison, *Spectator*, 565 (9 July 1714: ed. Bond, IV, 529).

described as "skillful" (*periti/quot calami legimus vestigia!* [107-108]).[27]
Interestingly, Addison reveals his awareness of the fact that the original
surface of the wall has been plastered over,[28] and presents in acute detail
the sequential stages whereby Fuller (unnamed in the poem, but alluded
to as *pictor* [10, 22, 82]) laid his prime coat, even commenting on the
rough texture of the paint he used. This is conveyed via a flashback to the
state of the surface prior to Fuller's painting. Thus whitewash (*albedo*
[8]) used to clothe the surface (*planitiem* [6]) with unprepossessing and
rude adornment (*inhonesto et simplice cultu* [7]), but lest any crack
should acknowledge its previous appearance (*priorem/... faciem* [8-9]),
the painter (*pictor* [10]) laid the foundations (*fundamenta .../substravit*
[9-10]) for his future painting, and drew the liquid (*umoremque
sequacem* [10]), presumably his prime coat, over the walls. Now the
walls are roughened (*squalent* [12]) by a thick coating (*velamine ...
crasso* [11]) and smeared with rougher paint. This contrast between a
former blank canvas, so to speak, and the present "picture," which is
"fertile in colors," is highlighted by a simile in which the microcosm of a
chapel mural is mirrored in the macrocosm of the universe itself. Thus in
a series of stunning equations Addison draws an implicit parallel
between the whitewashed wall of a chapel and a sky empty of stars
(13);[29] between a possible crack betraying a former surface and the mass
of the universe gaping wide open with an empty void throughout
heaven's vaults (14-15);[30] between the liquid coat of paint applied by the
artist and the interspersing ether that flowed all about the universe (16);[31]
and finally between the painter himself and those radiant forces which

---

[27] On the praise of a painter and his *calamus* as manifested by a work in an Oxford
chapel, cf. Peter Foulkes, *In Historiam Nativitatis Delineatam in Fenestra Orientali
Eccles. Cathed. Christi Oxon.*, 113-116: *quem, pictor, artis difficilem gradum/
timebis? aut quos non calamus tuus/felix vel in vitro colores/expediet teretive panno?*
(*Musae Anglicanae*, II, 185). Foulkes matriculated at Christ Church 16 June 1694,
aged 17. He received his BA in 1698; MA in 1701. See Foster, ed. *Alumni
Oxonienses*, II, 522. See also *DNB* sv.

[28] Cf. Bloxam, *Register*, II, cxxx: "The wall at the back of the Altar, disfigured by the
mutilated remains of Saintless niches, was rendered as level as possible, and then
plastered over and white-washed." Bloxam proceeds to cite lines 6-8 of Addison's
poem.

[29] *polo nondum stellis fulgentibus apto* (*Resurrectio* 13).

[30] *spatio moles immensa dehiscat inani,/per cava caelorum et convexa patentia late*
(*Resurrectio* 14-15).

[31] *hinc atque hinc interfusus fluitaverat aether* (*Resurrectio* 16).

illuminate the cosmos: the sun (Titan [18]), the moon (Cynthia [19]), and the Milky Way (*fulgor lacteus* [20]). Moreover, these points of equation are reinforced by syntactical parallels: *ne rima ulla .../agnoscat* (8-9) is mirrored by *ne ... moles ... dehiscat* (14); *mox fundamenta .../ substravit pictor* (9-10) by *mox radiante novum torrebat lumine mundum/Titan* (17-18). And details of the artist's painstaking methodology recur in the following lines. Thus while the wall is still in a raw state and "not proclaiming Apelles" (23),[32] the artist employs his pencils more carefully (24),[33] disturbing the sticky lime (24-25),[34] tempering its juices (25),[35] and eventually introducing all the outlines of the figures (26).[36]

In all of this the artist is the creator par excellence, who can transform a blank surface into a created universe of his own; he is an illuminating force in an empty vacuum, the bestower of light, life, and even immortality[37] upon his subject. Read on this level Addison's *Resurrectio* is essentially self-referential, proclaiming the resurrecting power of the artist as creator, a power reflecting that of the creator of the universe, an illuminating, life-bringing force, which mirrors its subject's centerpiece: the radiantly resurrected Christ. And this is reflected too in the power of another artist, the poet himself. Addison, the word-painter, can also give life to the inanimate, creating a "set-piece description" that

---

[32] *dum sordet paries nullumque fatetur Apellem* (*Resurrectio* 23). On Apelles as the epitome of the accomplished artist, cf. Foulkes, *In Historiam Nativitatis Delineatam*, 9-12: *vides quid audax finxerit in vitro/rite ordinatis dextra coloribus/Apellis, ut cunas tonantis/non humili refert tabella* (*Musae Anglicanae*, II, 181).

[33] *cautius exercet calamos* (*Resurrectio* 24).

[34] *arte tenacem/confundit viscum* (*Resurrectio* 24-25).

[35] *succosque attemperat* (*Resurrectio* 25).

[36] *omnes/inducit tandem formas* (25-26). As Sutton, ed. *The Latin Prose and Poetry of Joseph Addison, ad loc,* correctly notes, "That 'outlines' is here the correct translation of *formas* is shown by *picturarum vulgus inane* in the next line (the sketches have not yet been filled in)."

[37] The implicit identification between the revivifying powers of the artist, of the creator of the universe, and of the resurrected Christ recurs in Addison's simile of the Cadmus myth (*Resurrectio* 35-38) used of the resurrected dead emerging from the earth.

"brings the scene before our eyes,"[38] with the result that we have, in the words of Barthes, "the effect of the real."[39]

(i)   The Poet and the Painter

Where, as already observed, contemporary and later reactions to Fuller's painting were for the most part very negative, such is certainly not the case with the reception of Addison's neo-Latin ekphrastic recreation of the same. When his Latin poem was reprinted in 1719, with Burghers' engraving attached, it was hailed in the Preface as follows:

> The following lines are esteemed by the best judges to be the finest sketch of the Resurrection that any age or language has produced. Nor does their only excellence consist in being an accurate poem, but also on being an exact copy of the painter's original upon the altar in Magdalen College, but so much improved with all the strongest figures and most lively embellishments of a poetical description that the reader receives a double satisfaction in seeing the two sister-arts so useful to each other, in borrowing mutual helps and mutual advantages.
>
> It is indeed wonderful to find in the narrow compass of so few pages all the most dreadful circumstances of that last terrible crisis of time. The poem is a beautiful and succinct epitome of all that has or can ever be said on that important subject.[40]

Marked by its typically hyperbolic language, such praise is of course highly extravagant, but what does emerge from this near contemporary evidence of the piece's reception is the associated acknowledgement of the poet's powers of perception, the emphasis upon his ability to recreate and even surpass his model, to let the written text, and more specifically the neo-Latin text, mirror and enhance iconographical art. This concept of the marrying of "the two sister-arts" recurs in one of Addison's most self-conscious *Spectator* papers of 1712.[41] As Krieger notes, "Addison's

---

[38] Cf. Fowler, "Narrate and Describe," 26.

[39] Roland Barthes, "The Reality Effect," in *The Rustle of Language*, trans. R. Howard (New York, 1986), 141-148. Cf. Fowler, "Narrate and Describe," 26.

[40] *Poems on Several Occasions*, 81-82 (Preface).

[41] Addison, *Spectator*, 416 (27 June 1712: ed. Bond, III, 559): "Description runs yet further from the things it represents than painting, for a picture bears a real resemblance to its original, which letters and syllables are wholly void of. Colours speak all languages, but words are understood only by such a people or nation. ... It

spectrum of the arts, carrying an implicit hierarchy within it, seems to urge that poetry, reduced to verbal 'description' should look to the natural-sign 'sister arts' to define for it its representational function."[42]

Central to the *Resurrectio*'s verbal description is its couching of the whole in the language of Augustan Rome. Paradoxically, what is arguably the most vibrant recreation of Fuller's seventeenth-century mural is evinced in fact not by iconographical sketches or engravings, but by a poem composed in a dead language — a language, however, that in typical Addisonian fashion is both revivified and revivifying. And one of the ways in which this is achieved is through the appropriation and metamorphosis of Virgil.

(ii)   Linguistic Resurrection: From Virgil to Addison

In several respects the *Resurrectio* can be regarded as a poem characterized by the novelty and freshness of its treatment. In the opening lines the speaker highlights the innovative nature of his poem as he appeals to the Muse that she reveal his subject "in novel song" (*tu carmine, Musa,/pande novo* [4-5]). It will be seen that the novelty of that song is manifested in a variety of ways: in the terrifying nature of the scene which this ekphrasis is about to depict, in the skillful way in which that terror is counteracted by Addison's appropriation and inversion of a Virgilian underworld, and finally in the powers with which an ekphrastic artist goes beyond Virgil in enabling the literary to mirror the iconographical.

As the poem begins, the speaker's emphasis is upon the horror and terror of the Last Judgment: the blazing countenance (*ardentia ... ora* [2])[43] of an implicitly severe Judge – emotions mirrored on a poetic level in the "sacred fury" of inspiration which he asks the Muse to enkindle in the bard (*vatique sacros accende furores* [5]).[44] This atmosphere of terror

---

would be yet more strange to represent visible objects by sounds that have no ideas annexed to them and to make something like description in music."

[42] Cf. Krieger, *Ekphrasis*, 85.

[43] Addison is probably punning on the twofold meaning of *ardentia* as "raging" and "blazing (with light)." On the role of light and color in the mural and in Addison's representation of the same, see 108-112 above.

[44] Cf. Vida, *De Arte Poetica* 2. 395: *quid cum animis sacer est furor additus, atque potens vis*; Politian, *Nutricia* 139-140: *nunc age, qui tanto sacer hic furor incitet oestro/corda virum.* The theme recurs in Milton, *Elegia* 5. 12: *et furor et sonitus me*

and foreboding continues in a series of echoes and inversions of Virgil. Thus the ghostly images of the dead, images which are ghastly pale (*simulacra modis pallentia miris* [3]), are described in a phrase which is a verbatim echo of Virgil's catalogue in *Georgics* 1 of those eerie visions seen in the darkness of night, visions that formed part of a list of such terrifying omens as the eruption of Etna or the trembling of the Alps.[45] And these omens were evoked by the death of Julius Caesar.[46] In Addison, they are realized not on earth, but in the afterlife, in the visages of the dead. And later in the poem, the pseudo-gothic horror of the mural's and consequently the poem's depiction of a gruesome ill-formed specter rising up out of the earth is likewise conveyed through reminiscence of another eerie Virgilian scene: that of the mutilated ghost of Deiphobus as witnessed and encountered by Aeneas in the underworld of *Aeneid* 6. Deiphobus with his grotesque physical mutilations[47] has become in Addison's poem a specter with mangled countenance, deprived of its nose because of an unseemly wound, with much missing from its deformed body (46-47).[48] Similarly the description of the all-too-late regret exhibited by a soul cast out once more from Paradise by the sword-wielding *vindex* (99) recalls (at 103-104)[49] the wistful yearning of the suicides in Virgil's underworld.[50]

But if such Virgilian echoes can serve to recreate terror, so too perhaps can they offer some reassurance. In Virgil, Deiphobus' shade bore an uncanny resemblance to Aeneas' dream vision of the mutilated

---

sacer intus agit; 5. 22: *quid sacer iste furor?* See Haan, "Milton's Latin Poetry and Vida," 294-296.

[45] *Georgics* 1. 477. Virgil derived the phrase from Lucretius: *sed quaedam simulacra modis pallentia miris* (Lucr. 1.123). Lucretius is alluding to Ennius' depiction of hell as peopled not by our actual spirits or bodies, but by shadowy forms.

[46] Addison turns to *Georgics* 1 again later in the poem in his use of the phrase *longoque albescere tractu* (21) (of the Milky Way), which recalls Virgil's description of shooting stars (signs of a storm): *noctisque per umbram/flammarum longos a tergo albescere tractus* (*Georgics* 1.366-367).

[47] *lacerum crudeliter ora,/ora manusque ambas, populataque tempora raptis/auribus et truncas inhonesto vulnere nares* (*Aen.* 6. 495-497).

[48] *vultum truncata atque inhonesto vulnere nares/manca, et adhuc deest informi de corpore multum* (*Resurrectio* 46-47).

[49] *o! quantum vellet nunc aethere in alto/virtutem colere* (*Resurrectio* 103-104).

[50] *quam vellent aethere in alto/nunc et pauperiem et duros perferre labores!* (*Aen.* 6. 436-437).

Hector in the Trojan war of book 2. There, commenting on the stark change in Hector's physical appearance, Aeneas had exclaimed: *ei mihi, qualis erat, quantum mutatus ab illo/Hectore qui redit exuvias indutus Achilli ... (Aen. 2. 274-275).*[51] How changed was this grotesque image from the heroic Hector resplendent in the spoils of Achilles. Addison turns this statement upon its head in his description of the resurrected as opposed to the crucified Christ. Thus as Christ's majestic godhead shines forth in this ekphrasis, how different is he, how changed from the Christ who atoned for sins that were not his own (*quantum dissimilis, quantum o! mutatus ab illo/qui peccata luit cruciatus non sua* [59-60]). By means of such inversions the world of the pagan dead is transformed into that of Christian resurrection. And the methodology of inversion continues several lines later. Now even as Christ displays his pierced side, his hands, the wounds in his feet, the marks of the nails, the traces of the lance (66-68), around him hasten in search of his immortal gifts (*immortalia dona* [70]) throngs of holy souls (mothers, infants – their bodies now given over to a long life: young men, boys, and unwedded girls):

> umbrae huc felices tendunt, numerosaque caelos
> turba petunt atque immortalia dona capessunt.
> matres et longae nunc reddita corpora vitae
> infantum, iuvenes, pueri innuptaeque puellae
> stant circum, atque avidos iubar immortale bibentes,
> affigunt oculos in numine.
>
> (*Resurrectio* 69-74)

The lines echo and invert the description of those souls in *Aeneid* 6 flocking about Charon in their longing to be ferried across the river Styx:

> huc omnis turba ad ripas effusa ruebat,
> matres atque viri defunctaque corpora vita
> magnanimum heroum, pueri innuptaeque puellae,
> impositique rogis iuvenes ante ora parentum.
>
> (*Aen.* 6. 305-308)[52]

In Addison's ekphrasis the shades are blessed (*umbrae ... felices* [69]), while Virgil's shabbily clad Charon, the *portitor...horrendus* (6. 298), has been transmuted into the resurrected Christ, who can display the

---

[51] Cf. Satan's words to Beelzebub at *Paradise Lost* 1.84-87: "'If thou beest he; but oh how fallen! how changed/From him, who in the happy realms of light/Clothed with transcendent brightness didst outshine/Myriads though bright.'"

[52] Lines 306-308 are a verbatim echo of *Georgics* 4. 475-477 (of the souls in Orpheus' underworld).

wounds of his crucifixion amid radiant splendor. The souls themselves are endowed with, not bereft of, life, and eternal life at that – a contrast epitomized by the transformation of the Virgilian *defunctaque corpora vita* (6. 306) into *longae ... reddita corpora vitae* (71). The waters of the river Styx have become the immortal light of Christ's godhead, which is drunk in by the avid eyes of eager souls (*iubar immortale bibentes* [73]). And to reinforce this appropriation of the pagan to the Christian domain, the joy felt by these souls as they conceive of the love of Christ is depicted as surpassing the exultation experienced by Virgil's Sibyl when inspired by Apollo.[53] Thus can the onset of Christian love surpass that of pagan prophecy. Again Addison imitates, emulates and appropriates, as a pagan Virgilian underworld is transmuted into a Christian scene of resurrection.

(iii)   Iconographic Resurrection: From Virgil to Fuller

While reinventing Virgil, Addison simultaneously moves beyond his Augustan counterpart in recreating through ekphrastic description a work of seventeenth-century art.[54] As already noted, something of the quality of that iconographical inspiration has been preserved in an extant engraving and drawing. Close comparison of the *Resurrectio* with these iconographical representations reveals the fidelity of his ekphrastic description in general, especially in terms of its replication of the mural's individual sections/bands. As such, the youthful Addison emerges as a meticulously observant "spectator."

Burghers' engraving, the original of which survives in Magdalen College,[55] was attached to Addison's poem when it was reprinted in *Poems on Several Occasions* (London, 1719).[56] It has been described by

---

[53] Compare in general *Resurrectio* 78-80: *non aeque exsultat flagranti corde Sibylla/hospite cum tumet incluso et praecordia sentit/mota dei stimulis nimioque calentia Phoebo* with *Aeneid* 6. 46-51 and 6. 77-80.

[54] Cf. *Poems on Several Occasions*, xiii: "The *Resurrection* is a noble piece, drawn after the *Painter* with a masterly hand."

[55] Magdalen College Library and Archives: MC.FA1/9/28/56. At the bottom of the engraving there occurs: *Fuller Pinxit ad Alt:Coll: Magd:Oxon: Delin Mburg. sculpt. Univ.Oxon.* See Plate 3.

[56] The engraving is reproduced on 94, faced on 95 by "The Resurrection: A Poem" (i.e. Nicholas Amherst's English translation of Addison's *Resurrectio*).

Bloxam as "curious and interesting."[57] Part of this interest emerges from the fact that it portrays not just Fuller's Last Judgment mural, but also the entire eastern wall of the chapel at that time. This includes a grisaille hanging (painted by Richard Greenbury) of an altar table with candlesticks, tapers etc., behind which is depicted the Lord's Supper. The latter had also been observed and noted by Evelyn. According to Bloxam, in c. 1740 the tapestry was removed when a "finely carved wainscot of the grecian mode" was installed.[58] Positioned behind the altar was a reredos incorporating a painting of Christ carrying the cross. This was presented in 1745, is included in Cooper's drawing, and still remains today.[59] Indeed in terms of its wider perspective of the chapel, Cooper's drawing (in medium ink and sepia wash), dated c. 1817, is not without a "curiosity" and interest of its own in that it depicts a view of the chapel looking east, encapsulating its plaster vault, canopied niches between the windows, Jacobean stalls, and classical paneling. These are among the features that would eventually be swept away after 1828.[60] Common to both Burgers and Cooper, and hence of relevance to the present discussion, is of course the inclusion of Fuller's mural. For the most part, Burghers' engraving is rather more crude and narrow in its scope, while Cooper's is a much more gracefully talented work. However, both in different ways shed some light on Addison's poetic recreation of the whole: Burghers, in affording more close-up detail especially in terms of facial expression; Cooper in conveying a much wider perspective of the different bands in which the mural was organized, bands which, it will be argued, are reflected in the panoramic structure of Addison's poem.

What is immediately evident from both the engraving and the drawing is that Fuller's mural constituted to some degree an Anglicized pastiche of Michelangelo's famous equivalent. Liversidge, while acknowledging Fuller's contribution to religious painting in seventeenth-century England, has stated:

---

[57] Bloxam, *Register*, II, cxxxiii.

[58] In his brief account of a second visit which he paid to Magdalen Chapel (25 October 1664) Evelyn noted "the painting of Magdalens Chapel, which is on blue cloth in *chiaro oscuro*, by one Greenborough, being a *Coena Domini* " (*Diary*, ed. De Beer, III, 386). Cf. Bloxam, *Register*, II, cxxxiii.

[59] See Darwall-Smith and White, *The Architectural Drawings of Magdalen College*, xxxv.

[60] See the description provided by Darwall-Smith and White, *The Architectural Drawings of Magdalen College*, 21.

> The composition as a whole lacked coherence ...   A less imaginative interpretation of an apotheosis theme from the baroque period is difficult to envisage, and its deficiencies are such that even as a *pasticheur* of Michelangelo Fuller appears singularly inept.[61]

As noted above, such criticism is perhaps typical of the contemporary and modern reception which his piece has received. Nonetheless, even as a rather crude pastiche of Michelangelo, the work is not without some talent. In a general sense the very positioning of Fuller's mural behind the College's altar replicates, as do several other such Anglicized versions, the methodology of Michelangelo,[62] whose "positioning of his massively scaled Last Judgment behind the altar in the chapel's focal point was without precedent."[63] It is clear, moreover, that Fuller has structured his mural in accordance with the typical form of Last Judgment paintings, an internal structure manifested most supremely by Michelangelo.[64] Noteworthy also is the central emphasis which Fuller has given to Christ. Similarly in Michelangelo's work "never before had Christ so clearly initiated and controlled the drama."[65] More specifically, Fuller follows the typical structure of Last Judgment murals, which were traditionally divided into four horizontal bands. Thus, like Michelangelo, Fuller has as the bottom band a depiction of the resurrecting dead from breached tombs,[66] alongside a vision of Hell and the damned; as the second band the ascending elect in the company of trumpeting angels; the *ecclesia* group (in this instance Bishop Waynflete) as the third band, and, in the fourth, at the very top angels carrying the instruments of Christ's passion.[67]

---

[61] Liversidge, "Prelude to the Baroque," 318.

[62] Such, for example, is equally true of Fuller's Last Judgment which used to grace All Souls College Chapel.

[63] See Loren Partridge, *Michelangelo: The Last Judgment: A Glorious Restoration* (New York, 1997), 13.

[64] For detailed discussion, see Partridge, *Michelangelo*, 8-154.

[65] Partridge, *Michelangelo*, 22.

[66] Partridge, *Michelangelo*, 58, remarks that "Representations of the Last Judgment traditionally presented the breaching of the tombs near the bottom or lower left."

[67] See in general Partridge, *Michelangelo*, 13-17. For further examples, see Partridge, *Michelangelo*, Figure 3, descr., 13: "Anonymous, Last Judgment [below the *Crucifixion* and *Christ in Limbo*], mosaic, Torcello, Cathedral, west wall, twelfth century, second half." The fourth band depicts Christ enthroned in glory surrounded by angels. To the left are the Virgin, St. Peter, and five Apostles; to the right are John

In terms of its ekphrastic recreation Addison's description begins with the top of the mural, then proceeds to the bottom, and then to the center. The result is, as it were, a series of panoramic camera shots. The ekphrasis proper begins by stating that the extreme border of the mural (*ora suprema* [28]) contains angels: "winged messengers" (*aligeris ... ministris* [28]). Both Burghers' engraving (Plate 3) and Cooper's drawing (Plate 4) depict a host of angels along the upper part of the mural. The arched edge of the upper border is fringed, as it were, by eight cherubs, all positioned at key points; then beneath the arching façade are depicted two symmetrically positioned cherubs in the top center, with one arm extended as though heralding the risen Christ, who sits directly beneath. This pair of angels is flanked on either side by another angel blowing a trumpet, and their inflated cheeks are evident (in Cooper's drawing more so than in the engraving). This detail obviously underlies Addison's observation of a heavenly host blowing trumpets, and with visibly inflated cheeks (29-31).[68] Addison also remarks that this celestial band is scattered through the entire picture (*sparsaque per totam* [29]). Both the engraving and the drawing do indeed depict trumpet-blowing angels in another lower section of the mural: one of these to either side of the ascending Waynflete.[69] Both angels, flanking Waynflete, blow trumpets,

---

the Baptist, St. Paul, and five Apostles, with angels in the background. The third band depicts "a throne with book, cross, crown of thorns, reed with vinegar-soaked sponge, and lance, flanked by the kneeling Adam and Eve and angels; four trumpeting angels resurrecting the dead on land (left) and sea (right), one angel rolling up the heavens (right)." The second band represents "(center) St. Michael weighing souls; (left) ecclesiastics, martyrs, prophets, and ascetic women; (right) two angels forcing the proud into Hell, presided over by Satan." The first band depicts "(left) angel, St. Peter, door to paradise, Dismas, the Virgin, tree of life, and souls in the bosom of Abraham; (right) punishment of six of the seven deadly sins of lust, gluttony, sloth, envy, avarice, and anger (the seventh sin, pride, just above)." Cf. Partridge, *Michelangelo*, Figure 4, 13: "School of Coppo di Marcovaldo, *Last Judgment*, mosaic, Florence, Baptistry, vault, c. 1270-75: *Center*: Christ enthroned in glory. *Third band*: (left) angels with trumpet, cross, crown of thorns, and nails; (right) angels with trumpet, whips, lance, and reed with vinegar-soaked sponge. *Second band*: (left) the Virgin, St. Peter, and five Apostles; (right) John the Baptist, St. Paul, and five Apostles; (background) angels. *First band*: (center) resurrecting dead; (left) angels (one with banderole with Matthew 25:34), saved, door to paradise, souls in bosom of Abraham, tree of life; (right) demons, damned, Satan, torments of Hell."

[68] *caelestis turba tabellam/raucos inspirat lituos buccasque tumentes/inflat (Resurrectio* 29-31).

[69] William Waynflete (1395?-1486), Bishop of Winchester, Chancellor of England, and Founder in 1448 of Magdalen Hall, subsequently Magdalen College, Oxford. See among others Richard Chandler, *Life of William Wayneflete* (London, 1811).

by means of which they summon the dead, who rise from the depths of the earth. And the poem moves beyond the purely visual to encapsulate sound: these are *raucos ... lituos* (30), whose clangor permeates an astonished world (31),[70] penetrating, as it does, even the realms of the dead. Elsewhere avenging angels are visible: one forcefully dragging the accused; another brandishing a flaming sword as he evicts souls from a second paradise. In the mural then, as in Addison's albeit exaggerated *sparsaque per totam* (29),[71] cherubs occur in different realms or bands: at the top in the celestial zone above the figure of the seated Christ; at the bottom below the figure of Christ and in association with the fates of individual souls.

From the *ora suprema* (28) the poem now moves to a description of the bottom of the mural (*tabulamque per imam* [32]) as, in response to the trumpet blast, the ground swells (*picta gravescit humus* [33]), and from the opening earth (*terris ... apertis* [33]) there rise up the resurrected dead and many a specter (*progenies rediviva, et plurima ... imago* [34]). At the very bottom of both the engraving and the drawing figures are clearly visible climbing up out of an aperture in the earth. The physicality of the struggle of the rising dead as they emerge out of the earth in general and their tombs in particular, a struggle characteristic of Michelangelo's original,[72] is rather more obvious in Cooper than in Burghers. Just above them are depicted those summoning trumpet-blowing angels. Addison zooms in, as it were, upon the frequently grotesque details of the figures as the emerging bodies gradually take

---

[70] *et attonitum replet clangoribus orbem* (*Resurrectio* 31).

[71] Fuller has actually reduced the number of angels characteristic of Michelangelo's original. See Partridge, *Michelangelo*, 27-29: "Traditional representations of the Last Judgment usually employed two, at most four, symmetrically arranged trumpeters, who awaken the dead ... But Michelangelo's depiction – unprecedented in its dynamism – features eleven colourfully draped angels below Christ, eight with trumpets, as a secondary energy locus to intensify the drama and to serve as the fulcrum for the second band."

[72] For a parallel in Michelangelo, cf. Partridge, *Michelangelo*, Plates 42-45. Cf. 58: "At the left, nearly all of the souls give the impression of raising themselves and actively cooperating with the drama initiated by Christ and his angels. In the lower left foreground, for example, one soul strains to lift a heavy slab of rock, allowing another to crawl out vigorously." Elsewhere "three male nudes ... have each drawn one leg at a sharp angle out of the ground, planted both hands firmly on the earth, and begun to free the still entombed leg in order to stand up in response to the blare of the trumpeting angels toward whom they look."

shape, with limbs attaching to limbs (44),[73] a noseless *imago* (46-47),[74] whose body is not yet perfected; a stiff corpse into which life is gradually insinuated through its revived limbs which are scarcely moving (48-49).[75] Both Burghers and Cooper likewise capture something of the grotesque. Several of these reviving figures are only half-formed, their faces certainly missing features, while others press down their weight upon their elbows in an attempt to raise their still stiff bodies out of the ground.

From the bottom of the mural, the spectator is now invited to behold, if he can, the radiant center wherein is seated the Son of God. As noted above, the emphasis is very much on the light which surrounds and perfuses this divine image – flames about his brow, a very different image from the crucified Christ. Addison points out that it was in vain that Golgotha craved to bury Christ's divinity; instead He sought his native heaven and, borne above the ether, looked down upon a tiny moon and a smaller sun (52-65). This contrast between the crucified and the resurrected Christ may reflect the fact that at the very top of the mural is an image of angels transporting heavenwards the instruments of Christ's passion, most visibly the cross, but also the lance and crown of thorns.[76]

The description of Christ is likewise an accurate reflection of details of the mural in question: he displays his pierced side and both his hands (66),[77] the wound on his foot, the marks of the nails, and the traces of the lance that pierced him (67-68).[78] In both the engraving and the

---

[73] *aptanturque iterum coeuntia membra* (*Resurrectio* 44). Cf. Addison's description of the manufacture of puppets at *Machinae Gesticulantes* 78-79, on which see 85-87 above.

[74] *vultum truncata atque inhonesto vulnere nares/manca* (*Resurrectio* 46-47).

[75] *paulatim in rigidum hic vita insinuata cadaver/motu aegro vix dum redivivos erigit artus* (*Resurrectio* 48-49).

[76] For a parallel, see Partridge, *Michelangelo*, Figure 5, 14: "Pietro Cavallini, Last Judgment, fresco, Rome, S. Cecilia, 1290s *Top* (center) Christ enthroned in glory flanked by angels; (left) the Virgin, St. Paul, and five Apostles; (right) John the Baptist, St. Peter, and five Apostles. *Bottom* (center) altar with cross, nails, lance, reed with vinegar-soaked sponge, and vase surrounded by innocents; (left) two trumpeting angels, Saints Stephen and Lawrence (under trumpets), angels directing the elect (including women) toward Heaven; (right) two trumpeting angels, angels driving damned to Hell."

[77] *iam latus effossum et palmas ostendit utrasque* (*Resurrectio* 66).

[78] *vulnusque infixum pede clavorumque recepta/signa, et transacti quondam vestigia ferri* (*Resurrectio* 67-68).

drawing the marks in Christ's feet and side are clearly visible. In Cooper, however, Christ appears to be standing yet at the same time he almost sits upon a layer of clouds and (as in Burghers) he holds up his right hand, revealing the wound in his palm. This ambiguity of Christ's position, while not so prominent in Burgher's engraving, was indeed characteristic of Michelangelo's work.[79] In both, Christ holds in his left hand an orb, a detail unmentioned by Addison. In this centerpiece the risen Christ constitutes an important focal point. Thus blessed shades hasten towards him (69);[80] mothers, babies, young men, boys, unmarried girls, all gather round and gaze intently upon him (71-73).[81] In both Burghers and Cooper a throng of figures on the left veers towards Christ; on the right others gaze fixedly upon him, their bodies looking outwards, but their heads clearly turned intently towards him at such an angle that the eyes of the spectator are drawn in towards the center – towards Christ himself, a methodology found in Michelangelo's original.[82] Again, the whole progresses into the realm of sound, describing the ether thundering with praises, and heaven laughing with joyous triumph (74-75).[83]

The poem next turns to Wainfletus (William of Waynflete, Bishop of Winchester and founder of Magdalen College),[84] who is depicted as radiant, wearing a miter, rising from his tomb and supported by an angel

---

[79] Cf. Partridge, *Michelangelo*, 22: "At first sight Christ appears to be standing, lifting his right hand … he raises with his right hand – or so his movement implies – the saved souls on his right … Yet, at the same time he seemingly prepares to sit down on his celestial throne of clouds."

[80] *umbrae huc felices tendunt* (*Resurrectio* 69).

[81] *stant circum, atque avidos iubar immortale bibentes/affigunt oculos in numine* (*Resurrectio* 73-74).

[82] Cf. Partridge, *Michelangelo*, 38, on Michelangelo's original (though in this instance in relation to angels): "Simultaneously with its clockwise turning, the cross and the entire retinue of gesticulating, awestruck angels appear to be drawn toward Christ … The subsidiary group of angels to the right most clearly defines the diagonal thrust of their trajectory …These angels – most with outstretched arms, the foremost displaying the crown of thorns – align themselves like iron filings in a magnetic field and – drapery fluttering – glide toward Christ."

[83] *laudibus aether/intonat, et laeto ridet caelum omne triumpho* (*Resurrectio* 74-75).

[84] For Fuller's typical practice of inserting in his paintings relatively "modern" figures, cf. his copy of Dobson's *Beheading of John the Baptist*, in which he substituted for the heads portraits of his friends.

(82-83).[85] This captures well the mural's representation (likewise included in the engraving and the drawing) of the mitered Bishop rising with outstretched hands and supported in his ascent by angels on either side, who escort him upwards. Addison's observation that the bishop gazes without trepidation at the Judge (89)[86] is clearly evident in the iconographical representations.

From the rising dead Addison turns to hell, a horrible scene of fire and darkness: its molten rivers, the luminance of whose fire would seem to threaten the picture itself,[87] the gnashing of teeth, the hideously mangled faces, and the avenger raging at their backs, wielding his sword of lightning, and driving the sinners from Paradise (90-101). On the mural's bottom right-hand section, as recreated in the engraving and drawing, the avenging angel does indeed brandish a flaming sword at the backs of these evicted sinners, whose faces are horribly grotesque. Addison, however, focuses on one figure, an unnamed penitent who (in Virgilian terms)[88] would long all too late to cultivate virtue in the high ether, but is now reduced to tears of regret (102-106). In so doing he encapsulates the mood of that eviction scene in general.

It is a mood that is transformed in the poem's concluding lines, where having hymned the charms of this mural (107),[89] and its profusion of color,[90] the speaker addresses the *pictura* itself, praying that the glory of its beauty may never fade until the mural has witnessed the Last Day which it depicts:

> O fuci nitor, o pulchri durate colores!
> nec, pictura, tuae languescat gloria formae
> dum lucem videas, qualem exprimis ipsa, supremam.
> *(Resurrectio* 112-114)

Several years later the more mature Addison would make a rather pessimistic prediction in regard to the transitory nature of works of art:

---

[85] *quam mitra effigiem distinxit pictor honesto/surgentem e tumulo alatoque satellite fultam? (Resurrectio 82-83).*

[86] *impavidosque in iudice figit ocellos (Resurrectio 89).*

[87] Ironically much of Fuller's decorative work was destroyed in the Great Fire of 1666.

[88] See 114 above.

[89] *quam varias aperit veneres pictura! (Resurrectio 107).*

[90] See 108-111 above.

> Statues can last but a few thousands of years, edifices fewer, and colours still fewer than edifices. Michelangelo, Fontana and Raphael will hereafter be what Phidias, Vitruvius, and Apelles are at present; the names of great statuaries, architects and painters, whose works are lost.[91]

For Fuller's mural that Last Day (*lux ... suprema* [114]) has indeed come as a consequence of the vicissitudes of history, time, and taste, but something of its "glory" (*gloria* [113]) has indeed lived on. This has been rendered possible by Addison's skillful reworking of Virgil, by accurate iconographical recreation, and especially by the revivifying powers of a neo-Latin poem in general and of the artist/poet in particular. As such the very subject of the *Resurrectio Delineata* is mirrored in the poem's self-referential celebration of the resurrecting powers of art and of the artist himself.

---

[91] *Spectator*, 166 (10 September 1711: ed. Bond, II, 154).

CHAPTER 7

From Vigo to Vienna: *Addisoniana Rediviva*

In the late summer of 1699 Addison commenced his Grand Tour, proudly equipped with an erudite passport to foreign society. That passport took the form of his *Musae Anglicanae*, a volume which, as noted above, included all but one of his aforementioned Latin poems,[1] and was presented to Boileau in Paris.[2] As preparation for his subsequent travels through Italy Addison had reread classical Latin poetry, "and had made copious notes of passages which might lend interest to a journey through the scenes of classical antiquity."[3] It was a journey, moreover, that would inspire several of his vernacular works, most notably perhaps his *Remarks on Several Parts of Italy* (1705). This work is paved with illustrations from ancient authors,[4] whose comments enabled him to unite the classical and the contemporary. Such unification is equally evident in some hitherto unstudied Latin verses belonging to this period.

As part of his Grand Tour Addison visited Vienna, where he was hospitably received by George Stepney, diplomat, poet, and British minister at the Imperial Court.[5] The likely date of his arrival in Vienna is some time in October 1702 since in November 1702 Addison wrote to Stepney "in terms which suggest that he had already been at Vienna for at least a month."[6] It was during his sojourn in that city that he would write his *Dialogues Upon Ancient Medals*.

---

[1] The exception is *Tityrus et Mopsus* (published in 1689), which Addison did not anthologize in the *Musae Anglicanae*. See Chapter 1 above.

[2] See 8-9 above.

[3] Smithers, *The Life of Joseph Addison*, 46. Cf. Thackeray, *Essay on Addison*, in *Essays on Addison by Johnson, Macaulay, Thackeray*, ed. G.E. Hadow (Oxford, 1915), 94: "Addison had deeply imbued himself with the Latin poetical literature and had these poets at his fingers' ends when he travelled in Italy."

[4] Thus Courthope, *Addison*, 44: "His illustrations of his route from the Latin poets are remarkably happy and graceful."

[5] Smithers, *The Life of Joseph Addison*, 78, states that Addison "received many kindnesses" from Stepney. A friend of Lord Halifax, Stepney was a man of some erudition. A minor poet in his own right, he, like Addison, had been the victim of Wellington's literary piracy in the *Examen Poeticum Duplex*, on which see 5 above.

[6] Smithers, *The Life of Joseph Addison*, 76.

(i)   Addison's Vigo Epigrams

Also dated to this period, however, are Addison's Latin verses on the Vigo expedition of 1702. They survive in the British Library[7] among drafts or copies of Charles Whitworth's dispatches to James Vernon and (after 5 June 1702) Sir Charles Hedges, Secretaries of State;[8] Whitworth had been sent to Vienna during the temporary absence of Stepney. Oddly, however, these intriguing Latin verses seem to have escaped the notice of even the most meticulous of Addison's editors. Apparently unknown to Tickell and not previously printed, they are not included in the editions by Guthkelch or Sutton. And the enigma continues. By contrast it emerges that they *were* known to Thackeray, whose *The History of Henry Esmond*, II.5 ("On the Vigo Bay Expedition") announces:

> The latter was a bad business, though Mr Addison did sing its praises in Latin. That honest gentleman's muse had an eye to the main chance; and I doubt whether she saw much inspiration in the losing side.[9]

Modern scholarship has failed to shed light on this issue. Loofbourow in his study of Thackeray's novel does not identify the verses (or manuscript) in question.[10] Likewise Pantůčkova's perceptive analysis of Thackeray as literary critic, which does at least mention this reference in the novel, merely states that it demonstrates how Thackeray "openly dissociated himself from Addison's aesthetic relationship to reality."[11] The notebook in which he jotted down historical details and other facts while writing the novel does include an entry entitled "11 October 1702 Vigo. September Cadiz,"[12] but sheds no further light on the matter.

---

[7] BL Add.37349, ff 57-58 (Whitworth Papers). See Plates 5 and 6.

[8] See *The Correspondence of Charles Whitworth*, Vol. II, 3 Nov 1702-12.

[9] Text is that of *W.M. Thackeray: Henry Esmond* (Everyman: London, 1937), 182.

[10] John Loofbourow, *Thackeray and the Form of Fiction* (Princeton, 1964), 137.

[11] Lidmila Pantůčkova, *W.M. Thackeray as a Critic of Literature* (BRNO Studies in English 10-11, 1972), 70-71. There is no indication from her study that she is aware of the manuscript or indeed that she has actually read the Latin verses themselves.

[12] See John Sutherland, "Thackeray's Notebook for Henry Esmond," in *Costerus: Essays in English and American Language and Literature: Thackeray*, ed. P.L. Shillingsburg (Amsterdam, 1974), II, 193-215, at 210. The notebook was acquired by the New York Public Library in 1914. Sutherland, 210, makes the interesting observation that "Thackeray considered 1702 as an important juncture in his novel, and one about which he would have to make himself historically competent."

Although Thackeray was deeply familiar with Addison's Latin poetry,[13] how he came to know of these particular verses remains a mystery.

Irrespective of the history of the reception of the verses, their survival in manuscript is not only fortunate, but of particular interest to the present study. A close examination raises several issues that are of importance to a survey of Addison as a neo-Latin poet. Given the context in which they occur, it is clear that they are occasional verses celebrating the destruction by the Anglo-Dutch forces on 22 October 1702 of the Spanish Fleet at Vigo Bay, off the northwest coast of Spain.[14] It was a battle that reached a dramatic conclusion in the firing of the enemy ships, and the whole was seen as a huge British triumph, worthy of festive celebration in London. Thus a directive of 31 October 1702 proclaimed:

> The Queen has received news from the Duke of Ormond and Sir George Rooke that the fleet and land forces have seized and burnt the French men-of-war and Spanish galleons at Vigo. I am to tell you of this that you may give the necessary directions for rejoicings to be made in the City.[15]

---

[13] Thackeray's knowledge of Addison's Latin poetry in general shines through in *The History of Henry Esmond*. In II, cap. xi, entitled "The Famous Mr Joseph Addison", the following conversation takes place between Esmond and Richard Steele: "'Indeed' says Mr Esmond, with a bow, 'it is not from you only that I have learnt to admire Mr Addison. We loved good poetry at Cambridge as well as at Oxford, and I have some of yours by heart, though I have put on a red coat ... 'O qui canoro blandius Orpheo vocale ducis carmen'; shall I go on, sir? says Mr Esmond, who, indeed, had read and loved the charming Latin poems of Mr Addison, as every scholar of that time knew and admired them" (*Henry Esmond*, 228-229). Loofbourow, *Thackeray and the Form of Fiction*, 137; 142-143, argues that the "significance of artistic deviation from reality – the distinction between meaningful and meretricious illusion – is implicit ...; and the Orpheus allusion preludes a pastoral irony that pervades the poet's impersonation." Cf. Pantůčkova, *W.M. Thackeray as a Critic of Literature*, 71. The reference is to Addison's Ode to Dr Hannes. And allusions to Addison's vernacular poetry, in particular "The Campaign", figure elsewhere in the novel. Cf. Laurence Lerner, "The Unsaid in Henry Esmond," *Essays in Criticism* 45 (1995), 141-157, at 142-144, which argues that the function of "The Campaign" in *Henry Esmond* is "to show us what the Muse of History is normally concerned with" (143). Thus the novel is regarded "as an attempt to deconstruct *The Campaign*" (144).

[14] The British fleet was under the command of Sir George Rooke. Cf. *The Journal of Sir George Rooke, Admiral of the Fleet, 1700-1702*, ed. O. Browning (London, 1897), 228-234. Further details of the campaign are provided by *An Impartial Account of All the Material Transactions of the Grand Fleet ... In which is Included a Particular Relation of the Expedition at Cadiz, and the Glorious Victory at Vigo By an Officer that was Present in Those Actions* (London, 1703), 21-24. There is a copy of this rare work in the British Library, London.

[15] Cf. in general Hedges' Letters To the Lord Mayor of London.

Such celebrations, however, were not confined to England. Indeed Addison's participation in their Viennese counterpart is attested. It is known that on 30 November he, along with Edward Montagu and George Dashwood (son of the Lord Mayor of London), commoner of Magdalen,[16] accompanied Stepney to dine with the Prince of Liechtenstein and subsequently also attended at the Imperial Court an opera performed specifically in celebration of the Vigo victory.[17] This raises the possibility that his Latin verses were either written for, or inspired by, that celebration. If so, he may even have presented them formally to the Imperial Court. Alternatively he may have submitted the poems privately to Stepney (a talented Latinist),[18] as indeed he did with drafts of his *Dialogues Upon Ancient Medals*.[19] At the very least the performance in Vienna of an opera attended by Addison indicates not only that the Vigo Bay victory was being celebrated in the city during his sojourn there, but that he himself was a "spectator" at one such celebration.

The Vigo verses are of interest on a more literary level also: firstly, they are the only extant example of Addison's use of the elegiac meter;[20] secondly, their likely date of 1702 means that they represent his last surviving Latin verses, while also revealing that he continued to write Latin poetry much later than has previously been thought.[21] Thirdly, the

---

[16] Dashwood may have been Addison's former pupil. He matriculated at Magdalen College, Oxford in 1698 (aged 18). See Foster, *Alumni Oxonienses*, I, 374.

[17] Stepney-Hedges, State Papers 80/19: letter of 2/12/02. Cf. Smithers, *The Life of Joseph Addison*, 79.

[18] On Stepney as a Latinist, cf. *The Inscription Appointed to be Fix'd on A Marble Erected at Hochstadt: In Memory of that Glorious Victory: The Latin Written by Mr Stepney and Englished by a Gentleman of Oxon* (London, 1705).

[19] See Addison's letter to Stepney (sent from Vienna in November 1702) in Graham, ed. *The Letters of Joseph Addison*, 35-36. Interestingly, at the beginning of the letter Addison's comment reveals that he has already sent Stepney some verses, although he does not identify these (nor indeed whether they are in Latin or the vernacular): "That I may be as troublesome to you in prose *as in verse*, I take the liberty to send you the beginning of a work ..." (35). Italics are mine. Given the date of the current letter, it is possible that the "verses" in question were indeed the Vigo poems.

[20] With the exception of the Odes to Burnet and Hannes, Addison's other Latin poems are exclusively hexameter verses.

[21] Contrast Wiesenthal, *The Latin Poetry of the English Augustans*, 52: "The main bulk of Addison's Latin verse was composed between the years 1689-1694, and after this Addison is not known to have written any more."

lines demonstrate once more Addison's appropriation of the poetry of Virgil, by now one of the key hallmarks of his neo-Latin methodology.

The manuscript itself raises several questions. According to the BL Manuscripts catalogue index, folio 57 alone is attributed to Addison. It emerges however that several other Latin poems on folio 58, separated by Addison's verses by a mere #, are also in all likelihood by him.[22] Folio 57 begins with a quotation from Virgil, *Aeneid* 1.361-364, and the note: "Application: the affair of Vigo:"

> conveniunt, quibus aut odium crudele tyranni
> aut metus acer erat; naves, quae forte paratae,
> corripiunt onerantque auro. portantur avari
> Pygmalionis opes pelago; dux femina facti.[23]

Appended to these lines is the statement: "Verses made on the Expedition of Vigo by Mr Addison then at Vienna." There follow on that folio ten lines of Latin elegiac poetry. Depending upon the interpretation of the summary phrase "Verses," it could be argued that four further Latin poems, whose author or authors are not identified, are by Addison. And the composition of several neo-Latin epigrams upon a single given theme was a very common practice during the Renaissance and beyond.[24] The absence of attribution of the short poems that follow supports the argument that Addison was author of these also, an argument corroborated by internal evidence in the poems themselves, which constitute a series of variations upon a Virgilian passage.[25] These variations become increasingly intricate as each epigram dovetails into its successor. In short, it is very likely that the "Verses made on the Vigo Expedition" constitute five hitherto unnoticed Latin epigrams by Addison, all of which were transcribed in the same hand: that of Whitworth.[26]

---

[22] See Plates 5 and 6.

[23] British Museum BL Add. 37349, f 57. The opening line is incorrectly cited in the ms as verse 365.

[24] Compare, for example, Milton's five Latin epigrams on the Gunpowder Plot or his three Latin epigrams in praise of the Italian soprano, Leonora Baroni.

[25] See 134-137 below.

[26] It is interesting to note that the Vigo Bay victory is alluded to on folio 55 of the same manuscript in a letter to Hedges (dated Ratisbone 27 November 1702): "On the 21th [sic] Mr Stanhope sent me the happy news that the French and Spanish ships had been entirely destroyed at Vigo and on the 24th we received the confirmation and particulars thereof from all parts, which (all other business being laid aside) I took up

(ii)   Variations Upon a Virgilian Theme

As noted above, Addison's verses are prefaced by a quotation from
Virgil, *Aeneid* 1.361-364, and the statement "Application: the affair of
Vigo." The application of these lines is very pertinent given the context
in which they occur in *Aeneid* 1: Venus, in an introductory flashback of
Dido's past history, narrates to Aeneas her escape from her tyrannical
brother Pygmalion. Mustering her resources and seizing ships, she and
her followers load them with his gold. Thus is his wealth transported
across the sea, with a woman in charge of the enterprise. In terms of its
"application" to an early eighteenth-century military exploit, the lines
work on an allegorical level. Dido is here implicitly equated with Queen
Anne; consequentially the tyrannical Pygmalion symbolizes Louis XIV;
likewise the gold which Dido captured and carried across the sea[27] has
now become the enemy treasure won as a result of the expedition. The
manuscript continues with the heading "Verses made on the Expedition
of Vigo by Mr Addison then at Vienna"[28] and then the series of epigrams
in question. It is a series, it will be argued, that merits discussion as a
cohesive whole.

That the epigrams emphasize the theme of fire and its associated
literal and metaphorical images (e.g. the sun, the pyre, ardent passion)
need hardly come as a great surprise, given the fact that it was the firing

---

the whole thoughts and conversation of the Diette for that morning, and most of the
ministers sent to compliment me on the glorious progress of Her Majesty's arms by
sea and land, and I must do them the justice to own that the joy here was universal
particularly amongst those of the reformed religion in this place." Folio 56[v] proclaims:
"Here are letters from Italy of the 18th which say that Prince Eugene having posted his
army in their winter quarters, is gone privately to Vienna to give the Emperor an
account of the posture of affairs in those parts ..." There is no evidence from the
manuscript that Addison's Latin verses were sent to Hedges at Whitehall, although it
might not be unreasonable to assume that this was the case.

[27] According to Servius, *In Vergilii Carmina Commentarii*, ed. George Thilo (Leipzig,
1878), I, 124, Virgil's lines may hint at a tradition whereby Pygmalion had lined up a
number of ships laden with gold, which he aimed to trade for corn. These ships were
then seized by Dido and her party. In order to escape from her brother's emissaries
who were pursuing her in her flight, she hurled the gold into the sea, upon which they
turned and went after it: *sciendum autem quod clam tangit historiam. moris enim erat
ut de pecunia publica Phoenices misso a rege auro de peregrinis frumenta
conveherent. Dido autem a Pygmalione ad hunc usum paratas naves abstulerat: quam
cum fugientem a fratre missi sequerentur, aurum illa praecipitavit in mare, qua re
visa sequentes reversi sunt.*

[28] For an edition of all the Vigo verses included in the manuscript, see Appendix 2
below.

of the enemy ships that constituted the culmination of the Vigo battle.[29]
Thus in a poem published at London in 1702 Charles Tooke, hymning
the British success, proclaimed:

> While on the Eagle's outstretcht wings, like Jove
> With Bolts and Fire descending from above,
> The French Salmoneus rage Thou didst restrain,
> And shew'd the real Thund'rer of the Main:
> The Sea confest Thy pow'r; she open'd wide
> Her bosome, and in Flames the God enjoy'd.[30]

The first epigram (officially attributed to Addison) is marked by its
succinct wit and sardonic tone as it appropriates the Virgilian concept of
dux femina facti (1. 364)[31] to an early eighteenth-century context. In the
battle of Vigo a Queen of Carthage has now been reincarnated, as it were,
in a Queen of England, Anne, whose ultimately victorious resilience is
implicitly compared to that of Queen Elizabeth, and contrasted with the
audacious pride of her opponents. As such Addison's piece constitutes a
neo-Latin epigram on the power of a woman.

The piece begins with an implicit allusion to the overly proud
Philip II of Spain,[32] and the defeat of the Spanish Armada at the hands of
Elizabeth.[33] "By application" the criticism is telling: in terms of Philip of
Spain, Louis XIV has at Vigo suffered the same fate of humiliation at the
hands of an English Queen. And the dire consequences are highlighted.
Spain, because of her "immoderate ambition" (3) has had to unlearn
"huge thirst" (4).[34] Nor is Spain the only victim. Addressing France, the

---

[29] Cf. *An Impartial Account*: "One and soon after three of the French ships were set on
fire, and all abandoned the ship Monsieur Chateau-Renaud was in, being first afire,
and those near the boom."

[30] *To the Right Honourable Sir George Rooke, Vice Admiral of England &c, At His
Return from His Glorious Enterprise Near Vigo 1702* (London, 1702), 5.

[31] See W.R. Nethercut, "*Dux Femina Facti*: General Dido and the Trojans," *CB* 47
(1970), 26-30. Cf. J.P. Sullivan, "Dido and the Representation of Women in Vergil's
Aeneid," in *The Two Worlds of the Poet: New Perspectives on Vergil*, ed. R.M.
Wilhelm and H. Jones (Detroit, 1992), 64-73. See more generally Marilynn Desmond,
Reading Dido: Gender, Textuality, and the Medieval Aeneid (Minneapolis and
London, 1994).

[32] *cum nimio intumuit victrix Hispania fastu* (1).

[33] *olim infracta armis cessit, Elisa, tuis* (2).

[34] *immodica ambitio mundique capacia vota/ex illo ingentem dedidicere sitim* (3-4).

speaker proclaims that she too, whose ships have been fired (*combustis ... carinis* [5]), has experienced the power of a woman's hand.[35] The theme of the firing of ships and of a woman as instigating that deed may look back to and invert a scene from *Aeneid* 5, especially lines 641-663. There the angry goddess Juno sends Iris to incite the exhausted women of Troy to madness. Assuming the form of an aged woman Beroe, she urges them to set fire to their own ships, with the result that *furit immissis Volcanus habenis/transtra per et remos et pictas abiete puppis* (*Aen.* 5. 662-663).[36] But, as is frequently the case, the possible Virgilian parallel only lends irony to Addison's lines. In terms of the Vigo expedition the perpetrator of this firing is likewise female; however, the ships are not her own, but those of her enemy. And whereas in Virgil Ascanius eventually restores the women to their senses, and Jupiter in response to a prayer of Aeneas, extinguishes the fire, now there can be no such human or divine intervention. Instead an ironic question provides a panoramic vision of the scene, as the speaker asks if they can behold a fleet that is still smoldering on the Spanish shore – that *adhuc ... fumat* (7), indicating perhaps that Addison's lines were composed very soon after the event.

The irony continues as Addison reworks aspects of the *Aeneid* 1 lines prefixed to the whole. The wealth of the greedy Pygmalion transported over the sea by Dido (*portantur avari/Pygmalionis opes pelago* [*Aen.* 1. 363-364]) has now become the vast treasures secured by Britain in the course of the Vigo expedition, as "the whole of the Indies" flows towards the Britons (7-8).[37] According to Sir Cloudesly Shovel, this amounted to "about two millions in silver, and five in goods."[38] The

---

[35] *tu quoque sensisti combustis vana carinis,/Gallia, femineae quid potuere manus* (5-6).

[36] See in general S.G. Nugent, "Vergil's Voice of the Women in *Aeneid* V," *Arethusa* 25 (1992), 255-292; Karl Galinsky, "*Aeneid* V and the *Aeneid*," *AJP* 89 (1968), 157-185.

[37] *nonne vides ut adhuc in litore fumat Ibero/classis et ad Britonas India tota fluit?* (7-8). Cf. Jonathan Trelawny, Bishop of Exeter, *A Sermon Preach'd Before the Queen, and Both Houses of Parliament at the Cathedral Church of St Paul's, Nov. 12, 1702* (London, 1702), 29-30: "The French King ... reckon'd now the Treasure of the Indies surely his own ... But Providence laughed at him, and said: 'Not thy soul this night, but these things dearer to thee shall be taken from thee.'"

[38] "A Biographical Memoir of Sir Cloudesly Shovel", *The Naval Chronicle*, March 1815: "Of the galleons, the English took six, and the Dutch five, who likewise sunk. They had on board when they arrived, twenty million pieces of eight, and merchandise estimated of equal value, the greater part of which had been landed previous to the

poem concludes in an ironic reference to France's Salic Law (stating that persons descended from a previous sovereign through a female were excluded from the succession [9-10]).[39] The French refuse to be ruled by a woman, but now a woman ruling in England has humiliated them. And by the end of the poem this woman has been transformed into much more than a *dux femina facti*. Now as an English goddess brandishing thunderbolts (*Angliacae fulmina ... deae* [10]) she seems to usurp the role of Jupiter himself, king of the gods, epitomizing no doubt the domineering force and powerful success of a divinely inspired British campaign.[40]

In the second epigram the emphasis shifts from the defeat of both the Spanish and the French to singular concentration upon the French losses and attitude. In so doing it reworks aspects of Virgil's Dido episode in two ways. The first is in the development of the theme of deception. Addressing France, the lines convey that nation's pride in her refusal to admit defeat. This highly unrealistic attitude is criticized by means of skillfully contrasted clauses: hence the defeat of France (*vinceris* [1]) as opposed to her refusal to admit this (*numquam te victum ... fateris* [1]); the essentially "false" trophies (*falsa tropaea* [2]) which she proclaims, as opposed to the "true" defeat (*vera clade* [2]) which she suffers. The methodology of contrast continues in the ensuing lines, but this time the contrast is between individuals: thus although Mars favors Eugene of Savoy[41] (*Mars favet Eugenio* [3]), still his cousin, Vendôme,[42] celebrates a triumph (*sed tu, Vendôme, triumphas* [3]). And the pretence continues in the Basque's superficial concealment of wounds, in the

---

arrival of our force. Four millions of plate were destroyed, with ten millions of merchandise; about two millions in silver, and five in goods were brought away."

[39] *i nunc et ritu Salico muliebria temne/imperia, Angliacae fulmina passa deae* (9-10).

[40] The English viewed their victory not only as a great success and demonstration of power, but also as a consequence of divine favor. In 1703 there was minted at London a coin of Queen Anne with VIGO under the bust. On the obverse of the coin was inscribed *Anna Dei Gratia*. From the silver captured at Vigo a medal was minted to commemorate the victory, and bore the inscription: *CAPTA ET INCENSA GAL. ET HISP. CLASSE. AD VIGVM XII OCT MDCCII.* (The dating 12 October = 22 old style).

[41] Eugene of Savoy (1663-1736) was the chief Austrian commander in the War of the Spanish Succession.

[42] Louis Joseph, duc de Vendôme (1654-1712). In the War of the Spanish Succession he was appointed commander in Italy. He would decisively defeat his cousin Eugene of Savoy at Cassano in 1705.

parallel encomium of the very gods who have caused harm (5-6),[43] and
in the way in which the imperial court deceives the populace by means of
a joyous funeral pyre. It is in the combined notions of deception and the
funeral pyre that a Virgilian intertext is signaled. In *Aeneid* 4 Dido,
announcing that she has discovered a magical means whereby she can
wipe out everything that reminds her of Aeneas, requests that Anna build
a pyre (*Aen.* 4.478-498),[44] which her sister does, thereby unwittingly
assisting in Dido's suicide (*Aen.* 4. 500-503).[45] That pyre will become a
funeral pyre, a deception realized by Anna all too late:

> hoc illud, germana, fuit? me fraude petebas?
> hoc rogus iste mihi, hoc ignes araeque parabant?
> > *(Aen.* 4. 675-676)

In Addison, the imperial court (*aula* [8]) is implicitly identified
with the deceptive Dido, but the pyre is one that inspires joy (*laetifico ...
rogo* [8]), and the victim of this deception is not a sister but an entire
nation (*populos decipit* [8]).

In the following lines the theme of fire is further developed with a
reference to the firing of the enemy ships. On this occasion, however, the
focus is more on the remnants of fire. Now as though in a further *variatio*
upon Epigram 1, the wealth of the Indies does *not* flow to Britain, but
goes flying into ashes (*sed modo deletur flammis quae terruit
orbem/classis, et in cineres Indica gaza volat* [9-10]).[46] The whole
concludes in an ironic exhortation to France, which adopts the theme of
fire to a different level: since she boasts and turns losses into joys, then

---

[43] *vulnera Vasco tegit, palmasque ostentat inanes,/et laudat iustos, cum nocuere, deos*
[5-6])

[44] Cf. especially *Aen.* 4. 478-479 '*inveni, germana, viam (gratare sorori)/quae mihi
reddat eum vel eo me solvat amantem*'; 4. 494-498: '*tu secreta pyram tecto interiore
sub auras/erige, et arma viri thalamo quae fixa reliquit/impius exuviasque omnis
lectumque iugalem,/quo perii, super imponas: abolere nefandi/cuncta viri monimenta
iuvat monstratque sacerdos.*'

[45] *non tamen Anna novis praetexere funera sacris/germanam credit, nec tantos mente
furores/concipit aut graviora timet quam morte Sychaei./ergo iussa parat.* (*Aen.* 4.
500-503).

[46] *classis, et in cineres Indica gaza volat* (10) merits comparison with *Epigram* 1.8:
classis et ad Britonas India tota fluit. The shared opening *classis et*, followed by an
allusion to the wealth of the Indies (*India tota/Indica gaza*) and the personification of
such in a verb denoting swift movement (*fluit*; *volat*), surely suggest that both were
composed by the same person, and thus perhaps provides additional internal evidence
that Addison is indeed author of all five Latin epigrams on the subject.

let her add these torches to her festive fires: *Gallia iactatrix, quae damna in gaudia vertis,/has quoque festivis ignibus adde faces* [11-12]). The concept of fire underlying the first epigram (*combustis ... carinis* [5]; *fumat ... classis* [7-8]) is hereby developed threefold into: the fire of a funeral pyre, the consequential ashes, and the ironic allusion to celebratory torches.

In Epigram 3 fire once again provides the underlying theme, now cleverly linked to the fact that Louis XIV was known as the Sun-King. The lines are prefixed by the heading: "Le soleil est la dévise du Roy et Phaeton voulait s'égaler au soleil." The opening lines depict the sea-god Neptune beholding the defeat in the Spanish sea, and remarking that Jupiter has taken up arms against the French also, a development perhaps of the equation of Queen Anne with the thunder-brandishing Jupiter in Epigram 1. Similarly the firing of French ships, described in that epigram in the succinct *combustis ... carinis* (5), is developed through balanced repetition of *combusserat* (3) and *combusta* (4) as the fire suffered by France is now seen as her punishment for inflicting a similar fate upon innocent citadels (3-4).[47] And as if to encapsulate the entire theme, the concluding lines, mirroring the poem's French heading, equate King Louis XIV with Phaeton, who, thinking that he was equal to the sun (5),[48] suffered the fate of burning in the middle of the sea (5-6).[49] Addison's summary of Phaeton's fate is essentially selective, a fate described by Ovid in *Metamorphoses* 2. As a consequence of his daring attempt to ride his father's chariot towards the sun, he was burnt and, with his hair on fire (*flamma populante capillo* [*Met.* 2.319]), fell headlong, like a shooting star, into the river Eridanus (*quem procul a patria diverso maximus orbe/excipit Eridanus fumantiaque abluit ora.* [*Met.* 2. 323-324]).[50] And Addison's knowledge of the Phaeton story is indicated by the fact that only two years later (1704) his own English verse-translation of that particular episode from Ovid's poem would appear in *Poetical*

[47] *illa tot innocuas quae iam combusserat arces/combusta ultori classis ab igne perit* (3-4).

[48] *se soli ratus esse parem* (5).

[49] *cum perderet orbem,/in mediis Phaeton taliter arsit aquis* (5-6).

[50] For the appropriation of the Phaeton myth as an allegory of overwielding military ambition against Queen Anne, cf. George Stepney, "The Austrian Eagle" in *The Works of the Most Celebrated Minor Poets* (London, 1749), II, 20: "At Anna's call the Austrian eagle flies,/Bearing her thunder to the southern skies;/Where a rash prince with an unequal sway,/Inflames the region and misguides the day;/'Til the usurper from his chariot hurl'd/Leaves the true monarch to command the world."

Miscellanies.[51] He translates Ovid's description of Phaeton's final end as follows:

> The breathless Phaeton, with flaming hair,
> Shot from the chariot, like a falling star,
> That in a summer's evening from the top
> Of heaven drops down, or seems at least to drop;
> 'Till on the Po his blasted corps was hurl'd,
> Far from his country, in the western world.[52]

In the Latin epigram Louis' fate as Phaeton is mirrored in that of the French fleets burning in the middle of the sea.

Epigram 4 turns the theme of fire upon its head by applying it to the winning rather than the losing side. Thus Queen Anne is equated with the phoenix famed for its resurrection from the ashes, a development of the ash motif of Epigram 2. Just as fire indicates eternal life for the phoenix, so does the ash afford perpetual glory to Anne.[53]

It is in Epigram 5, however, that the themes of fire, ash, and the role of Anne herself coalesce in a highly skillful epilogue to the series. This four-line poem takes the variations on the theme back full circle to that Virgilian quotation prefixed to the whole, and to several aspects of the Dido story already reworked in the preceding epigrams. And it does so by picking up the felicitous coincidence between the name of Dido's sister and that of England's Queen. Anna, that unwitting builder of Queen Dido's funeral pyre, is contrasted with another Anne, the Queen of England, who is preparing funeral pyres of an altogether different sort: *iam soror Anna pyram moriturae construxit Elisae;/nunc regina novos praeparat Anna rogos* (1-2).[54] The language is highly Virgilian, as

---

[51] "The Story of Phaeton, Beginning the Second Book of Ovid's *Metamorphoses*, translated by Mr Joseph Addison," *Poetical Miscellanies: The Fifth Part* (London, 1704). Cf. Guthkelch, ed. *Miscellaneous Works*, I, 63-77.

[52] Guthkelch, ed. *Miscellaneous Works*, I, 77. Cf. Addison's "Notes" accompanying his translation of the episode: "The story of Phaeton is told with a greater air of majesty and grandeur than any other in all Ovid. It is indeed the most important subject he treats of, except the deluge." (Guthkelch, ed. *Miscellaneous Works*, I, 133).

[53] *phoenici aeternam praebent incendia vitam,/hic tibi perpetuum dat cinis, Anna, decus.* It is noteworthy that one of the English ships at Vigo was named the "Phoenix." See *An Impartial Account*, 29.

[54] Compare the reference to the construction of the *pyra* (1) with *Aen.* 4.494-495: *tu secreta pyram tecto interiore sub auras/erige*; *Aen.* 4.504-505: *at regina pyra penetrali in sede sub auras/erecta.*

denoted, for example, by the phrase *soror Anna*[55] or (of Dido) the future participle *moritura*.[56] But the verses also engage intertextually with Epigram 2. Where the French court constructed deceptive funeral pyres for its own people, Anne has done the same, but significantly the victim of her "new pyres" (*novos praeparat Anna rogos* [2]) is the enemy (including the French). Moreover, the use of the Punic term Elissa for Dido (*moriturae ... Elisae* [1]),[57] while finding a parallel in Virgil,[58] would also seem to look back to the use of *Elisa* (for Queen Elizabeth) in Addison's first Latin epigram, now perhaps surpassed by Queen Anne herself. And those celebratory torches of Epigram 2.12 have become the deadly torches (*ferales ... faces* [4]) applied to the enemy fleet by an Anne who both embodies and transcends the roles of a Carthaginian queen, her sister, and perhaps even Queen Elizabeth (*Elisa*) herself.

The world of Virgil's Carthage and the tragedy of its queen, a tragedy assisted by Anna, have indeed "by application to the affairs of Vigo" been reborn in a series of poetic recreations of an eighteenth-century naval battle.

And perhaps indeed it is precisely in terms of such appropriation of Virgil that Addison engendered the rebirth of the greatest poet of Augustan Rome.

> Oh could the Muse my ravish'd breast inspire
> With warmth like yours, and raise an equal fire,
> Unnumber'd beauties in my verse should shine,
> And Virgil's Italy should yield to mine![59]

---

[55] Cf. *Anna soror* (*Aen.* 4.9); *Annam ... huc siste sororem* (*Aen.* 4.634).

[56] Cf. *nec moritura tenet crudeli funere Dido?* (*Aen.* 4.308); *ne quid inexpertum frustra moritura relinquat* (*Aen.* 4.415); *testatur moritura deos* (*Aen.* 4. 519); *quem metui moritura?* (*Aen.* 4. 604).

[57] On Dido as Elissa, cf. Servius (on *Aen.* 1.340), *Commentary*, ed. Thilo, I, 120: *Dido vero nomine Elissa ante dicta est, sed post interitum a Poenis Dido appellata, id est virago Punica lingua, quod cum a suis sociis cogeretur cuicumque de Afris regibus nubere et prioris mariti caritate teneretur, forti se animo et interfecerit et in pyram iecerit, quam se ad expiandos prioris mariti manes exstruxisse fingebat."* Cf. Servius (on *Aen.* 4.335), *Commentary*, ed. Thilo, I, 523: *'Elissae' autem Didonis, quae appellata est lingua Punica virago, cum se in pyram sponte misisset, fingens placare manes prioris mariti, cum nubere se velle Iarbae mentiretur.*

[58] Cf. *nec me meminisse pigebit Elissae* (*Aen.* 4. 335); *di morientis Elissae* (*Aen.* 4. 610); *moenia ... quae iam infelicis Elissae/conlucent flammis* (*Aen.* 5. 3-4).

[59] Addison, "A Letter From Italy," 51-54 (Guthkelch, ed. *Miscellaneous Works*, I, 53-55).

It is a rebirth moreover that is mirrored in the themes of artistic recreation and renewal (of both the animate and the inanimate) that can be seen to characterize Addison's own Latin poetry. Thus did the resurrection of Virgil signal the birth of another author, a neo-Latin poet, who could thereby emerge phoenix-like as a *Vergilius Redivivus* in late seventeenth-century England.

Plate 1

Joshua Barnes, *Gerania: A New Discovery of A Little Sort of People ... Called Pygmies* (London, 1675): Frontispiece
By Permission of the British Library (Shelfmark 1080h.35)

Plate 2

GERANIA:

A NEW

DISCOVERY

OF A

Little sort of PEOPLE

Anciently Discoursed of, called

PYGMIES.

With a lively Description

Of their Stature, Habit,

Manners, Buildings, Know-

ledge, and Government, being

very delightful and profitable.

By *JOSHUA BARNES,*

of *Emanuel College, Cambridge.*

Ingentes animos angusto in Corpore versant. Virg.

"Ἴδμεν ψεύδεα πολλὰ λέγειν ἐτύμοισιν

ὁμοῖα. Hesiod.

LONDON,

Printed by *W. G.* for *Obadiah Blagrave,*

at the Sign of the *Printing-press,* over

against the *Pump* in *Little-Britain,* 1675.

Joshua Barnes, *Gerania: A New Discovery of A Little Sort of People ... Called Pygmies* (London, 1675): Title-Page
By Permission of the British Library (Shelfmark 1080h.35)

Plate 3

Isaac Fuller's Mural on the Last Judgment, Magdalen College Chapel, Oxford
(Engraving by Michael Burghers)
By Permission of the President and Fellows, Magdalen College, Oxford

142

Plate 4

Isaac Fuller's Mural on the Last Judgment, Magdalen College Chapel, Oxford
(Drawing by G.C. Cooper [c. 1817])
By Permission of the President and Fellows, Magdalen College, Oxford.

Plate 5

Latin Verses on the Vigo Expedition
BL Add. 37349, folio 57 (Whitworth Papers)
By Permission of the British Library

144

Plate 6

Latin Verses on the Vigo Expedition
BL Add. 37349, folio 58 (Whitworth Papers)
By Permission of the British Library

APPENDIX 1

Addison's Latin Poems[1]

---

[1] Text of the *Tityrus et Mopsus* is that of the *Vota Oxoniensia Pro Serenissimis Guilhelmo Rege et Maria Regina M. Britanniae &c Nuncupata* (Oxford, 1689). Texts of the *Barometri Descriptio*, *Proelium Inter Pygmaeos et Grues Commissum*, *Machinae Gesticulantes*, *Sphaeristerium*, and *Resurrectio Delineata* are those printed in *Musarum Anglicanarum Analecta* (Oxford, 1699), Vol. II. I have modernized spelling and punctuation.

Tityrus et Mopsus

TITYRUS MOPSUS

T. Hic inter corylos, umbrosa cacumina, densas
    nos cantare pares quoniam convenimus ambo,
    dicamus laudes heroum ut, Mopse, solemus;
    tempora transibunt sic laeta canentibus; et nunc
    dic, age, quos nostro celebrari carmine sumes.   5

M. Tityre, nunc reddantur eis pia munera laudum
    otia qui dederint nobis placidamque quietem;
    scilicet illorum resonent encomia silvae
    qui dignabantur regni fulcire ruinas.

T. Tanta haud conveniunt humili tenuique cicutae,   10
    sed quoniam in magnis, dicunt, voluisse sat esse,
    ipse tuas, Gulielme, canam laudesque Mariae,
    nam quos iunxit amor nemo seiungere debet. ·

M. Tunc mihi, Phoebe, fave, Musaeque favete canenti
    ne culpa ingenii illorum minuantur honores.   15

T. Ast ego nec Phoebum curo Phoebive sorores,
    carmina namque mihi cedit nunc lemma canenti.

M. Sint licet illustri proavorum stemmate clari,
    sunt magis ornati propriis virtutibus ambo.

T. Si rex est regit immanes qui pectoris aestus,   20
    tum quot regna tenet Gulielmus quotque Maria!

M. Inclitus hic Mavors, sapiens haec altera Pallas;
    vulnerat ille armis, forma sed vulnerat illa.

T. Quando vias pelagi tentarunt, mole superbum
    sustulit ad nubes mare se fastuque tumebat.   25

M. Quando tellurem tetigerunt, Arcades omnes
    Pani deo Arcadiae tenerum mactavimus agnum.

T. Tunc iterum totus resonat modulamine campus,
    miscent pastores iterum nymphaeque choreas.

M. Laetus gramineis lusit tunc agnus in agris,   30
    floribus atque novis haedi insiluere petulci.

T. Quantus erat victor Gulielmus quando popelli
    vicit corda, hostes vicit, vicitque seipsum!

M. Participat sponsi virtutem et regna Maria,
    digna tribus regnis et tanto digna marito.   35

T. Primus hic imperio, nulli est virtute secundus:
    sic sol quam stellae maiori luce refulget.

M. Sed qualis stellas micat inter luna minores,
    talis, cum cincta est sociis, regina videtur.

T. At quae nos illis nunc, Tityre, digna precemur   40
    ludere qui pecori pecorisque dedere magistris?

M. Aeternam inveniant quam donavere quietem!

T. et sero caelos exornet sidus utrumque!

Tityrus and Mopsus

TITYRUS MOPSUS

T.   Since we have come together here amid the dense hazels with their shady summits, both of us, equally matched in singing, let us speak of the praises of heroes, Mopsus, as we are accustomed to do; thus will the time pass by happily for us as we sing; and now, come on: say whom you will undertake to be celebrated in our song.

M.   Tityrus, now let dutiful gifts of praise be rendered unto those who have granted us leisure and quiet repose. That is to say, let the woods resound the encomia of those who deigned to fortify the ruins of a kingdom.

T.   Things so great do not suit the humble, thin reed. But since, so they say, to have had the will suffices in mighty matters, I myself will sing of your praises, William, and those of Mary. For those whom love has joined together, no one ought to separate.

M.   Then, Phoebus, look with favor upon me, and Muses, look with favor upon me as I sing, lest the fault of my talent diminish their honors.

T.   But I care neither for Phoebus nor for Phoebus' sisters, for now the very subject matter yields songs to me as I sing.

M.   Although famous through an illustrious ancestral lineage, both of them are more adorned by virtues of their own.

T.   If a king is one who rules the vast tides of the heart, then how many kingdoms does William, how many does Mary hold!

M.   He is Mars the famous, she is another Pallas in her wisdom; he wounds with weapons, but she wounds with her beauty.

T.   When they made trial of the ocean's ways the haughty sea reared itself up to the clouds and swelled with pride.

M.   When they touched land, all of us Arcadians sacrificed a tender lamb to Pan, god of Arcadia.

T.   Thereupon the whole field resounds once more with music; once more shepherds and nymphs join together in dancing.

M.   Thereupon the happy lamb sported in the grassy fields and the wanton kids trampled upon the fresh flowers.

T.   How great a conqueror was William when he overcame the hearts of his people, overcame the enemy, overcame his very self!

M.   Mary has a share in the virtue and kingdoms of her spouse, she who is worthy of three kingdoms, and worthy of a husband so great.

T.   He is first in dominion; he is second to none in virtue: thus does the sun shine with a light greater than that of a star.

M.   But just as the moon gleams amid lesser stars, so does the Queen seem when she is surrounded by her companions.

T.   But what prayers may we now utter, Tityrus, that are worthy of those who have granted sport to the flock and to the masters of the flock?

M.   May they have the eternal peace which they themselves have bestowed!

T.   And may each of their stars be tardy in adorning the heavens!

Barometri Descriptio

Qua penetrat fossor terrae caeca antra metallo
fecunda informi rudibusque nitentia venis,
dum stupet occultas gazas nummosque futuros,
eruit argenti latices nitidumque liquorem;
qui nullo effusus prodit vestigia tractu   5
nec terram signo revolubilis imprimit udo,
sed fractus sparsim in globulos formam usque rotundam
servat et in teretes lapsans se colligit orbes.
　　　Incertum qua sit natura: an negligat ultra
perficier iubar et maturus inutile temnat,   10
an potius solis vis imperfecta relinquat
argentum male coctum divitiasque fluentes.
quicquid erit, magno se iactat nobilis usu.
nec deus effulsit magis aspectabilis olim
dum Danaen flavo circum pretiosus amictu   15
ambiit, et gratam suadente libidine formam,
depluit irriguo liquefactum numen in auro.
　　　Quin age, sume tubum fragilem cui densior aer
exclusus; fundo vitri subsidat in imo
argenti stagnum ut pluvia impendente metallum   20
mobile descendat, vel contra ubi postulat aestus,
prodeat hinc liquor emergens et rursus inane
occupet ascensu tubulumque excurrat in omnem.
　　　Iam caeli faciem tempestatesque futuras
conscia lympha monet, brumamque et frigora narrat.   25
nam quoties liquor insurgit vitreoque canali
sublatum nequeunt ripae cohibere priores,
tum laetos sperare dies licet, arva fatentur
aestatem et large diffuso lumine rident.
sin sese immodicum attollens argenteus umor   30
et nimium oppressus contendat ad ardua vitri,
iam sitiunt herbae, iam succos flamma feraces
excoquit, et languent consumpto prata virore.
　　　Cum vero tenues nebulas spiracula terrae
fundunt et madidi fluitant super aequora fumi,   35
pabula venturae pluviae, tum fusile pondus
inferiora petit. nec certior ardea caelos
indicat umentes medias quando aetheris oras
tranando crassa fruitur sublimius aura,
discutit et madidis rorantia nubila pennis.   40
nunc guttae agglomerant, dispersas frigora stipant
particulas, rarusque in nimbum cogitur umor:
prata virent, segetem fecundis imbribus aether
irrigat et bibulae radici alimenta ministrat.
　　　Quin ubi plus aequo descendens unda metalli   45
fundum amat, impatiens pluviae metuensque procellam,

A Description of the Barometer

Where the miner penetrates earth's hidden hollows fertile in formless metal and glittering with virginal veins, while he is astounded at concealed treasures and future coins, he digs up liquid silver and a gleaming fluid. Poured forth, this does not betray its track with any trail nor as it rolls does it imprint the earth with the seal of its wetness, but broken dispersedly into little globules, it completely preserves its circular shape, and as it flows, it gathers itself into smooth circles.

Unable to determine its nature – whether it disregards the possibility of further perfection – prematurely he despises its radiance as useless – or perhaps rather the imperfect strength of the sun leaves the silver poorly ripened, and its riches flowing. Whatever the case, it boasts that it is noble for a mighty purpose. Nor did the god once upon a time shine more visibly when, expensive in his golden raiment, he encircled Danae all about and, his lust urging upon him the pleasantness of her shape, he rained his liquefied divinity in a golden shower.

Come on then: take up a brittle tube, from which denser air has been shut out. Let a pool of silver sink to the very bottom of the glass so that when rain is impending, the mobile metal may descend, or, on the other hand, when heat demands, the liquid may issue forth from this point and, seizing again the vacuum as it ascends, it may rush and extend into the entire tube.

Now the conscious liquid warns of the sky's aspect and of future storms, and it tells of wintry weather and cold. For as often as the fluid rises and the edges cannot hold back, as they did before, its ascent in the glass tube, then one may hope for propitious days; the fields acknowledge the summer, and smile amid the abundantly diffused light. But if the silvery moisture rears itself immoderately, and excessively squeezed, it presses forward towards the heights of the glass, now the grass is parched, now the flame bakes the once fertile juices, and the meadows languish, their verdure consumed.

But when the fissures of the earth pour forth thin mists, and moist vapor flows over the seas, fodder for rain to come, then the liquefied weight seeks the lower regions. With no greater certainty does the heron indicate moist heavens, when swimming across the mid shores of ether, it enjoys the dense breeze on high, and scatters the dewy clouds from its seeping wings. Now drops mass together, cold compresses the scattered particles, and the sparse moisture is compacted into a cloud: the meadows become verdant, and the ether waters the crops with fertile showers, and affords nourishment to the thirsty root.

Moreover when the liquid metal descends more than is fitting, and embraces the bottom, with no tolerance of rain, and

agricolae caveant. non hoc impune colonus
aspicit: ostendet mox feta vaporibus aura
collectas hiemes tempestatemque sonoram.
at licet argentum mole incumbente levatum   50
subsidat penitusque imo se condat in alveo,
cetera quaeque tument: eversis flumina ripis
exspatiata ruunt, spumantibus aestuat undis
diluvium, rapidique effusa licentia ponti.
    Nulla tacet secreta poli mirabile vitrum   55
quin varios caeli vultus et tempora prodit:
ante refert quando tenui velamine tutus
incedes, quando sperabis frigidus ignem.
    Augurio hoc fretus, quamquam atri nubila caeli
dirumpunt obscura diem pluviasque minantur,   60
machina si neget et sudum promittat apertum,
audax carpat iter nimbo pendente viator.
nec metuens imbrem poscentes messor aristas
prosternat. terrae iam bruma incumbit inermis,
frigoraque haud nocitura cadunt feriuntque paratos.   65

Pugmaio-Geranomachia
Sive
Proelium Inter Pygmaeos et Grues Commissum

Pennatas acies et lamentabile bellum
Pygmeadum refero. parvas tu, Musa, cohortes
instrue: tu gladios mortemque minantia rostra
offensosque grues indignantesque pusillam
militiam celebra, volucrumque hominumque tumultus.   5
    Heroum ingentes animos et tristia bella
Pieridum labor exhausit versuque sonoro
iussit et aeterna numerorum assurgere pompa.
quis lectos Graium iuvenes et torva tuentem
Thesea; quis pedibus velocem ignorat Achillem?   10
quem dura Aeneae certamina, quem Gulielmi
gesta latent? fratres Thebani et flebile fatum
Pompeii quem non delassavere legentem?
primus ego intactas acies gracilemque tubarum
carmine depingam sonitum, nova castra secutus,   15
exiguosque canam pugiles gruibusque malignos
heroas, nigrisque ruentem e nubibus hostem.
    Qua solis tepet ortu primitiisque diei
India laeta rubet, medium inter inhospita saxa
(per placidam vallem et paucis accessa vireta)   20
Pygmaeum quondam steterat, dum fata sinebant,

fearing a storm, then let farmers beware: it is not with impunity that the husbandman beholds this; soon the breeze abounding in vapors will reveal its gathered storms and resounding tempest. But even if the silver, relieved of its pressing mass, should subside and utterly bury itself in the channel-bottom, everything else swells up; rivers rush beyond their bounds, their banks overthrown, the flood seethes with foaming waves, and the waywardness of the rapid deep is poured forth.

The amazing glass keeps silent about none of heaven's secrets; on the contrary, it reveals the various aspects and climates of the sky: it relates in advance when you may safely go forth in a thin garment; when, feeling the cold, you will hope for the fire.

Relying on this augury, even though the clouds of a black sky burst asunder and in their darkness threaten a rainy day, if the device denies this and promises clear weather, then let the traveler daringly pluck his way although a cloud is impending; let the reaper with no fear of a shower lay low crops in need of reaping; now winter looms unarmed upon the earth, while the chills that fall will not cause harm, striking, as they do, those who are prepared.

Pugmaio-Geranomachia
or
The Battle Engaged Between Pygmies and Cranes

I tell of winged battle lines and of the deplorable war of the Pygmies. You, o Muse, draw up small cohorts: you celebrate swords and beaks threatening death, and cranes resentful and indignant at a puny warfare: the uprisings of both birds and men.

The Muses' effort has exhausted the huge spirits and grim wars of heroes, and has commanded them to rise in high-sounding verse and in an eternal procession of meter. Who does not know of the choice youths of the Greeks, and the fiercely glaring Theseus? Who does not know of fleet-footed Achilles? From whom do the harsh battles of Aeneas, from whom do the exploits of William lie hidden? Who as he reads has not been tired out by the Theban brothers and Pompey's lamentable death? I shall be the first to represent in song untouched battle lines and the graceful sound of trumpets, following a new campaign; and I shall sing of tiny competitors, and of heroes ill-disposed towards cranes, and of an enemy charging out of black clouds.

Where fertile India becomes warm at the rising of the sun and glows red at the beginning of the day, in the midst of inhospitable rocks there once stood the Pygmy empire, while the fates permitted (along a tranquil valley and greenswards accessible to few).

imperium. hic varias vitam excoluere per artes
seduli et assiduo fervebant arva popello.
nunc si quis dura evadat per saxa viator,
desertosque lares et valles ossibus albas   25
exiguis videt et vestigia parva stupescit.
desolata tenet victrix impune volucris
regna, et securo crepitat grus improba nido.
non sic dum multos stetit insuperabilis annos
parvula progenies. tum si quis comminus ales   30
congredi et immixtae auderet se credere pugnae,
miles atrox aderat sumptisque feroculus armis
sternit humi volucrem moribundam umerisque reportat
ingentem praedam caesoque epulatur in hoste.
saepe improvisas mactabat, saepe iuvabat   35
diripere aut nidum aut ulcisci in prole parentem.
nempe larem quoties multa construxerat arte
aut uteri posuisset onus volucremque futuram,
continuo vultu spirans immane minaci
omnia vastaret miles fetusque necaret   40
immeritos vitamque abrumperet imperfectam,
cum tepido nondum maturuit hostis in ovo.
        Hinc causae irarum, bella hinc, fatalia bella,
atque acies leto intentae, volucrumque virumque
commissae strages confusaque mortis imago.   45
        Non tantos motus nec tam memorabile bellum
Maeonius quondam sublimi carmine vates
lusit ubi totam strepituque armisque paludem
miscuit: hic (visu miserabile!) corpora murum
sparsa iacent iuncis transfixa, hic gutture rauco   50
rana dolet pedibusque abscisso poplite ternis
reptat humi, solitis nec sese saltibus effert.
        Iamque dies Pygmaeo aderat quo tempore caesi
paenituit fetus intactaque maluit ova.
nam super his accensa graves exarsit in iras   55
grus stomachans, omnesque simul, quas Strymonis unda
aut stagnum Mareotidis imi aut uda Caystri
prata tenent, adsunt; Scythicaque excita palude
et coniurato volucris descendit ab Istro
stragesque immensas et vulnera cogitat absens,   60
exacuitque ungues ictum meditata futurum,
et rostrum parat acre fugaeque accommodat alas.
tantus amor belli et vindictae arrecta cupido.
ergo ubi ver nactus proprium, suspensus in alto
aere concussis exercitus obstrepit alis   65
terraeque immensos tractus semotaque longe
aequora despiciunt, Boreamque et nubila tranant
innumeri; crebro circum ingens fluctuat aether
flamine et assiduus miscet caelum omne tumultus.

Here they painstakingly enhanced their lives by means of various skills, and the fields were a ferment of activity with a busy little people. Now if any traveler escapes along the harsh rocks, he sees deserted dwellings, and valleys white with tiny bones, and is astounded at the small tracks. A victorious bird occupies with impunity the desolate kingdom, and the wicked crane cackles in the safety of its nest. It was not so when the tiny race stood invincible for many years. At that time if any bird dared to engage in close combat and to entrust himself to the confusion of battle, a fierce soldier was at hand and, taking up arms, ferociously he lays the bird low upon the ground to die, and carries back his huge booty upon his shoulders, and feasts upon his slaughtered foe. Frequently he slew them, caught off their guard; frequently he took delight in either tearing down their nest or in taking revenge against a parent by slaying its offspring. To be sure, as often as it had built its home with great skill or had deposited the weight of its womb, a future bird, immediately the soldier, emanating cruelty with his threatening expression, would lay waste to everything and would kill the innocent brood, and cut short their uncompleted lives when the enemy has not yet matured in its warm egg.

Hence the causes of anger, hence wars, deadly wars, and battle lines intent on death, the conjoined slaughter of birds and of men, and the disorderly image of death.

Not so great were the revolts nor so memorable the war of which the Maeonian bard once sported in sublime song when he confounded an entire marsh with din and warfare: here (miserable to behold!) there lie scattered the corpses of mice pierced by reeds; here a frog cries out in pain from its croaking throat, and with a knee cut off, creeps on the ground upon three feet, and does not rear itself up with its customary hopping.

And now the day was at hand for the Pygmy when he regretted slaughtering the brood, and preferred that the eggs had remained untouched. For incensed on their account, the crane boiled with rage, and flared up with grave wrath; and all those contained by Strymon's water or the Mareotic marsh or the moist meadowlands of the Cayster's depths are at hand together, and from its ally, the Danube, the bird descends, roused from its Scythian marsh. Though absent, it contemplates huge slaughter and wounds, and sharpens its talons, planning a future strike, gets its sharp beak ready, and adapts its wings to flight. So great is the passion for war and their aroused desire for vengeance. And so when it has obtained its own springtime, the army, hanging in the heights of the air, makes a din by shaking its wings, and they look down upon the vast tracts of the earth and the far-distant seas; in their countless numbers they swim across the North and the clouds. All about the vast ether surges with frequent blasts, and a constant tumult throws the entire heavens into confusion.

Nec minor in terris motus dum bella facessit   70
impiger instituitque agmen firmatque phalanges
et furit arreptis animosus homuncio telis,
donec turma duas composta excurrat in alas
ordinibusque frequens et marte instructa perito.
Iamque acies inter medias sese arduus infert   75
Pygmeadum ductor, qui maiestate verendus
incessuque gravis reliquos supereminet omnes
mole gigantea mediamque assurgit in ulnam.
torvior aspectu (hostilis nam insculpserat unguis
ore cicatrices) vultuque ostentat honesta   80
rostrorum signa et crudos in pectore morsus.
immortali odio aeternisque exercuit iris
alituum gentem. non illum impune volucris
aut ore aut pedibus peteret confisus aduncis.
fatalem quoties gruibus destrinxerat ensem   85
truncavitque alas celerique fugam abstulit hosti!
quot fecit strages! quae nudis funera pullis
intulit, heu! quoties implevit Strymona fletu!

Iamque procul sonus auditur, piceamque volantum
prospectant nubem bellumque hostesque ferentem.   90
crebrescit tandem atque oculis se plurimus offert
ordinibus structus variis exercitus ingens
alituum, motisque eventilat aera pennis.
turba polum replet specieque immanis obumbrat
agmina Pygmaeorum et densa in nubibus haeret;   95
nunc densa at patriis mox reddita rarior oris.
belli ardent studio Pygmaei et lumine saevo
suspiciunt hostem, nec longum tempus et ingens
turba gruum horrifico sese super agmina lapsu
praecipitat gravis et bellum sperantibus infert.   100
fit fragor: avulsae volitant circum aera plumae.
mox defessa iterum levibus sese eripit alis
et vires reparata iterum petit impete terras.
armorum pendet fortuna: hic fixa volucris
cuspide sanguineo sese furibunda rotatu   105
torquet agens circum rostrumque intendit in hostem
imbelle et curvos in morte recolligit ungues.
Pygmaei hic stillat lentus de vulnere sanguis
singultusque ciet crebros pedibusque pusillis
tundit humum, et moriens unguem exsecratur acutum.   110

Aestuat omne solum strepitu tepidoque rubescit
sanguine, sparguntur gladii, sparguntur et alae
unguesque et digiti, commixtaque rostra lacertis.

Pygmeadum saevit mediisque in millibus ardet
ductor quem late hinc atque hinc pereuntia cingunt   115
corpora fusa gruum; mediaque in morte vagatur
nec plausu alarum nec rostri concidit ictu.

No less is the commotion on earth while the energetic dwarf wages war, draws up his column, and strengthens his infantry-lines, and full of spirit, seizes his weapons, and rages until the organized squadron extends into two flanks and, packed in its ranks, is drawn up with military skill.

And now, towering in between the battle lines, there charges the Pygmy leader, who fearful in his majesty and authoritative in his gait, stands out above all the rest in his gigantic bulk, and rises up to the height of half a cubit. More savage in appearance (for the enemy's talon had carved scars upon his face), he displays honorable beak-marks upon his countenance, and raw bite marks upon his chest. He has harassed the race of winged creatures with eternal hatred and unceasing anger. No bird trusting either in his beak or in his curved feet, would attack him with impunity. How often had he drawn his death-dealing sword upon the cranes, lopped the wings and removed the means of flight from his swift enemy! How much slaughter has he caused! What deaths has he inflicted, alas, upon the unarmed chicks! How often has he filled the Strymon with lamentation!

And now a sound is heard in the distance, and they see in front of them a pitch-black cloud of flying creatures, bearing both war and the enemy. At last it spreads out and in great numbers a huge army of winged creatures, comprised of various ranks, presents itself before their eyes and fans the air with the movement of their wings. The throng fills the sky, and vast in its appearance, it overshadows the Pygmy army, and lingers dense among the clouds; dense now but soon to be returned more sparse to its native shores. The Pygmies are ablaze with enthusiasm for war and with fierce glance they look up at the enemy; and in a short time the huge throng of cranes with an horrific swoop hurls itself down heavily upon their army and inflicts war upon those who hope for it. There is a din: feathers torn off float about in the air. Soon, though exhausted, a bird rears itself up again upon its light wings, and having renewed its strength, again it makes for the earth in an assault. The fortune of arms hangs poised: here a bird, transfixed by a spear, turns itself around in frenzy in a bloody twisting, and aims its unwarlike beak at the enemy, and contracts its curved talons in death; here blood drips slowly from a Pygmy's wound as he summons up frequent sobs and stamps the ground with his puny feet, and, as he dies, he curses the sharp talon.

The whole ground seethes with din, and grows red with warm blood; swords are scattered, scattered are wings, talons and fingers, and beaks confounded with arms.

The Pygmy leader rages, and is ablaze in the midst of thousands, around whom on a broad front are gathered the dying and strewn bodies of cranes; he wanders in the midst of death, and does not fall either by the strike of wings or by the blow of a beak.

Ille gruum terror, illum densissima circum
miscetur pugna et bellum omne laborat in uno,
cum subito appulsus (sic di voluere) tumultu   120
ex inopino ingens et formidabilis ales
comprendit pedibus pugnantem et (triste relatu)
sustulit in caelum; bellator ab unguibus haeret
pendulus, agglomerat strepitu globus undique densus
alituum; frustra Pygmaei lumine maesto   125
regem inter nubes lugent, solitoque minorem
heroem aspiciunt gruibus plaudentibus escam.
    Iamque recrudescit bellum; grus desuper urget
Pygmaeum rostro atque hostem petit ardua morsu;
tum fugit alta volans. is sursum bracchia iactat   130
vulneris impatiens et inanes saevit in auras.
talis erat belli facies cum Pelion ingens
mitteret in caelum Briareus solioque tonantem
praecipitem excuteret: sparguntur in aethere toto
fulminaque scopulique; flagrantia tela deorsum   135
torquentur Iovis acta manu, dum vasta Gigantum
corpora fusa iacent semiustaque sulphure fumant.
    Viribus absumptis penitus Pygmeïa tandem
agmina languescunt; ergo pars vertere terga
horribili perculsa metu, pars tollere vocem   140
exiguam; late populus cubitalis oberrat.
instant a tergo volucres lacerantque trahuntque
immites, certae gentem exstirpare nefandam.
    Sic Pygmaea domus multos dominata per annos
tot bellis defuncta, gruum tot laeta triumphis,   145
funditus interiit: nempe exitus omnia tandem
certus regna manet; sunt certi denique fines
quos ultra transire nefas; sic corruit olim
Assyriae imperium, sic magnae Persidis imis
sedibus eversum est et maius utroque Latinum.   150
    Elysii valles nunc agmine lustrat inani
et veterum heroum miscetur grandibus umbris
plebs parva, aut si quid fidei mereatur anilis
fabula, pastores per noctis opaca pusillas
saepe vident umbras, Pygmaeos corpore cassos,   155
dum secura gruum et veteres oblita labores
laetitiae penitus vacat indulgetque choreis,
angustosque terit calles viridesque per orbes
turba levis salit et lemurum cognomine gaudet.

He is the cranes' terror; about him is fought a most dense battle, and in him alone the whole war exerts itself; when summoned by a sudden uproar (thus the gods willed), unexpectedly a huge and terrifying bird seizes him with his feet while he is fighting and (sad to relate) lifted him up into the heavens; the warrior hangs dangling from its talons and on every side a dense flock of birds swarms together in clamor; in vain the Pygmies with grief-stricken expression mourn their king amongst the clouds, and behold their hero smaller than usual, as the cranes applaud their food.

And now war breaks out again: from above a crane presses upon a Pygmy with his beak, and poised on high, attacks the enemy with his biting; then flying on high, he escapes. He tosses his arms upwards, unable to endure the wound, and he rages into thin air. Such was the aspect of war when Briareus the huge would have hurled Pelion into the sky and shaken the thunderer headlong from his throne. Lightning and rocks are scattered over the whole ether, and blazing weapons, driven by the hand of Jove, are hurled downwards, while the huge bodies of giants lie strewn, and half-burnt they reek of sulphur.

Utterly bereft of their strength, at last the Pygmy troops languish; and so some turn their backs, stricken by terrible fear; others raise their tiny voices; the cubit race wanders about far and wide. The birds press upon them from behind; cruelly they tear them apart, and drag them, resolved to extirpate the heinous race.

Thus the Pygmy dynasty which had held dominion for many years, having carried out so many wars, having rejoiced in so many triumphs over the cranes, utterly died off: indeed an assured end eventually awaits all kingdoms; in short there are set limits beyond which it is wrong to cross; thus did the Assyrian empire once collapse; thus was the empire of mighty Persia uprooted from the depths of its foundations, and the kingdom of Latium, greater than both.

Now the tiny people in its insubstantial troop surveys the Elysian valleys, and intermingles with the mighty shades of ancient heroes. Or if old wives' tales merit any credence, shepherds often see in the darkness of night tiny shades, Pygmies without bodies, as with no fear of cranes and with no memory of the struggles of old, this people is utterly free for jollity, and indulges in dancing, and treads narrow paths, while along green circles the insubstantial throng dances and rejoices in the name of fairies.

Machinae Gesticulantes
Anglice: A Puppet Show

Admiranda cano levium spectacula rerum,
exiguam gentem et vacuum sine mente popellum,
quem non surreptis caeli de fornice flammis
innocua melior fabricaverat arte Prometheus.
    Compita qua risu fervent, glomeratque tumultum   5
histrio delectatque inhiantem scommate turbam,
quotquot laetitiae studio aut novitate tenentur
undique congressi permissa sedilia complent.
nec confusus honos: nummo subsellia cedunt
diverso et varii ad pretium stat copia scamni.   10
tandem ubi subtrahitur velamen lumina passim
angustos penetrant aditus qua plurima visum
fila secant, ne cum vacuo datur ore fenestra,
pervia fraus pateat. mox stridula turba penates
ingreditur pictos et moenia squalida fuco.   15
hic humiles inter scaenas angustaque claustra
quicquid agunt homines, concursus, bella, triumphos,
ludit in exiguo plebecula parva theatro.
    Sed praeter reliquos incedit homuncio rauca
voce strepens; maior subnectit fibula vestem   20
et referunt vivos errantia lumina motus;
in ventrem tumet immodicum; pone eminet ingens
a tergo gibbus; Pygmaeum territat agmen
maior et immanem miratur turba gigantem.
hic magna fretus mole imparibusque lacertis   25
confisus gracili iactat convicia vulgo
et crebro solvit, lepidum caput, ora cachinno.
quamquam res agitur sollemni seria pompa,
spernit sollicitum intractabilis ille tumultum
et risu importunus adest atque omnia turbat;   30
nec raro invadit molles, pictamque protervo
ore petit nympham invitoque dat oscula ligno.
    Sed comitum vulgus diversis membra fatigat
ludis et vario lascivit mobile saltu.
    Saepe etiam gemmis rutila et spectabilis auro   35
lignea gens prodit nitidisque superbit in ostris.
nam quoties festam celebrat sub imagine lucem,
ordine composito nympharum incedit honestum
agmen et exigui proceres parvique Quirites.
Pygmaeos credas positis mitescere bellis,   40

Miming Contraptions
In English: A Puppet Show

I sing of the wonderful spectacles of slight matters, a small race and an empty, mindless little people, whom a superior Prometheus had fashioned not from flames stolen from heaven's furnace, but by a harmless skill.

Where the crossroads are aglow with laughter, and the actor gathers together a tumultuous crowd, delighting the gaping throng with his buffoonery, as many as are possessed by their enthusiasm for jollity or novelty come together from all sides, and fill the seats which are provided. Nor is there lack of differentiation in regard to precedence: benches yield to a variety of prices, and a supply of different forms of seating is available at a price. At last when the curtain is raised, their eyes ranging in every direction penetrate the narrow openings where numerous threads bisect their vision, lest if the accessible gap is presented with its empty façade, the deception may be apparent and unimpeded. Soon the shrill-sounding throng enters the decorated dwelling with its walls rough with paint. Here amid humble scenery and the confines of a narrow space this little race mimes in its tiny theatre whatever men do – their assemblies, wars, triumphs.

But surpassing the rest there advances a little man shouting in a hoarse voice; a larger brooch fastens his garment, and his eyes as they roll resemble the movements of live ones. His belly is immoderately swollen; behind, a vast protuberance sticks out from his back; in his larger size he terrifies the Pygmy troop, and that throng marvels at the huge giant. Relying on his mighty mass, and trusting in his arms that outmatch theirs, he hurls abuse at the puny populace and, amusing individual that he is, opens his mouth in frequent laughter. Even though serious business is being conducted with solemn ceremony, that unmanageable creature scorns the restless commotion, marks his untimely presence with laughter, and throws everything into confusion. And not infrequently he attacks gentlewomen, and assails a painted nymph with his wanton lips, and plies kisses upon the wood against its will.

But the crowd of his companions weary their limbs with various forms of entertainment, and nimbly frolic with different types of dancing.

Frequently the wooden race also comes forward gleaming with jewels and outstanding in gold, and taking pride in shining purple. For as often as it celebrates an imaginary feast day, there advances in orderly procession an honorable troop of nymphs, and tiny lords and small citizens. You would believe that the Pygmies had cast aside war and were growing mild, and that now

iamque infensa gruum temnentes proelia, tutos
indulgere iocis tenerisque vacare choreis.
       Tales cum medio labuntur sidera caelo
parvi subsiliunt lemures, populusque pusillus
festivos, rediens sua per vestigia, gyros   45
ducit et angustum crebro pede pulsitat orbem.
mane patent gressus; hinc succos terra feraces
concipit, in multam pubentia gramina surgunt
luxuriem, tenerisque virescit circulus herbis.
       At non tranquillas nulla abdunt nubila luces: 50
saepe gravi surgunt bella, horrida bella, tumultu.
arma cient truculenta cohors placidamque quietem
dirumpunt pugnae; usque adeo insincera voluptas
omnibus et mixtae castigant gaudia curae.
iam gladii tubulique ingesto sulphure feti,   55
protensaeque hastae fulgentiaque arma minaeque
telorum ingentes subeunt; dant claustra fragorem
horrendum, ruptae stridente bitumine chartae
confusos reddunt crepitus et sibila miscent.
sternitur omne solum pereuntibus; undique caesae   60
apparent turmae, civilis crimina belli.
       Sed postquam insanus pugnae deferbuit aestus
exuerintque truces animos, iam Marte fugato,
diversas repetunt artes curasque priores.
nec raro prisci heroes quos pagina sacra   65
suggerit atque olim peperit felicior aetas
hic parva redeunt specie; cano ordine cernas
antiquos prodire, agmen venerabile, patres.
rugis sulcantur vultus prolixaque barbae
canities mento pendet: sic tarda senectus   70
Tithonum minuit cum moles tota cicadam
induit in gracilem sensim collecta figuram.
       Nunc tamen unde genus ducat, quae dextra latentes
suppeditet vires, quem poscat turba moventem,
expediam: truncos opifex et inutile lignum   75
cogit in humanas species et robore natam
progeniem telo efformat, nexuque tenaci
crura ligat pedibus umerisque accommodat armos,
et membris membra aptat et artubus insuit artus.
tunc habiles addit trochleas quibus arte pusillum   80
versat onus molique manu famulatus inerti
sufficit occultos motus vocemque ministrat.
his structa auxiliis iam machina tota peritos
ostendit sulcos duri et vestigia ferri.
hinc salit atque agili se sublevat incita motu   85
vocesque emittit tenues et non sua verba.

spurning the hostile battles of the cranes, they were safely indulging in jesting, and were free for gentle dancing.

Such are the small fairies who, when the constellations sink down from the middle of the heaven, jump about, a tiny people dancing in festive rings, returning along their own footprints, and stamping a narrow circle with their frequent footsteps. In the morning their tracks are evident; from this the earth conceives abundant juices, the growing grass rises in great fruitfulness, and the little circle grows green with tender plants.

But tranquil days are concealed by clouds: often amid grave tumult there arise wars, terrible wars. The aggressive cohort summons arms, and battles disrupt the peaceful quiet; to such a degree is everyone's pleasure corrupted, and the admixture of anxieties neutralizes joy. Now there follow swords and muskets packed with a heap of gunpowder, outstretched spears, gleaming arms, and the huge threat of weaponry; the doors make an horrific crash; crackers bursting asunder with hissing bitumen produce confused rattling with whistling intermingled. The whole ground is strewn with the dying; on all sides there appear slaughtered bands, the crimes of civil war.

But after the mad tide of battle has cooled off, and they have cast aside their ferocity of spirit with Mars now put to flight, they seek once more their various arts and former preoccupations. Not infrequently heroes of old supplied by Holy Writ, and the product of an age more blessed, return here in miniature form; you could see the ancient fathers, a venerable troop, advancing in white procession: their countenances are furrowed with wrinkles, and upon their chins there hangs the luxuriant whiteness of a beard. Thus did tardy old age shrink Tithonus when his entire mass assumed the form of the cicada, gradually concentrated into a slight shape.

But now I shall unfold whence he, whose movement the throng demands, derives his birth; what right hand supplies his hidden strength. A craftsman compresses bits of trees and useless wood into human forms, and with his tool he fashions a race born of wood, and with binding fastenings he ties the legs to the feet and fits the arms to the shoulders, and matches limbs to limbs, and sews joints to joints. Then he adds maneuverable pulleys, by which he artfully turns his tiny work, and manipulating with his hand, he supplies the inert mass with hidden movements, and produces a voice. Constructed by means of this assistance, now the whole contraption reveals skillful carvings and the traces of the tough tool. Hence it leaps about and elevates itself, impelled by an agile movement, and utters slight tones, and words that are not its own.

Sphaeristerium

Hic ubi graminea in latum sese explicat aequor
planities vacuoque ingens patet area campo,
cum solem nondum fumantia prata fatentur
exortum et tumidae pendent in gramine guttae,
improba falx noctis parva incrementa prioris   5
desecat, exiguam radens a caespite messem;
tum motu assiduo saxum versatile terram
deprimit exstantem et surgentes atterit herbas.
lignea percurrunt vernantem turba palaestram
uncta, nitens oleo, formae quibus esse rotundae   10
artificis ferrum dederat facilisque moveri.
ne tamen offendant incauti errore globorum
quaeque suis incisa notis stat sphaera; sed unus
hanc vult quae infuso multum inclinata metallo
vertitur in gyros et iniquo tramite currit;   15
quin alii diversa placet, quam parcius urget
plumbea vis motuque sinit procedere recto.
      Postquam ideo in partes turbam distinxerat aequas
consilium aut sors, quisque suis accingitur armis.
evolat orbiculus, quae cursum meta futurum   20
designat; iactique legens vestigia, primam,
qui certamen init, sphaeram demittit at illa
leniter effusa exiguum quod ducit in orbem
radit iter, donec sensim primo impete fesso
subsistat; subito globus emicat alter et alter.   25
      Mox ubi funduntur late agmina crebra minorem
sparsa per orbiculum stipantque frequentia metam
atque negant faciles aditus, iam cautius exit
et leviter sese insinuat revolubile lignum.
at si forte globum qui misit spectat inertem   30
serpere et impressum subito languescere motum,
pone urget sphaerae vestigia et anxius instat,
obiurgatque moras currentique imminet orbi.
atque ut segnis honos dextrae servetur, iniquam
incusat terram ac surgentem in marmore nodum.   35
      Nec risus tacuere globus cum volvitur actus
infami iactu aut nimium vestigia plumbum
allicit et sphaeram a recto trahit insita virtus.
tum qui proiecit strepitus effundit inanes
et variam in speciem distorto corpore, falsos   40
increpat errores et dat convicia ligno.
sphaera sed irarum temnens ludibria, coeptum
pergit iter nullisque movetur surda querelis.
      Illa tamen laudes summumque meretur honorem
quae non dirumpit cursum absistitque moveri,   45

The Bowling Green

Here where the grassy surface extends into an expansive plain and a huge space lies exposed in an empty field, when the misty meadows do not yet acknowledge that the sun has risen, and the swollen drops hang upon the grass, the relentless sickle reaps the previous night's slight growth, clipping from the turf a small harvest; next the stone, revolving in its constant motion, presses down the protruding earth, and wears down the rising blades of grass. Across the verdant sports ground there races a wooden throng, anointed, gleaming with oil, to whom the craftsman's tool had afforded a round shape and an ability to be moved easily. But in case the careless break the rules through mistaking the balls, each bowl stands inscribed with its own markings. But one competitor wants this one, which being greatly unbalanced by an infusion of metal, spins in a circle and runs in an uneven path; whereas another is pleased by a different sort, whose quantity of lead renders its momentum more moderate, thereby allowing it to proceed in a straight line.

Therefore after choice or chance had divided the throng into equal sides, each man girds himself with his own arms. Out flies a little ball, which, as the marker, indicates the future course. The man who begins the contest, following the tracks of the thrown ball, casts the first bowl, but being discharged with gentle force, this traces a journey which veers towards a small curve until, its initial impetus gradually exhausted, it comes to a standstill; suddenly one bowl after another dashes forth.

Soon when numerous troops have rushed out all about, scattering over a smaller circle, being closely packed, they crowd around the marker, and deny easy access; now a revolving wood sets out on a more cautious path, and makes its way in with little force. But if by chance the man who cast a lifeless bowl watches it winding its way and the momentum thrust upon it suddenly languishing, from behind he urges on the bowl's path and anxiously he hovers over it, cursing its delays, and bending over the bowl as it runs. And so that his sluggish hand's reputation may be saved, he blames the unevenness of the ground and a nodule rising on the bowl's surface.

Nor have they silenced their laughter when a bowl rolls forth, impelled by a shameful pitch, or when the lead lures it too much off its track and its innate strength drags the bowl from its straight line. Then the man who cast it utters useless clamorings, and twisting his body into a variety of shapes, he rebukes its erroneous wanderings and hurls abuse at the wood. But the bowl, spurning the derision of his wrath, proceeds upon the journey it has begun and in its deafness is unmoved by any protests.

However that bowl deserves the chief praises and honor which does not break its course or stop its movement until

donec turbam inter crebram dilapsa supremum
perfecit stadium et metae inclinata recumbit.
hostis at haerentem orbiculo detrudere sphaeram
certat, luminibusque viam signantibus omnes
intendit vires et missile fortiter urget: 50
evolat adducto non segnis sphaera lacerto.
    Haud ita prosiliens Eleo carcere pernix
auriga invehitur cum raptus ab axe citato
currentesque domos videt et fugientia tecta.
    Si tamen in duros, obstructa satellite multo,   55
impingat socios confundatque orbibus orbes,
tum fervet bilis, fortunam damnat acerbam,
atque deos atque astra vocat crudelia.
    Si vero incursus faciles aditumque patentem
inveniat partoque hostis spolietur honore,   60
turba fremit confusa, sonisque frequentibus, 'euge,'
exclamant socii; plausu strepit omne viretum.
    Interea fessos inimico Sirius astro
corripit et salsas exsudant corpora guttas;
lenia iam zephyri spirantes frigora et umbrae   65
captantur, vultuque fluens abstergitur umor.

Resurrectio Delineata ad Altare Coll. Magd. Oxon.

Egregios fuci tractus calamique labores
surgentesque hominum formas ardentiaque ora
iudicis et simulacra modis pallentia miris,
terribilem visu pompam, tu carmine, Musa,
pande novo vatique sacros accende furores.   5
    Olim planitiem (quam nunc fecunda colorum
insignit pictura) inhonesto et simplice cultu
vestiit albedo, sed ne rima ulla priorem
agnoscat faciem, mox fundamenta futurae
substravit pictor tabulae umoremque sequacem   10
per muros traxit. velamine moenia crasso
squalent obducta et rudioribus illita fucis.
    Utque (polo nondum stellis fulgentibus apto)
ne spatio moles immensa dehiscat inani,
per cava caelorum et convexa patentia late   15
hinc atque hinc interfusus fluitaverat aether;
mox radiante novum torrebat lumine mundum
Titan, et pallens alienos mitius ignes
Cynthia vibrabat; crebris nunc consitus astris
scintillare polus, nunc fulgor lacteus omne   20
diffluere in caelum longoque albescere tractu.

slipping in between the packed throng, it has reached the end of its final track, and comes to rest, leaning upon the marker. But an opponent endeavors to dislodge the bowl as it clings to the little ball, and, his eyes marking the path, he applies all his strength and strongly hurls his missile; out flies the energetic bowl as he thrusts forward his arm.

Not so rapidly is the charioteer borne as he rushes forth from the starting point at Elis when, whirled along in his speeding chariot, he sees houses running by and buildings as they fly past.

However, if, being obstructed by its many accomplices, it dashes against its tough companions, and throws bowl upon bowl into confusion, then anger boils up; he damns his bitter fortune, and calls gods and stars cruel.

But if it finds an easy advance and open access, the opponent will be despoiled of the honor he has won. The disordered throng roars out, and with constant noise his companions shout 'Hurrah!' The whole green resounds with applause.

Meanwhile Sirius with his baneful star lays hold of the weary, and their bodies sweat salted drops; now are sought the zephyrs breathing gentle cool, and the shades, and from the brow is wiped the flowing moisture.

The Resurrection Depicted Near the Altar of Magd. College, Oxford

The excellent expanses of paint, and the labors of the pencil, the rising forms of men, the blazing countenance of the Judge and images pallid in wondrous ways, a procession terrible to behold, reveal, o Muse, in novel song, and inflame in the bard the sacred furies.

Once upon a time whitewash with its unprepossessing and rude adornment covered the surface (which is now decorated by a picture abundant in colors), but lest any crack should declare its previous appearance, the artist soon laid the foundations for his future mural and drew the tractable liquid across the walls. The walls are rough, overlaid with a thick coating and smeared with cruder paint marks.

As when (the sky not yet being studded with gleaming stars), lest the immense mass should gape open through the empty void, ether was poured in here and there, and had flowed through the vaults of heaven and its widely expansive dome; soon Titan scorched the newly created universe with his radiant light, and pale Cynthia was emitting more gently fires that were not her own. Now glittered the sky, sown with a multitude of stars; now a milky brightness flowed into the entire heavens, and glowed with white light in its long expanse.

Sic operis postquam lusit primordia pictor,
dum sordet paries nullumque fatetur Apellem,
cautius exercet calamos atque arte tenacem
confundit viscum succosque attemperat; omnes   25
inducit tandem formas. apparet ubique
muta cohors et picturarum vulgus inane.
    Aligeris muri vacat ora suprema ministris,
sparsaque per totam caelestis turba tabellam
raucos inspirat lituos buccasque tumentes   30
inflat, et attonitum replet clangoribus orbem.
defunctis sonus auditur, tabulamque per imam
picta gravescit humus, terris emergit apertis
progenies rediviva, et plurima surgit imago.
    Sic dum fecundis Cadmus dat semina sulcis,   35
terra tumet praegnans animataque gleba laborat,
luxuriatur ager segete spirante, calescit
omne solum, crescitque virorum prodiga messis.
    Iam pulvis varias terrae dispersa per oras,
sive inter venas teneri concreta metalli   40
sensim diriguit, seu sese immiscuit herbis,
explicata est; molem rursus coalescit in unam
divisum funus, sparsos prior alligat artus
iunctura, aptanturque iterum coeuntia membra.
hic nondum specie perfecta resurgit imago   45
vultum truncata atque inhonesto vulnere nares
manca, et adhuc deest informi de corpore multum.
paulatim in rigidum hic vita insinuata cadaver
motu aegro vix dum redivivos erigit artus.
inficit his horror vultus, et imagine tota   50
fusa per attonitam pallet formido figuram.
    Detrahe quin oculos, spectator, et ora nitentem
si poterint perferre diem, medium inspice murum
qua sedet orta Deo proles, Deus ipse, sereno
lumine perfusus radiisque inspersus acutis.   55
circum tranquillae funduntur tempora flammae,
regius ore vigor spirat, nitet ignis ocellis,
plurimaque effulget maiestas numine toto.
quantum dissimilis, quantum o! mutatus ab illo
qui peccata luit cruciatus non sua, vitam   60
quando luctantem cunctata morte trahebat!
sed frustra voluit defunctum Golgotha numen
condere, dum victa fatorum lege triumphans
nativum petiit caelum et super aethera vectus
despexit lunam exiguam solemque minorem.   65
    Iam latus effossum et palmas ostendit utrasque
vulnusque infixum pede clavorumque recepta
signa, et transacti quondam vestigia ferri.
umbrae huc felices tendunt, numerosaque caelos

Thus after the painter had sported with the elementary stages, while the wall is still coarse and does not proclaim Apelles, he works his pencil strokes more carefully, and skillfully disturbs the sticky lime; he adjusts its juices, and at last he introduces all the shapes. Everywhere there appears a silent cohort, and an empty throng of outlines.

The wall's uppermost edge is allocated to winged servants, while, scattered across the entire picture, a heavenly host blows upon raucous trumpets and puffs their swelling cheeks, and fills an astounded world with their blare. The sound is heard by the dead, and the ground depicted along the bottom of the picture swells up, as from the opening earth a revived offspring emerges, and many a specter rises.

Thus while Cadmus gave seeds to the fertile furrows, the pregnant earth swelled up and the clod of soil, quickened with life, labored, the field flourished with a living crop, the whole soil grew warm, and a lavish harvest of men came into existence.

Now their dust extends, scattered across the various regions of the earth (whether being compacted amid the veins of soft metal it has gradually become stiff, or whether it has merged with plants); the dismembered corpse is joined together once more into a single mass, and the erstwhile joint binds together severed limbs, while the members as they come together are fitted once more. Here there rises up again a specter, its form not yet perfected, with mangled face and a nose disfigured by an unseemly wound, and still a great deal is missing from the deformed body. Here life has gradually made its way into a stiff corpse while in its difficulty in moving, it can hardly raise its revived limbs. Horror imbues the faces of these, and in the entire representation fear, infusing the astonished figure, emits pallor.

But drag your eyes away, viewer, and if your face is able to endure the glaring light of day, look at the middle of the mural where is seated God's begotten Son, God himself, suffused in unclouded light and besprinkled with pointed rays. Tranquil flames are poured about his temples, a kingly vitality breathes in his countenance, fire shines in his eyes, and the greatest majesty beams in all his divinity. How different, o how changed, from him who by his crucifixion atoned for sins not his own when he dragged out a struggling life with death delaying! But vain was Golgotha's wish to bury his dead divinity, as triumphant in his victory over the law of the fates, he sought his native heaven, and borne above the ether, he looked down upon the tiny moon and a smaller sun.

Now he shows his pierced side and both his palms and the wound implanted in his foot, and the nail marks he received, and the traces of the lance that once transfixed him. Shades of the blessed make their way to this point, and an abundant throng

turba petunt atque immortalia dona capessunt.   70
matres et longae nunc reddita corpora vitae
infantum, iuvenes, pueri innuptaeque puellae
stant circum, atque avidos iubar immortale bibentes,
affigunt oculos in numine; laudibus aether
intonat, et laeto ridet caelum omne triumpho.   75
his amor impatiens conceptaque gaudia mentem
funditus exagitant imoque in pectore fervent.
non aeque exsultat flagranti corde Sibylla
hospite cum tumet incluso et praecordia sentit
mota dei stimulis nimioque calentia Phoebo.   80
     Quis tamen ille novus perstringit lumina fulgor?
quam mitra effigiem distinxit pictor honesto
surgentem e tumulo alatoque satellite fultam?
agnosco faciem: vultu latet alter in illo
Wainfletus: sic ille oculos, sic ora ferebat.   85
eheu quando animi par invenietur imago!
quando alium similem virtus habitura!
irati innocuas securus numinis iras
aspicit impavidosque in iudice figit ocellos.
     Quin age et horrentem commixtis igne tenebris   90
iam videas scaenam; multo hic stagnantia fuco
moenia flagrantem liquefacto suphure rivum
fingunt, et falsus tanta arte accenditur ignis
ut toti metuas tabulae ne flamma per omne
livida serpat opus tenuesque absumpta recedat   95
pictura in cineres propriis peritura favillis.
huc turba infelix agitur turpisque videri
infrendet dentes et rugis contrahat ora.
vindex a tergo implacabile saevit, et ensem
fulmineum vibrans acie flagrante scelestos   100
iam Paradiseis iterum depellit ab oris.
heu! quid agat tristis? quo se caelestibus iris
subtrahat? o! quantum vellet nunc aethere in alto
virtutem colere! at tandem suspiria ducit
nequicquam et sero in lacrimas effunditur: obstant   105
sortes non revocandae et inexorabile numen.
     Quam varias aperit veneres pictura! periti
quot calami legimus vestigia! quanta colorum
gratia se profert! tales non discolor Iris
ostendat vario cum lumine floridus imber   110
rore nitet toto et gutta scintillat in omni.
     O fuci nitor, o pulchri durate colores!
nec, pictura, tuae languescat gloria formae
dum lucem videas, qualem exprimis ipsa, supremam.

seeks the heavens in quest of his immortal gifts. About him stand mothers and the bodies of infants now restored to long life: young men, boys, and unmarried girls, and drinking his immortal radiance, they fix their eager eyes upon his divinity; the ether thunders with praises, and the entire sky smiles in its triumphal joy. An impatient love and the joys they have conceived utterly rouse their minds, and they are aflame in the depths of their hearts. Not equally did the Sibyl exult in her burning heart when she swelled with the guest shut within her, and felt her heart moved by the goads of a god, and growing warm with Phoebus' very great presence.

But what is that new brilliance that dazzles the eyes? What image has the painter distinguished with a miter as he rises from his honorable tomb, supported by a winged attendant? I recognize his face: in that countenance there lies concealed a second Waynflete: he had the same eyes, the same face. Alas, when will be found an image that equals his mind! When will virtue possess another like him! Immune to God's anger, he beholds wrath that cannot harm him as he fixes his fearless eyes upon the Judge.

But come, and now you may see a dreadful scene of darkness intermingled with fire: here the walls, drenched with an abundance of paint, depict a stream blazing with liquefied sulphur, while an imaginary fire is enkindled with such skill that you would fear for the whole painting, lest the livid flame might creep through the entire work and lest the picture, consumed and reduced into fine ashes, might be on the point of perishing in its own embers. Hither is driven an unhappy throng which, shameful to behold, gnashes its teeth and scowls with wrinkles. At their backs the avenger rages relentlessly, and brandishing his sword of lightning, now with blazing blade he drives the wicked away once more from the shores of Paradise. Alas! What is the sad man to do? Whither may he withdraw from the heavenly wrath? O how greatly now would he wish to foster virtue in the high ether! But at last he emits sighs in vain, and too late he dissolves into tears. In his way stand irrevocable fate and an inexorable divinity.

How various are the charms that the picture reveals! How many traces of the skillful pencil do we peruse! What attractiveness of colors is put on view! Multicolored Iris does not display such hues when her bright shower gleams in its radiance with varied light and shines in all its moisture, glistening in every droplet.

O splendor of paint, o beautiful colors, endure! Nor, o picture, may the glory of your beauty languish until you behold the Last Day which you yourself depict.

APPENDIX 2

Addison's Latin Verses on the Vigo Expedition[1]

---

[1] Text of the Vigo epigrams is that of BL Add. 37349, ff 57-58 (Charles Whitworth Papers, Volume II). See Plates 5 and 6. The writing is in faint brown ink (on paper measuring 8 inches long x 13 inches wide). The hand is that of Whitworth, whose transcription of the Latin poems is much neater than the annotations on the same page (likewise in Whitworth's hand). This apparent discrepancy is actually characteristic of the manuscript collection as a whole. In the following edition I have modernized spelling and punctuation.

BL Add. 37349, ff 57-58

Application: The Affair of Vigo

Virg: *Aeneid*: Lib i. vers. 365

Conveniunt quibus aut odium crudele tyranni
aut metus acer erat; naves, quae forte paratae,
corripiunt onerantque auro. <u>portantur avari</u>
<u>Pygmalionis opes pelago; dux femina facti.</u>

Verses made on the Expedition at Vigo
by Mr Addison then at Vienna

Cum nimio intumuit victrix Hispania fastu;
   olim infracta armis cessit, Elisa, tuis.
immodica ambitio mundique capacia vota
   ex illo ingentem dedidicere sitim.
tu quoque sensisti combustis vana carinis,   5
   Gallia, femineae quid potuere manus.
nonne vides ut adhuc in litore fumat Ibero
   classis et ad Britonas India tota fluit?
i nunc et ritu Salico muliebria temne
   imperia, Angliacae fulmina passa deae.   10

Vinceris et nunquam te victum, Galle, fateris,
   falsa sed in vera clade tropaea canis.
Mars favet Eugenio, sed tu, Vendôme, triumphas;
   Teuto fugat Celtam, Celta fugatus ovat;
vulnera Vasco tegit, palmasque ostentat inanes,   5
   et laudat iustos, cum nocuere, deos.
maesta triumphatas quoties flent castra phalanges
   laetifico populos decipit aula rogo.
sed modo deletur flammis quae terruit orbem
   classis, et in cineres Indica gaza volat.   10
Gallia iactatrix, quae damna in gaudia vertis,
   has quoque festivis ignibus adde faces.

Virg: Aen. Titulus: vers. 365 *sic BL*   *re vera est vers.* 361   3-4   *BL haec verba ita*
delineantur Epig 1 1 intumuit *BLcorr* : intimuit *BL*   fastu *BLcorr* : fasti *BL*   Epigr 2 2
clade *BLcorr* : dade *BL*   5 ostendat *BL*   ostentat *scripsi*

BL Add. 37349, ff 57-58

Application: The Affair of Vigo

Virg: *Aeneid*: Bk 1 vers. 365

There come together those who had either cruel hatred towards, or intense fear of, the tyrant: they seize ships which by chance had been prepared, and they pile them up with gold. The wealth of the greedy Pygmalion is carried upon the sea, with a woman as leader of the action.

Verses made on the Expedition at Vigo by Mr Addison then at Vienna

Victorious Spain swelled with excessive pride; she who was once unbroken yielded to your arms, Elizabeth. As a consequence her immoderate ambition and her rapacious desire for the world have unlearned huge thirst. You too, vacuous France, your boats burnt, have experienced the power of female hands. Don't you see how the fleet is still smoldering on the Iberian shore, and the whole of the Indies flows towards Britain? Go now and in Salic custom spurn the dominion of a woman, you who have suffered the lightning-bolts of an English goddess.

You are conquered and, O Frenchman, you never admit that you have been conquered, but you sing of false trophies in a real defeat. Mars favors Eugenius, but you, Vendôme, are celebrating a triumph. The German puts the Celt to flight; the routed Celt is rejoicing; the Basque covers his wounds and shows his empty palms, and praises the gods as just at the very moment when they have harmed him. As often as the mourning camp laments phalanxes that have been triumphed over, the court deceives the people with a joyous pyre. But recently the fleet which terrified the world is destroyed by flames, and the treasure of the Indies goes flying into ashes. O boastful France, who turn losses into joys, add these torches also to your festive fires.

Le soleil est la dévise du Roy et Phaeton voulait s'égaler au soleil

Vidit ut Hispano Neptunus in aequore cladem,
    'haec,' ait, 'in Gallos Iuppiter arma movet;
illa tot innocuas quae iam combusserat arces
    combusta ultori classis ab igne perit.
se soli ratus esse parem, cum perderet orbem,   5
    in mediis Phaethon taliter arsit aquis.'

Phoenici aeternam praebent incendia vitam,
    hic tibi perpetuum dat cinis, Anna, decus.

Iam soror Anna pyram moriturae construxit Elisae;
    nunc regina novos praeparat Anna rogos.
funere ne careat peritura potentia regum
    ferales classi subdidit Anna faces.

Epig 3 Titulus voulait *BLcorr* : voloit *BL* voloit *trans duas lineas scriptum deletum est et voulait superscriptum est*

The sun is the emblem of the King, and Phaeton wished to equate himself with the sun.

When Neptune saw the defeat in the Spanish sea, he said: 'Jupiter is stirring up these arms against the French. That fleet which had already burnt so many harmless citadels, now itself burnt, perishes by a fire of vengeance. Thus did Phaethon burn in the middle of the sea when, thinking he was a match for the sun, he lost the world.'

Conflagrations portend eternal life for the phoenix. This ash gives perpetual glory to you, Anne.

Now Anna, her sister, constructed a pyre for Elissa on the point of death; now Anne the Queen prepares new funeral pyres. Lest the power of kings, a power on the point of perishing, should lack death, Anne placed deadly firebrands beneath the fleet.

APPENDIX 3

A Translation of All Virgil's Fourth *Georgic*
Except the Story of Aristaeus
By Mr Jo. Addison, of Magdalen College OXON

Appendix 3

A Translation of All Virgil's Fourth Georgic
Except the Story of Aristaeus
By Mr Jo. Addison of Magdalen College OXON.[1]

Ethereal sweets shall next my Muse engage,
and this, Maecenas, claims your patronage.
Of little creatures' wondrous acts I treat;
the ranks and mighty leaders of their state,
their laws, employments, and their wars relate.   5
A trifling theme provokes my humble lays:
trifling the theme, not so the poet's praise,
if great Apollo and the tuneful Nine
join in the piece to make the work divine.

First, for your bees a proper station find   10
that's fenc'd about and shelter'd from the wind,
for winds divert 'em in their flight, and drive
the swarms, when loaden homeward, from their hive.
Nor sheep nor goats must pasture near their stores
to trample underfoot the springing flowers;   15
nor frisking heifers bound about the place
to spurn the dew-drops off, and bruise the rising grass;
nor must the lizard's painted brood appear
nor wood-pecks nor the swallow harbour near.
They waste the swarms, and as they fly along   20
convey the tender morsels to their young.

Let purling streams and fountains edg'd with moss
and shallow rills run trickling through the grass;
let branching olives o'er the fountain grow
or palms shoot up and shade the streams below;   25
that when the youth, led by their princes, shun
the crowded hive, and sport it in the sun,
refreshing springs may tempt 'em from the heat,
and shady coverts yield a cool retreat.

Whether the neighbouring water stands or runs,   30
lay twigs across, and bridge it o'er with stones,
that if rough storms or sudden blasts of wind
should dip or scatter those that lag behind,
here they may settle on the friendly stone
and dry their reeking pinions at the sun.   35

---

[1] Text is that printed in *The Annual Miscellany* (London, 1694), 58-86. I have modernized spelling and punctuation.

Plant all the flowery banks with lavender,
with store of sav'ry scent the fragrant air;
let running betony the field o'erspread
    and fountains soak the violet's dewy bed.

    Tho' barks or plaited willows make your hive,   40
a narrow inlet to their cells contrive,
for colds congeal and freeze the liquors up
and, melted down with heat, the waxen buildings drop.
The bees, of both extremes alike afraid,
their wax around the whistling crannies spread,   45
and suck out clammy dews from herbs and flow'rs
to smear the chinks and plaster up the pores;
for this they hoard up glue whose clinging drops
like pitch or bird-lime hang in stringy ropes.
They oft, 'tis said, in dark retirements dwell   50
and work in subterraneous caves their cell;
at other times th' industrious insects live
in hollow rocks or make a tree their hive.

    Point all their chinky lodgings round with mud,
and leaves must thinly on your work be strow'd,   55
but let no baleful yew-tree flourish near
nor rotten marshes send out steams of mire
nor burning crabs grow red and crackle in the fire
nor neighb'ring caves return the dying sound
nor echoing rocks the doubled voice rebound.   60
Things thus prepar'd——
when th' under-world is seiz'd with cold and night,
and summer here descends in streams of light,
the bees thro' woods and forests take their flight.
They rifle every flow'r, and lightly skim   65
the crystal brook, and sip the running stream;
and thus they feed their young with strange delight
and knead the yielding wax, and work the slimy sweet.
But when on high you see the bees repair,
borne on the winds thro' distant tracts of air,   70
and view the winged cloud all blackning from afar,
while shady coverts and fresh streams they choose,
milfoil and common honeysuckles bruise,
and sprinkle on their hives the fragrant juice.
On brazen vessels beat a tinkling sound   75
and shake the cymbals of the goddess round;
then all will hastily retreat and fill
the warm resounding hollow of their cell.

    If e're two rival kings their right debate,
and factions and cabals embroil the state,   80

the people's actions will their thoughts declare:
all their hearts tremble and beat thick with war;
hoarse, broken sounds, like trumpets' harsh alarms,
run thro' the hive and call 'em to their arms;
all in a hurry spread their shiv'ring wings   85
and fit their claws and point their angry stings;
in crowds before the king's pavilion meet
and boldly challenge out the foe to fight.
At last, when all the heavens are warm and fair,
they rush together out and join; the air   90
swarms thick and echoes with the humming war.
All in a firm round cluster mix and strow
with heaps of little corps the earth below,
as thick as hailstones from the floor rebound
or shaken acorns rattle on the ground.   95
No sense of danger can their kings control,
their little bodies lodge a mighty soul:
each obstinate in arms pursues his blow
'till shameful flight secures the routed foe.
This hot dispute and all this mighty fray   100
a little dust flung upward will allay.

        But when both kings are settled in their hive,
mark him who looks the worst, and lest he live
idle at home in ease and luxury,
the lazy monarch must be doom'd to die;   105
so let the royal insect rule alone
and reign without a rival in his throne.

        The kings are different: one of better note,
all speckt with gold and many a shining spot,
looks gay and glistens in a gilded coat;   110
but love of ease and sloth in one prevails
that scarce his hanging paunch behind him trails.
The people's looks are different as their king's:
some sparkle bright, and glitter in their wings;
others look loathsome and diseas'd with sloth,   115
like a faint traveller, whose dusty mouth
grows dry with heat and spits a mawkish froth.
The first are best——
from their o'erflowing combs you'll often press
pure luscious sweets that mingling in the glass   120
correct the harshness of the racy juice,
and a rich flavour through the wine diffuse.
But when they sport abroad and rove from home,
and leave the cooling hive, and quit th' unfinish'd comb,
their airy ramblings are with ease confin'd,   125
clip their king's wings, and if they stay behind,
no bold usurper dares invade their right

nor sound a march nor give the sign for flight.
Let flow'ry banks entice 'em to their cells,
and gardens all perfum'd with native smells;　　　　　130
where carv'd Priapus has his fix'd abode,
the robber's terror, and the scarecrow god.
Wild thyme and pine-trees from their barren hill
transplant, and nurse 'em in the neighbouring soil;
set fruit-trees round, nor e'er indulge thy sloth,　　　135
but water 'em, and urge their shady growth.

　　And here, perhaps, were not I giving o'er
and striking sail and making to the shore,
I'd show what art the gardener's toils require,
why rosy pæstum blushes twice a year;　　　　　　140
what streams the verdant succory supply,
and how the thirsty plant drinks rivers dry;
with what a cheerful green does parsley grace,
and writhes the bellying cucumber along the twisted grass;
nor wou'd I pass the soft acanthus o'er,　　　　　　145
ivy nor myrtle-trees that love the shore,
nor daffodils that late from earth's slow womb
unrumple their swoln buds and show their yellow bloom.

　　For once I saw in the Tarentine vale,
where slow Galesus drencht the washy soil,　　　　　150
an old Corician yeoman, who had got
a few neglected acres to his lot,
where neither corn nor pasture grac'd the field
nor wou'd the vine her purple harvest yield,
but savoury herbs among the thorns were found,　　155
vervain and poppy-flowers his garden crown'd,
and drooping lilies whiten'd all the ground.
Blest with these riches he cou'd empires slight,
and when he rested from his toils at night,
the earth unpurchas'd dainties wou'd afford,　　　　160
and his own garden furnish out his board.
The spring did first his op'ning roses blow;
first ripening autumn bent his fruitful bough.
When piercing colds had burst the brittle stone,
and freezing rivers stiffen'd as they run,　　　　　165
he then wou'd prune the tender'st of his trees,
chide the late spring, and lingring western breeze.
His bees first swarm'd, and made his vessels foam
with the rich squeezings of the juicy comb.
Here lindens and the sappy pine increas'd;　　　　　170
here, when gay flow'rs his smiling orchard drest,
as many blossoms as the spring cou'd show,
so many dangling apples mellow'd on the bough.
In rows his elms and knotty pear-trees bloom,

and thorns ennobled now to bear a plum,   175
and spreading plane-trees, where, supinely laid,
he now enjoys the cool and quaffs beneath the shade.
But these for want of room I must omit
and leave for future poets to recite.

    Now I'll proceed their natures to declare,   180
which Jove himself did on the bees confer
because, invited by the timbrel's sound,
lodg'd in a cave, th' almighty babe they found,
and the young god nurst kindly under ground.

    Of all the wing'd inhabitants of air   185
these only make their young the public care;
in well-dispos'd societies they live,
and laws and statutes regulate their hive;
nor stray like others unconfin'd abroad,
but know set stations and a fix'd abode: 190
each provident of cold in summer flies
thro' fields and woods to seek for new supplies,
and in the common stock unlades his thighs.
Some watch the food, some in the meadows ply,
taste ev'ry bud, and suck each blossom dry;   195
whilst others, lab'ring in their cells at home,
temper Narcissus' clammy tears with gum
for the first groundwork of the golden comb;
on this they found their waxen works, and raise
the yellow fabric on its gluey base.   200
Some educate the young or hatch the seed
with vital warmth, and future nations breed;
whilst others thicken all the slimy dews
and into purest honey work the juice;
then fill the hollows of the comb, and swell   205
with luscious nectar ev'ry flowing cell.
By turns they watch, by turns with curious eyes
survey the heav'ns, and search the clouded skies
to find out breeding storms, and tell what tempests rise.
By turns they ease the loaden swarms or drive   210
the drone, a lazy insect, from their hive.
The work is warmly ply'd through all the cells,
and strong with thyme the new-made honey smells.

    So in their caves the brawny Cyclops sweat,
when with huge strokes the stubborn wedge they beat   215
and all th' unshapen thunderbolt complete;
alternately their hammers rise and fall,
whilst griping tongs turn round the glowing ball.
With puffing bellows some the flames increase,
and some in waters dip the hissing mass;   220

their beaten anvils dreadfully resound,
and Aetna shakes all o'er, and thunders under ground.

    Thus, if great things we may with small compare,
the busy swarms their diff'rent labours share.
Desire of profit urges all degrees.   225
The aged insects, by experience wise,
attend the comb and fashion every part,
and shape the waxen fret-work out with art;
the young at night, returning from their toils,
bring home their thighs clog'd with the meadows' spoils. 230
On lavender and saffron buds they feed;
on bending osiers and the balmy reed;
from purple violets and the teile they bring
their gather'd sweets, and rifle all the spring.

    All work together, all together rest;   235
the morning still renews their labours past.
Then all rush out, their different tasks pursue,
sit on the bloom, and suck the rip'ning dew;
again, when ev'ning warns 'em to their home,
with weary wings and heavy thighs they come   240
and crowd about the chink, and mix a drowsy hum.
Into their cells at length they gently creep;
there all the night their peaceful station keep,
wrapt up in silence and dissolv'd in sleep.
None range abroad when winds and storms are nigh   245
nor trust their bodies to a faithless sky,
but make small journeys with a careful wing,
and fly to water at a neighb'ring spring;
and lest their airy bodies should be cast
in restless whirls, the sport of every blast,   250
they carry stones to poise 'em in their flight,
as ballast keeps th' unsteady vessel right.

    But of all customs that the bees can boast
'tis this may challenge admiration most:
that none will Hymen's softer joys approve   255
nor waste their spirits in luxurious love,
but all a long virginity maintain
and bring forth young without a mother's pain:
from herbs and flow'rs they pick each tender bee,
and cull from plants a buzzing progeny;   260
from these they choose out subjects, and create
a little monarch of the rising state;
then build wax kingdoms for the infant prince,
and form a palace for his residence.

But often in their journeys, as they fly,   265
on flints they tear their silken wings or lie
grov'ling beneath their flowery load and die.
Thus love of honey can an insect fire,
and in a fly such gen'rous thoughts inspire.
Yet by repeopling their decaying state,   270
tho' sev'n short springs conclude their vital date,
their ancient stocks eternally remain,
and in an endless race their children's children reign.

No prostrate vassal of the East can more
with slavish fear his haughty prince adore;   275
his life unites 'em all; but when he dies,
all in loud tumults and distractions rise;
they waste their honey and their combs deface,
and wild confusion reigns in every place.
Him all admire, all the great guardian own,   280
and crowd about his courts and buzz about his throne.
Oft on their backs their weary prince they bear,
oft in his cause, embattl'd in the air,
pursue a glorious death in wounds and war.

Some from such instances as these have taught: 285
"the bees' extract is heav'nly; for they thought
the universe alive, and that a soul,
diffus'd throughout the matter of the whole,
to all the vast unbounded frame was giv'n,
and ran through earth, and air, and sea, and all   290
the deep of heav'n;
that this first kindled life in man and beast,
life, that again flows into this at last;
that no compounded animal could die,
but when dissolv'd, the spirit mounted high,
dwelt in a star, and settl'd in the sky."   295

Whene'er their balmy sweets you mean to seize
and take the liquid labours of the bees,
spurt draughts of water from your mouth, and drive
a loathsome cloud of smoke amidst their hive.

Twice in the year their flow'ry toils begin,   300
and twice they fetch their dewy harvest in:
once when the lovely Pleiades arise
and add fresh lustre to the summer skies;
and once when hast'ning from the watry sign,
they quit their station and forbear to shine.   305

The bees are prone to rage and often found
to perish for revenge, and die upon the wound;

their venom'd sting produces aching pains,
and swells the flesh, and shoots among the veins.

When first a cold hard winter's storms arrive   310
and threaten death or famine to their hive,
if now their sinking state and low affairs
can move your pity and provoke your cares,
fresh burning thyme before their cells convey,
and cut their dry and husky wax away;   315
for often lizards seize the luscious spoils
or drones that riot on another's toils;
oft broods of moths infest the hungry swarms
and oft the furious wasp their hive alarms
with louder hums and with unequal arms   320
or else the spider at their entrance sets
her snares, and spins her bowels into nets.

When sickness reigns (for they as well as we
feel all th' effects of frail mortality),
by certain marks the new disease is seen: 325
their colour changes, and their looks are thin;
their funeral rites are form'd, and ev'ry bee
with grief attends the sad solemnity;
the few diseas'd survivors hang before
their sickly cells, and droop about the door   330
or slowly in their hives their limbs unfold,
shrunk up with hunger and benumb'd with cold;
in drawling hums the feeble insects grieve,
and doleful buzzes echo thro' the hive,
like winds that softly murmur thro' the trees,   335
like flames pent up or like retiring seas.
Now lay fresh honey near their empty rooms
in troughs of hollow reeds, whilst frying gums
cast round a fragrant mist of spicy fumes.
Thus kindly tempt the famish'd swarm to eat,   340
and gently reconcile 'em to their meat:
mix juice of galls, and wine, that grow in time
condens'd by fire, and thicken to a slime;
to these, dry'd roses, thyme, and centaury join,
and raisins ripen'd on the Psythian vine.   345

Besides, there grows a flow'r in marshy ground,
its name amellus, easy to be found;
a mighty spring works in its root and cleaves
the sprouting stalk and shows itself in leaves:
the flow'r itself is of a golden hue,   350
the leaves inclining to a darker blue;
the leaves shoot thick about the flow'r and grow
into a bush, and shade the turf below;

the plant in holy garlands often twines
the altars' posts, and beautifies the shrines;   355
its taste is sharp, in vales new-shorn it grows
where Mella's stream in watery mazes flows.
Take plenty of its roots and boil them well
in wine, and heap 'em up before the cell.

But if the whole stock fail and none survive   360
to raise new people, and recruit the hive,
I'll here the great experiment declare
that spread th' Arcadian shepherd's name so far:
how bees from blood of slaughter'd bulls have fled,
and swarms amidst the red corruption bred.   365

For where th' Egyptians yearly see their bounds
refresh'd with floods, and sail about their grounds,
where Persia borders, and the rolling Nile
drives swiftly down the swarthy Indian's soil
'till into sev'n it multiplies its stream   370
and fattens Egypt with a fruitful slime,
in this last practice all their hope remains,
and long experience justifies their pains.

First then a close contracted space of ground
with straiten'd walls and low-built roof they bound;   375
a narrow shelving light is next assign'd
to all the quarters, one to every wind;
through these the glancing rays obliquely pierce.
Hither they lead a bull that's young and fierce,
when two years' growth of horn he proudly shows,   380
and shakes the comely terrors of his brows;
his nose and mouth, the avenues of breath,
they muzzle up, and beat his limbs to death;
with violence to life and stifling pain
he flings and spurns, and tries to snort in vain;   385
loud heavy blows fall thick on ev'ry side
till his bruis'd bowels burst within the hide;
when dead, they leave him rotting on the ground,
with branches, thyme, and cassia, strow'd around.
All this is done when first the western breeze   390
becalms the year and smooths the troubled seas;
before the chatt'ring swallow builds her nest
or fields in spring's embroidery are dress'd.
Meanwhile the tainted juice ferments within,
and quickens as its works: and now are seen   395
a wond'rous swarm, that o'er the carcass crawls,
of shapeless, rude, unfinish'd animals.
No legs at first the insect's weight sustain;

at length it moves its new-made limbs with pain;
now strikes the air with quiv'ring wings, and tries   400
to lift its body up, and learns to rise;
now bending thighs and gilded wings it wears
full grown, and all the bee at length appears;
from every side the fruitful carcass pours
its swarming brood, as thick as summer showers   405
or flights of arrows from the Parthian bows,
when twanging strings first shoot 'em on the foes.

        Thus have I sung the nature of the bee,
while Caesar, tow'ring to divinity,
the frighted Indians with his thunder aw'd   410
and claim'd their homage and commenc'd a god.
I flourish'd all the while in arts of peace,
retir'd and shelter'd in inglorious ease;
I who before the songs of shepherds made,
when gay and young my rural lays I play'd,   415
And set my Tityrus beneath his shade.

APPENDIX 4

Joseph Addison,
An Essay on Virgil's *Georgics*

Appendix 4

Joseph Addison,
An Essay on Virgil's Georgics[1]

Virgil may be reckoned the first who introduced three new kinds of
poetry among the Romans, which he copied after three of the greatest
masters of Greece. Theocritus and Homer have still disputed for the
advantage over him in *Pastoral* and *Heroics*, but I think all are
unanimous in giving him the precedence to Hesiod in his *Georgics*. The
truth of it is: the sweetness and rusticity of a *Pastoral* cannot be so well
expressed in any other tongue as in the Greek, when rightly mixed and
qualified with the Doric dialect; nor can the majesty of an heroic poem
anywhere appear so well as in this language, which has a natural
greatness in it, and can be often rendered more deep and sonorous by the
pronunciation of the Ionians. But in the Middle style, where the writers in
both tongues are on a level, we see how far Virgil has excelled all who
have written in the same way with him.

   There has been abundance of criticism spent on Virgil's *Pastorals*
and *Aeneids,* but the *Georgics* are a subject which none of the critics have
sufficiently taken into their consideration, most of them passing it over in
silence or casting it under the same head with *Pastoral* – a division by no
means proper unless we suppose the style of a husbandman ought to be
imitated in a *Georgic* as that of a shepherd is in *Pastoral.* But though the
scene of both these poems lies in the same place, the speakers in them are
of a quite different character since the precepts of husbandry are not to be
delivered with the simplicity of a ploughman, but with the address of a
poet. No rules therefore that relate to *Pastoral* can any way affect the
Georgics since they fall under that class of poetry which consists in
giving plain and direct instructions to the reader: whether they be moral
duties, as those of Theognis and Pythagoras, or philosophical
speculations, as those of Aratus and Lucretius, or rules of practice, as
those of Hesiod and Virgil. Among these different kinds of subjects, that
which the *Georgics* go upon is, I think, the meanest and least improving,
but the most pleasing and delightful. Precepts of morality, besides the
natural corruption of our tempers, which makes us averse to them, are so
abstracted from ideas of sense that they seldom give an opportunity for
those beautiful descriptions and images which are the spirit and life of
poetry. Natural philosophy has indeed sensible objects to work upon, but
then it often puzzles the reader with the intricacy of its notions, and
perplexes him with the multitude of its disputes. But this kind of poetry I
am now speaking of addresses itself wholly to the imagination. It is

---

[1] Text is that prefixed to *The Works of Virgil, Containing his Pastorals,
Georgics and Aeneis Translated into English Verse by Mr Dryden*
(London, 1697). I have modernized spelling and punctuation.

altogether conversant among the fields and woods, and has the most delightful part of nature for its province. It raises in our minds a pleasing variety of scenes and landscapes, whilst it teaches us and makes the driest of its precepts look like a description. A *Georgic* therefore is some part of the science of husbandry put into a pleasing dress, and set off with all the beauties and embellishments of poetry. Now since this science of husbandry is of a very large extent, the poet shows his skill in singling out such precepts to proceed on as are useful, and at the same time most capable of ornament. Virgil was so well acquainted with this secret that to set off his first *Georgic* he has run into a set of precepts which are almost foreign to his subject, in that beautiful account he gives us of the signs in nature, which precede the changes of the weather.

And if there be so much art in the choice of fit precepts, there is much more required in the treating of them that they may fall in after each other by a natural unforced method, and show themselves in the best and most advantageous light. They should all be so finely wrought together in the same piece that no coarse seam may discover where they join; as in a curious brede of needlework one colour falls away by such just degrees, and another rises so insensibly that we see the variety without being able to distinguish the total vanishing of the one from the first appearance of the other. Nor is it sufficient to range and dispose this body of precepts into a clear and easy method unless they are delivered to us in the most pleasing and agreeable manner. For there are several ways of conveying the same truth to the mind of man, and to choose the pleasantest of these ways is that which chiefly distinguishes poetry from prose, and makes Virgil's rules of husbandry pleasanter to read than Varro's. Where the prose-writer tells us plainly what ought to be done, the poet often conceals the precept in a description, and represents his country-man performing the action in which he would instruct his reader. Where the one sets out as fully and distinctly as he can all the parts of the truth which he would communicate to us, the other singles out the most pleasing circumstance of this truth, and so conveys the whole in a more diverting manner to the understanding. I shall give one instance out of a multitude of this nature that might be found in the *Georgics* where the reader may see the different ways Virgil has taken to express the same thing, and how much pleasanter every manner of expression is than the plain and direct mention of it would have been. It is in the second *Georgic*, where he tells us what trees will bear grafting on each other:

> et saepe alterius ramos impune videmus
> vertere in alterius, mutatamque insita mala
> ferre pirum et pruinis lapidosa rubescere corna.[2]

> ... steriles platani malos gessere valentis,
> castaneae fagos; ornusque incanuit albo
> flore piri glandemque sues fregere sub ulmis.[3]

---

[2] *Georgics* 2. 32-34.
[3] *Georgics* 2. 70-72.

>   nec longum tempus, et ingens
>   exit ad caelum ramis felicibus arbos,
>   miraturque novas frondes et non sua poma.[4]

Here we see the poet considered all the effects of this union between trees of different kinds, and took notice of that effect which had the most surprise, and by consequence the most delight in it, to express the capacity that was in them of being thus united. This way of writing is everywhere much in use among the poets, and is particularly practised by Virgil, who loves to suggest a truth indirectly and, without giving us a full and open view of it, to let us see just so much as will naturally lead the imagination into all the parts that lie concealed. This is wonderfully diverting to the understanding: thus to receive a precept that enters, as it were, through a by-way, and to apprehend an idea that draws a whole train after it. For here the mind, which is always delighted with its own discoveries, only takes the hint from the poet, and seems to work out the rest by the strength of her own faculties.

But since the inculcating precept upon precept will at length prove tiresome to the reader, if he meets with no entertainment, the poet must take care not to encumber his poem with too much business, but sometimes to relieve the subject with a moral reflection or let it rest awhile for the sake of a pleasant and pertinent digression. Nor is it sufficient to run out into beautiful and diverting digressions (as it is generally thought) unless they are brought in aptly and are something of a piece with the main design of the *Georgic*. For they ought to have a remote alliance at least to the subject, that so the whole poem may be more uniform and agreeable in all its parts. We should never quite lose sight of the country, though we are sometimes entertained with a distant prospect of it. Of this nature are Virgil's descriptions of the original of agriculture, of the fruitfulness of Italy, of a country life, and the like, which are not brought in by force, but naturally rise out of the principal argument and design of the poem. I know no one digression in the *Georgics* that may seem to contradict this observation, besides that in the latter end of the first book, where the poet launches out into a discourse of the battle of Pharsalia and the actions of Augustus. But it is worth while to consider how admirably he has turned the course of his narration into its proper channel and made his husbandman concerned even in what relates to the battle in those inimitable lines:

>   scilicet et tempus veniet, cum finibus illis
>   agricola incurvo terram molitus aratro
>   exesa inveniet sacabra robigine pila,
>   aut gravibus rastris galeas pulsabit inanis
>   grandiaque effossis mirabitur ossa sepulchris.[5]

---

[4] *Georgics* 2. 80-82.
[5] *Georgics* 1. 493-497.

And afterwards, speaking of Augustus's actions, he still remembers that agriculture ought to be some way hinted at throughout the whole poem:

non ullus aratro
dignus honos, squalent abductis arva colonis,
et curvae rigidum falces conflantur in ensem.[6]

We now come to the style which is proper to a *Georgic*; and indeed this is the part on which the poet must lay out all his strength that his words may be warm and glowing, and that everything he describes may immediately present itself, and rise up to the reader's view. He ought in particular to be careful of not letting his subject debase his style and betray him into a meanness of expression, but everywhere to keep up his verse in all the pomp of numbers and dignity of words.

I think nothing which is a phrase or saying in common talk should be admitted into a serious poem because it takes off from the solemnity of the expression and gives it too great a turn of familiarity. Much less ought the low phrases and terms of art that are adapted to husbandry have any place in such a work as the *Georgic*, which is not to appear in the natural simplicity and nakedness of its subject, but in the pleasantest dress that poetry can bestow on it. Thus Virgil, to deviate from the common form of words, would not make use of *tempore* but *sidere* in his first verse, and everywhere else abounds with metaphors, Graecisms, and circumlocutions to give his verse the greater pomp, and preserve it from sinking into a plebeian style. And herein consists Virgil's masterpiece, who has not only excelled all other poets, but even himself in the language of his *Georgics*, where we receive more strong and lively ideas of things from his words than we could have done from the objects themselves; and find our imaginations more affected by his descriptions than they would have been by the very sight of what he describes.

I shall now, after this short scheme of rules, consider the different success that Hesiod and Virgil have met with in this kind of poetry, which may give us some further notion of the excellence of the *Georgics*. To begin with Hesiod: if we may guess at his character from his writings, he had much more of the husbandman than the poet in his temper. He was wonderfully grave, discreet and frugal; he lived altogether in the country, and was probably for his great prudence the oracle of the whole neighbourhood. These principles of good husbandry ran through his works and directed him to the choice of tillage and merchandise, for the subject of that which is the most celebrated of them. He is everywhere bent on instruction, avoids all manner of digressions, and does not stir out of the field once in the whole *Georgic*. His method in describing month after month with its proper seasons and employments is too grave and simple; it takes off from the surprise and variety of the poem, and makes the whole look but like a modern almanac in verse. The reader is carried through a course of weather, and may beforehand guess whether he is to meet with snow or rain, clouds or sunshine in the next description. His

---

[6] *Georgics* 1. 506-508.

descriptions indeed have abundance of nature in them, but then it is nature in her simplicity and undress. Thus when he speaks of January: 'The wild beasts,' says he, 'run shivering through the woods with their heads stooping to the ground and their tails clapped between their legs; the goats and oxen are almost flea'd with cold, but it is not so bad with the sheep because they have a thick coat of wool about them. The old men too are bitterly pinched with the weather, but the young girls feel nothing of it, who sit at home with their mothers by a warm fireside.' Thus does the old gentleman give himself up to a loose kind of tattle, rather than endeavour after a just poetical description. Nor has he shown more of art or judgment in the precepts he has given us, which are sown so very thick that they clog the poem too much and are often so minute and full of circumstances that they weaken and unnerve his verse. But after all we are beholden to him for the first rough sketch of a *Georgic* where we may still discover something venerable in the antiqueness of the work; but if we would see the design enlarged, the figures reformed, the colouring laid on, and the whole piece finished, we must expect it from a greater master's hand.

Virgil has drawn out the rules of tillage and planting into two books, which Hesiod has dispatched in half a one, but has so raised the natural rudeness and simplicity of his subject with such a significancy of expression, such a pomp of verse, such variety of transitions, and such a solemn air in his reflections that if we look on both poets together, we see in one the plainness of a downright countryman, and in the other something of a rustic majesty like that of a Roman dictator at the plough-tail. He delivers the meanest of his precepts with a kind of grandeur; he breaks the clods and tosses the dung about with an air of gracefulness. His prognostications of the weather are taken out of Aratus, where we may see how judiciously he has picked out those that are most proper for his husbandman's observation; how he has enforced the expression and heightened the images which he found in the original.

The second book has more wit in it and a greater boldness in its metaphors than any of the rest. The poet with a great beauty applies oblivion, ignorance, wonder, desire and the like to his trees. The last *Georgic* has indeed as many metaphors, but not so daring as this: for human thoughts and passions may be more naturally ascribed to a bee than to an inanimate plant. He who reads over the pleasures of a country life, as they are described by Virgil in the latter end of this book, can scarce be of Virgil's mind in preferring even the life of a philosopher to it.

We may, I think, read the poet's clime in his description, for he seems to have been in a sweat at the writing of it:

> o quis me gelidis sub montibus Haemi
> sistat, et ingenti ramorum protegat umbra![7]

---

[7] *Georgics* 2. 488-489.

and is everywhere mentioning among his chief pleasures the coolness of his shades and rivers, vales and grottos, which a more northern poet would have omitted for the description of a sunny hill and fireside.

The third *Georgic* seems to be the most laboured of them all: there is a wonderful vigour and spirit in the description of the horse and chariot-race. The force of love is represented in noble instances and very sublime expressions. The Scythian winter-piece appears so very cold and bleak to the eye that a man can scarce look on it without shivering. The Murrain at the end has all the expressiveness that words can give. It was here that the poet strained hard to out-do Lucretius in the description of his plague, and if the reader would see what success he had, he may find it at large in Scaliger.

But Virgil seems nowhere so well pleased as when he is got among his bees in the fourth *Georgic*, and ennobles the actions of so trivial a creature with metaphors drawn from the most important concerns of mankind. His verses are not in a greater noise and hurry in the battles of Aeneas and Turnus than in the engagement of two swarms. And as in his *Aeneis* he compares the labours of his Trojans to those of bees and pismires, here he compares the labours of the bees to those of the Cyclops. In short, the last *Georgic* was a good prelude to the *Aeneis*, and very well showed what the poet could do in the description of what was really great by his describing the mock-grandeur of an insect with so good a grace. There is more pleasantness in the little platform of a garden, which he gives us about the middle of this book, than in all the spacious walks and waterworks of Rapin. The speech of Proteus at the end can never be enough admired, and was indeed very fit to conclude so divine a work.

After this particular account of the beauties in the *Georgics*, I should in the next place endeavour to point out its imperfections, if it has any. But though I think there are some few parts in it that are not so beautiful as the rest, I shall not presume to name them, as rather suspecting my own judgment, than I can believe a fault to be in that poem which lay so long under Virgil's correction, and had his last hand put to it. The first *Georgic* was probably burlesqued in the author's lifetime; for we still find in the scholiasts a verse that ridicules part of a line translated from Hesiod: *nudus ara, sere nudus*. And we may easily guess at the judgment of this extraordinary critic, whoever he was, from his censuring this particular precept. We may be sure Virgil would not have translated it from Hesiod had he not discovered some beauty in it; and indeed the beauty of it is what I have before observed to be frequently met with in Virgil: the delivering the precept so indirectly, and singling out the particular circumstance of sowing and ploughing naked to suggest to us that these employments are proper only in the hot season of the year.

I shall not here compare the style of the *Georgics* with that of Lucretius, which the reader may see already done in the preface to the second volume of *Miscellany Poems*, but shall conclude this poem to be the most complete, elaborate, and finished piece of all antiquity. The *Aeneis* indeed is of a nobler kind, but the *Georgic* is more perfect in its kind. The *Aeneis* has a greater variety of beauties in it, but those of the

Georgic are more exquisite. In short, the *Georgic* has all the perfection that can be expected in a poem written by the greatest poet in the flower of his age, when his invention was ready, his imagination warm, his judgment settled, and all his faculties in their full vigour and maturity.

BIBLIOGRAPHY

1. MANUSCRIPTS
British Library, London

BL Add.37349, ff 57-58 (Whitworth Papers).

2. ADDISON: EDITIONS

Nova Philosophia Veteri Praeferenda Est in *Theatri Oxoniensis Encaenia Sive Comitia Philologica Julii 7 Anno 1693 Celebrata* (Oxford, 1693), L2^v-M1^v.

A Translation of All Virgil's Fourth Georgic, Except the Story of Aristaeus, The Annual Miscellany (London, 1694), 58-86.

An Essay on Virgil's Georgics prefixed to *The Works of Virgil, Containing his Pastorals, Georgics and Aeneis Translated into English Verse by Mr Dryden* (London, 1697).

Latin Poems in *Examen Poeticum Duplex* (London, 1698).

Latin Poems in *Musarum Anglicanarum Analecta*, II (Oxford, 1699).

A Dissertation Upon the Most Celebrated Roman Poets (London, 1718).

Poems on Several Occasions with a Dissertation Upon the Roman Poets by Mr. Addison (London, 1719).

The Works of the Right Honourable Joseph Addison, ed. Thomas Tickell (London, 1721), 4 vols.

The Tatler: A Corrected Edition, ed. Alexander Chalmers (London, 1806), 4 vols.

The Miscellaneous Works of Joseph Addison, ed. A.C. Guthkelch (London, 1914), 2 vols.

The Letters of Joseph Addison, ed. Walter Graham (Oxford, 1941).

The Spectator, ed. D.F. Bond (Oxford, 1965), 5 vols.

The Tatler, ed. D.F. Bond (Oxford, 1987), 3 vols.

The Latin Prose and Poetry of Joseph Addison: A Hypertext Edition, ed. D.F. Sutton (http://eee.uci.edu/~papyri/Addison/ The Philological Museum: California, 1997; revised ed. 1998).

3. OTHER PRIMARY TEXTS AND ANTHOLOGIES

"A Biographical Memoir of Sir Cloudesly Shovel," *The Naval Chronicle*, March 1815.

ALDRICH, Henry, *Inauguratio Regis Gulielmi et Reginae Mariae, Musarum Anglicanarum Analecta* (Oxford, 1699), II, 32-34.

An Impartial Account of all the Material Transactions of the Grand Fleet ... In which is Included a Particular Relation of the Expedition at Cadiz, and the Glorious Victory at Vigo By an Officer that was Present in those Actions (London, 1703).

ARISTOTLE, *History of Animals*, trans. D.M. Balme (Loeb Classical Library: Harvard, 1991).

BARLAEUS, Caspar, *Poemata* (Amsterdam, 1645).

BARNES, Joshua, *Gerania: A New Discovery of a Little Sort of People Called Pygmies With a Lively Description of their Stature, Habit, Manner, Buildings, Knowledge, and Government* (London, 1675).

BISSE, Thomas, *Microscopium*, *Musarum Anglicanarum Analecta* (Oxford, 1699), II, 163-168.

——————, *Lusus Poetici* (London, 1720).

BROWNE, Sir Thomas, *Pseudodoxia Epidemica*, ed. Robin Robbins (Oxford, 1981).

BUCHANAN, George, *Rerum Scoticarum Historia* (Frankfurt, 1584).

BUCKERIDGE, Bainbrigg, *An Essay Towards an English School of Painters*, appended to Richard Graham, trans., Roger de Piles, *The Art of Painting and the Lives of the Painters* (London, 1706).

BURNET, Thomas, *A Second Tale of a Tub or The History of Robert Powel the Puppet-Show-Man* (London, 1715).

CALPURNIUS SICULUS, *Eclogues*, ed. C.H. Keene (London, 1887).

CATULLUS, *Poems*, ed. C.J. Fordyce (Oxford, 1961).

CICERO, *Pro Caelio*, ed. R.G. Austin (Oxford, 1952).

DILLINGHAM, William, *Poemata Varii Argumenti, Partim e Georgio Herberto Latine (Utcunque) Reddita, Partim Conscripta a Wilh. Dillingham S.T.D.* (London, 1678).

——————, *Sphaeristerium* in *Examen Poeticum Duplex* (London, 1698), 29-33.

EVELYN, John, *Diary*, ed. E.S. De Beer (Oxford, 1955).

FRIEND, Joseph, *Pugna Gallorum Gallinaceorum*, *Musarum Anglicanarum Analecta* (Oxford, 1699), II, 85-90.

FROWDE, Philip, *Cursus Glacialis*, *Musarum Anglicanarum Analecta* (Oxford, 1699), II, 145-147.

GARTH, Samuel, *The Dispensary* (London, 1699).

GRAY, Thomas, *Luna Habitalis* in Estelle Haan, *Thomas Gray's Latin Poetry: Some Classical, Neo-Latin and Vernacular Contexts* (Collection Latomus 257: Brussels, 2000), 168-173.

HESIOD, *Works and Days*, ed. M.L. West (Oxford, 1978).

HOBART, Nicolaus, *Dioptrices Laus*, *Musarum Anglicanarum Analecta* (Oxford, 1699), I, 94-98.

HOMER, *Iliad*, trans. A.T. Murray; rev. W.F. Wyatt (Loeb Classical Library: Harvard, 1999).

——————, *Odyssey*, trans. A.T. Murray; rev. G.E. Dimock (Loeb Classical Library: Harvard, 1995).

HORACE, *Opera*, ed. Stephanus Borzsák (Leipzig, 1984).

JOHNSON, Samuel, *Works*, ed. Donald Greene (Oxford, 1984).

JUVENAL, *Satires Book 1*, ed. Susanna Morton Braund (Cambridge, 1996).

KNAPP, Francis, *Taurus in Circo*, *Musarum Anglicanarum Analecta* (Oxford, 1699), II, 80-84.

LELAND, John, *Principum ac Illustrium Aliquot et Eruditorum in Anglia Virorum Encomia, Trophaea, Genethliaca et Epithalamia a Ioanne Lelando Antiquario Conscripta* (London, 1589).

LIVY, *Ab Urbe Condita*, trans. B.O. Foster et al (Loeb Classical Library: Harvard, 1959).

LLUELYN, Martin, *Men Miracles* (London, 1646).

LUCRETIUS, *De Rerum Natura*, ed. Cyril Bailey; rev. Louis Roberts (Oxford, 1977).

MACAULAY, Thomas Babington, "The Life and Writings of Addison," in *Critical and Historical Essays Contributed to The Edinburgh Review* (London, 1877), 736 (July, 1843).

MASTERS, Thomas, *Mensa Lubrica, Musarum Anglicanarum Analecta* (Oxford, 1699), I, 17-19.

MILTON, John, *Complete Shorter Poems*, ed. John Carey (London and New York, 1971; rev. 1997).

————, *Paradise Lost*, ed. Alastair Fowler (London and New York, 1971; rev. 1998).

Musarum Anglicanarum Analecta (Oxford, 1699).

NEWEY, Thomas, *Inauguratio Regis Gulielmi et Reginae Mariae, Musarum Anglicanarum Analecta* (Oxford, 1699), II, 52-55.

OLDHAM, John, *Poems and Translations* (London, 1683).

OVID, *Metamorphoses*, trans. F.J. Miller (Loeb Classical Library: Harvard, 1916).

————, *Tristia*, ed. J.B. Hall (Stuttgart, 1995).

PLAUTUS, *Bacchides*, ed. John Barsby (Warminster, 1986).

————, *Poenulus*, ed. Gregor Maurach (Heidelberg, 1975).

PLINY, the Elder, *Natural History*, trans. H. Rackham (Loeb Classical Library: Harvard, 1938).

PLINY, the Younger, *Letters*, ed. A.N. Sherwin-White (Oxford, 1966).

POLIZIANO, ANGELO, *Prose Volgari Inedite e Poesie Latine e Greche Edite e Inedite*, ed. Isidoro del Lungo (New York, 1976).

ROOKE, Sir George, *Journal*, ed. O. Browning (London, 1897).

ROSS, Alexander, *Arcana Microcosmi* (London, 1652).

SENECA, *Epistulae*, ed. C.D.N. Costa (Warminster, 1988).

————, *Octavia*, ed. Lucile Yow Whitman (Stuttgart, 1978).

SERVIUS, *In Vergilii Carmina Commentarii*, ed. George Thilo (Leipzig, 1878).

SMITH, Edmund, *Works* (London, 1714).

SMITH, Robert Percy, *Early Writings* (London, 1851).

STATIUS, *Opera*, trans. J.H. Mosley (Loeb Classical Library: Harvard, 1928).

STEPNEY, George, "The Austrian Eagle" in *The Works of the Most Celebrated Minor Poets* (London, 1749), II, 20.

————, *The Inscription Appointed to be Fix'd on A Marble Erected at Hochstadt: In Memory of that Glorious Victory: The Latin Written by Mr Stepney and Englished by a Gentleman of Oxon* (London, 1705).

STRUTT, Joseph, *Sports and Pastimes of the People of England* (London, 1801).

SUETONIUS, *Divus Augustus*, ed. J.M. Carter (Bristol, 1982).

SWIFT, Jonathan, *Gulliver's Travels*, ed. Robert Demaria (Penguin, 2001).

THACKERAY, W.M., *Essay on Addison*, in *Essays on Addison by Johnson, Macaulay, Thackeray*, ed. G.E. Hadow (Oxford, 1915).

————, *Henry Esmond* (Everyman: London, 1937).

The Annual Miscellany (London, 1694).

Theatri Oxoniensis Encaenia, Sive Comitia Philologica Julii 7 Anno 1693 Celebrata (Oxford, 1693).

TIBULLUS, *Carmina*, ed. George Luck (Stuttgart, 1988).

TOOKE, Charles, *To the Right Honourable Sir George Rooke, Vice Admiral of England &c, At His Return from His Glorious Enterprise Near Vigo 1702* (London, 1702).

TRELAWNY, Jonathan, Bishop of Exeter, *A Sermon Preach'd Before the Queen, and Both Houses of Parliament at the Cathedral Church of St Paul's, Nov. 12, 1702 Being the Day of Thanksgiving for the Signal Successes Vouchsafed to Her Majesty's Forces by Sea and Land ... and Sir George Rooke, Admiral at Vigo* (London, 1702).

VIDA, Marco Girolamo, *De Arte Poetica*, ed. R.G. Williams (New York, 1976).

————, *Scacchia Ludus*, ed. with introduction and notes by M.A. Di Cesare (*Bibliotheca Humanistica & Reformatorica* 13: Nieuwkoop, 1975).

VIRGIL, *Opera*, ed. R.A.B. Mynors (Oxford, 1969).

————, *Georgics*, ed. R.F. Thomas (Cambridge, 1988), 2 vols.

————, *Georgics*, ed. R.A.B. Mynors (Oxford, 1990).

VOLTAIRE, *Essay on Epic Poetry*, ed. F.D. White (Albany, New York, 1915).

Vota Oxoneniensia Pro Serenissimis Guilhelmo Rege et Maria Regina M. Britanniae &c Nuncupata (Oxford, 1689).

WALPOLE, Horace, *Anecdotes of Painting in England*, ed. R.N. Wornum (London, 1888).

WATSON, Thomas, *Amintae Gaudia* (London, 1592).

WERESMARTI, Petrus, *Dissertatio Philosophica ... de Phaenomenis Barometricis* (Frankfurt, 1712).

4.   WORKS OF REFERENCE

ANONYMOUS, *The New Oxford Guide or Companion Through the University* (Oxford, 1759).

BLOXAM, John Rouse, *A Register of the Presidents, Demies ... of Saint Mary Magdalen College in the University of Oxford* (Oxford, 1857).

CHALMERS, Alexander, *History of the Colleges, Halls and Public Buildings Attached to the University of Oxford* (Oxford, 1810).

Dictionary of National Biography.

FOSTER, Joseph, ed. *Alumni Oxonienses: The Members of the University of Oxford 1500-1866*, 4 vols. (London, 1891; rpt Nendeln, Liechtenstein, 1968).

Oxford Latin Dictionary.

ROSCHER, W.H. and ZIEGLER, K., *Ausführliches Lexicon der Griechischen und Römischen Mythologie* (Teubner, 1884-1937).

VENN, John and VENN, J.R. eds. *Alumni Cantabrigienses* (Cambridge, 1922).

5.   SECONDARY LITERATURE

AIKIN, Lucy, *The Life of Joseph Addison* (London, 1843).

AITKEN, Robert, "Virgil's Plough," *Journal of Roman Studies* 46 (1956), 97-106.

AURIGEMMA, Salvatore, *The Baths of Diocletian and the Museo Nazionale Romano*, trans. J. Guthrie (Fifth edition Rome: Istituto Poligrafico Dello Stato, 1963).

BARTHES, Roland, "The Reality Effect," in *The Rustle of Language*, trans. R. Howard (New York, 1986), 141-148.

BEARE, William, *The Roman Stage* (London, 1950).

BINNS, J.W., ed. *The Latin Poetry of English Poets* (London, 1974).

BLOOM, L.D., "Addison's Popular Aesthetic: The Rhetoric of the *Paradise Lost* Papers," in L.L. Martz, Aubrey Williams, P.M. Spacks, eds. *The Author in His Work: Essays on a Problem in Criticism* (Yale, 1978), 263-281.

BRADNER, Leicester, "The Composition and Publication of Addison's Latin Poems," *Modern Philology* 35 (1938), 359-367.

——————, *Musae Anglicanae: A History of Anglo-Latin Poetry 1500-1925* (Oxford, 1940).

BYROM, Michael, *Punch and Judy: Its Origin and Evolution* (Aberdeen, 1972; rpt. London, 1979).

——————, *Punch in the Italian Puppet Theatre* (London, 1983).

——————, *Puppet Theatre in Antiquity* (Bicester, 1996).

CHALKER, John, *The English Georgic* (London, 1969).

CHANDLER, Richard, *Life of William Wayneflete* (London, 1811).

CHEEK, Macon, "Milton's *In Quintum Novembris*: An Epic Foreshadowing," *Studies in Philology* 54 (1957), 172-184.

CLARK, D.L., *John Milton at St Paul's School: A Study of Ancient Rhetoric in English Renaissance Education* (New York, 1948; rpt Hamden, 1964).

CONNOR, P.J., "The *Georgics* as Description: Aspects and Qualifications," *Ramus* 8 (1979), 34-58.

CORSE, Taylor, "An Echo of Dryden in Addison's *Cato*," *Notes & Queries* 38.2 (1991), 178.

COSTELLO, W.T., *The Scholastic Curriculum at Early Seventeenth-Century Cambridge* (Cambridge, 1958).

COURTHOPE, W.J., *Addison* (London, 1889; rpt 1911).

CROFT-MURRAY, Edward, *Decorative Painting in England 1537-1837* (London, 1962).

CRUIKSHANK, George, *Punch and Judy* (London, 1828).

DALZELL, Alexander, *The Criticism of Didactic Poetry* (Toronto, 1996).

DAMROSCH, Leopold, "The Significance of Addison's Criticism," *Studies in English Literature* 19 (1979), 421-430.

DARWALL-SMITH, Robin and WHITE, Roger, *The Architectural Drawings of Magdalen College — A Catalogue* (Oxford, 2001).

DESMOND, Marilynn, *Reading Dido: Gender, Textuality, and the Medieval Aeneid* (Minneapolis and London, 1994).

DI CESARE, M.A., "From Virgil to Vida to Milton," *Acta Conventus Neo-Latini Turonensis*, 1976 (Paris: Librairie Philosophique, 1980), I, 153-161.

DOWNES, Kerry, "Fuller's 'Last Judgement,'" *Burlington Magazine* cii (1960), 451-452.

DRAKE, Gertrude, "Satan's Councils in the *Christiad*, *Paradise Lost* and *Paradise Regained*," *Acta Conventus Neo-Latini Turonensis*, 979-989.

DRUCE, Robert and HUNT, J.D., eds. "Poems on Pictures," *Word & Image* 2.1 (1986), 45-103.

DUCKWORTH, G.E., *The Nature of Roman Comedy* (Princeton, 1952).

EDDY, W.A., *Gulliver's Travels: A Critical Study* (Princeton, 1923).

ELIOSEFF, L.A., *The Cultural Milieu of Addison's Literary Criticism* (Austin, 1963).

ELLISON, Julie, "Cato's Tears," *English Literary History* 63.3 (1996), 571-601.

FOWLER, D.P.,"Narrate and Describe: The Problem of Ekphrasis," *Journal of Roman Studies* 81 (1991), 25-35.

FREEMAN, L.A., "What's Love Got to Do With Addison's Cato?" *Studies in English Literature* 39.3 (1999), 463-482.

GALE, M.R, *Virgil on The Nature of Things: The Georgics, Lucretius and the Didactic Tradition* (Cambridge, 2000).

GALINSKY, Karl, "*Aeneid* V and the *Aeneid*," *American Journal of Philology* 89 (1968), 157-185.

GOW, A.S.F., "The Ancient Plough," *Journal of Hellenic Studies* 34 (1914), 249-275.

HAAN, Estelle, *John Milton's Latin Poetry: Some Neo-Latin and Vernacular Contexts* (PhD thesis: The Queen's University of Belfast, 1987).

————, "Milton's *Paradise Regained* and Vida's *Christiad*," *From Erudition to Inspiration: Essays in Honour of M.J. McGann*, (Belfast: Belfast Byzantine Texts and Translations, 1992), 53-77.

————, "From Helicon to Heaven: Milton's Urania and Vida," *Renaissance Studies* 7.1 (1993), 86-107.

————, "Heaven's Purest Light: *Paradise Lost* 3 and Vida," *Comparative Literature Studies* 30.2 (1993), 115-136.

————, "Milton's Latin Poetry and Vida," *Humanistica Lovaniensia: Journal of Neo-Latin Studies* 44 (1995), 282-304.

————, "Milton's *Naturam Non Pati Senium* and Hakewill," *Medievalia et Humanistica* 24 (1997), 147-167.

————, *From Academia to Amicitia: Milton's Latin Writings and the Italian Academies* (Transactions of the American Philosophical Society 88.6: Philadelphia, 1998).

————, *Thomas Gray's Latin Poetry: Some Classical, Neo-Latin and Vernacular Contexts* (Collection Latomus 257: Brussels, 2000).

————, *Andrew Marvell's Latin Poetry: From Text to Context* (Collection Latomus 275: Brussels, 2003).

————, "From Neo-Latin to Vernacular: Celestial Warfare in Vida and Milton," *Hommages à Carl Deroux: Christianisme et Moyen Âge: Néo-Latin et Survivance de la Latinité*, ed. Paul Defosse (Collection Latomus 279: Brussels, 2003), 408-419.

————, "Twin Augustans: Addison's Neo-Latin Poetry and Horace," *Notes & Queries*, forthcoming.

HEFFERNAN, James, "Ekphrasis and Representation," *New Literary History* 22.2 (Spring 1991), 297-316.

————, *Museum of Words: The Politics of Ekphrasis from Homer to Ashberry* (Chicago, 1992).

HINDS, Stephen, *Allusion and Intertext: Dynamics of Appropriation in Roman Poetry* (Cambridge, 1998).

HOLLANDER, John, "The Poetics of Ekphrasis," *Word & Image* 4.1 (1988), 209-219.

JOHNSON, Barbara, "Les Fleurs du Mal Armé: Some Reflections on Intertextuality," in *Lyric Poetry*, eds. Chaviva Hošek and Patricia Parker (Ithaca and London, 1985), 264-280.

JOHNSTON, P.A., *Vergil's Agricultural Golden Age: A Study of the Georgics* (Mnem. Supp. 60: Brill, 1980).

KELSALL, M.M., "The Meaning of Addison's *Cato*," *Review of English Studies* 17 (1966), 149-162.

KRIEGER, Murray, *Ekphrasis: The Illusion of the Natural Sign* (Johns Hopkins, 1991).

KRISTEVA, Julia, *Desire in Language: A Semiotic Approach to Literature and Art*, trans. Thomas Gora, Alice Jardine and L.S. Roudiez (New York, 1980).

LEACH, E.W., *Virgil's Eclogues: Landscapes of Experience* (Ithaca, 1974).

LE COMTE, E.S., *Yet Once More: Verbal and Psychological Pattern in Milton* (New York, 1953).

LERNER, Laurence, "The Unsaid in Henry Esmond," *Essays in Criticism* 45 (1995), 141-157.

LIVERSIDGE, M.J.H., "Prelude to the Baroque: Isaac Fuller at Oxford," *Oxoniensia* 57 (1992), 311-329.

LOOFBOUROW, John, *Thackeray and the Form of Fiction* (Princeton, 1964).

MITCHELL, W.J.T., "Ekphrasis and the Other," *Picture Theory and Essays on Verbal and Visual Representation* (Chicago, 1994), chap. 5.

MORGAN, Llewelyn, *Patterns of Redemption in Virgil's Georgics* (Cambridge, 1999).

MUELLNER, Leonard, "The simile of the Cranes and Pygmies: A Study of Homeric Metaphor," *Harvard Studies in Classical Philology* 93 (1990), 59-101.

NETHERCUT, W.R., "*Dux Femina Facti*: General Dido and the Trojans," *Classical Bulletin* 47 (1970), 26-30.

NIELSEN, Inge, *Thermae Et Balnea* (Denmark, 1993).

NUGENT, S.G., "Vergil's Voice of the Women in *Aeneid* V," *Arethusa* 25 (1992), 255-292.

PANTŮČKOVA, Lidmila, *W.M. Thackeray as a Critic of Literature* (BRNO Studies in English 10-11, 1972).

PARKER, Deborah, *Lectura Dantis: Inferno* X, in *Lectura Dantis*, I, No. 1 (Fall) (1987), 37-47.

PARTRIDGE, Loren, *Michelangelo: The Last Judgment: A Glorious Restoration* (New York, 1997).

PUTNAM, M.C.J., *Virgil's Pastoral Art: Studies in the Eclogues* (Princeton, 1970).

—————————, *Virgil's Poem of the Earth: Studies in the Georgics* (Princeton, 1979).

RAND, E.K., *The Magical Art of Virgil* (Harvard, 1931).

ROSENTHAL, L.J., "Juba's Roman Soul: Addison's *Cato* and Enlightenment Cosmopolitanism," *Studies in the Literary Imagination* 32.2 (1999), 63-76.

ROYAL, S.J., "Joseph Addison (1672-1719): A Checklist of Works and Major Scholarship," *Bulletin of the New York Public Library* 77 (1974), 236-250.

SACCAMANO, Neil, "The Sublime Force of Words in Addison's *Pleasures*," *English Literary History* 58.1 (1991), 83-106.

SCHUCH, Gerhard, *Addison und die Lateinischen Augusteer: Studien zur Frage der Literarischen Abhängigkeit des Englischen Klassizismus* (PhD thesis, University of Köln, 1962).

SESSIONS, W.A., "Milton's *Naturam*," *Milton Studies* 19 (1984), 53-72.

SMITHERS, Peter, *The Life of Joseph Addison* (Oxford, 1968).

SPEAIGHT, George, "'Powell From the Bath': An Eighteenth-Century London Puppet Theatre," *Studies in English Theatre History in Memory of Gabrielle Enthoven* (London, 1952), 38-51.

SULLIVAN, J.P., "Dido and the Representation of Women in Vergil's *Aeneid*," in *The Two Worlds of the Poet: New Perspectives on Vergil*, ed., R.M. Wilhelm and H. Jones (Detroit, 1992), 64-73.

SUTHERLAND, John, "Thackeray's Notebook for Henry Esmond" in *Costerus: Essays in English and American Language and Literature: Thackeray*, ed. P.L. Shillingsburg (Amsterdam, 1974), II, 193-215.

VOLK, Katharina, *The Poetics of Latin Didactic* (Oxford, 2002).

WALKER, William, "Ideology and Addison's Essays on the Pleasures of the Imagination," *Eighteenth-Century Life* 24.2 (2000), 65-84.

WARD, John, *Roman Era in Britain* (Methuen: London, 1911).

WATERHOUSE, Ellis, *Painting in Britain 1530 to 1790* (London, 1978).

WIESENTHAL, A.J., *The Latin Poetry of the English Augustans* (PhD thesis, Virginia, 1979).

WILLIAMS, R.D. and KELSALL, Malcolm, "Critical Appreciations V: Joseph Addison, *Pax Gulielmi Auspiciis Europae Reddita*, 1697, lines 96-132 and 167-end," *Greece & Rome* 27 (1980), 48-59.

INDEX NOMINUM